AN ANTHOLOGY

OF IRISH

LITERATURE

AN ANTHOLOGY OF IRISH LITERATURE

EDITED, WITH AN INTRODUCTION, BY

David H. Greene, NEW YORK UNIVERSITY

VOLUME II

New York University Press
New York   1971

CONTENTS

Part II: Myth, Saga, and Romance

TRANSLATIONS FROM THE GAELIC

Part III: The Bardic Tradition

COURT POETRY TRANSLATED FROM THE GAELIC

Part IV: Modern Irish Poetry

TRANSLATIONS FROM THE GAELIC

Part V : Irish Literature in English (VOLUME II)

Contents

AN ANTHOLOGY
OF IRISH
LITERATURE

Irish Literature in English

The Irish Dancer

I am of Ireland,
And of the holy land
    Of Ireland.
Good Sir, pray I thee,
For of *saint charité*
Come and dance with **me**
    In Ireland.

14TH CENTURY.

A Rhyme-beginning Fragment[1]

Love hath me brought in evil thought,
    Thought I have to blinne;[2]
Blinne to think it is for nought,
    Nought is love of sin.

Sin me hath in care ibrought,
    Brought in much unwinne;[3]
Winne to weld[4] I had ithought,
    Thought is that I am in.

In me is care, how I shall fare,
    Fare I will and funde;[5]
Funde I with outen are,[6]
    Ere I be brought to ground.

14TH CENTURY.

Cokaygne[7]

Far in sea, west of Spain,
Is a land that's named Cokaygne,
There is no land under heavenriche[8]

---

1 See Bibliographical Notes, p. 589. The poem may be paraphrased thus. *Love has led me to sinful thoughts. I have intended to stop. But merely to intend is to do nothing, and nothing is the love of sin. Sin, in turn, has brought me only worry and much unhappiness. I thought I could achieve happiness but have got no farther than the thought. And now I am worried about how I shall go on. But go on I must and fare. I shall go on without honor until I perish.*   2 Stop.
3 Unhappiness.   4 Happiness.   5 Go.   6 Honor.
7 See Bibliographical Notes, p. 589.   8 The kingdom of heaven.

Of wealth, of goodness, it iliche,[1]
Though Paradise be merry and bright
Cokaygne is of fairer sight.
What is there in Paradise
But grass, and flowers, and green ris?[2]
Though there be joy and great dute[3]
There is no food only fruit;
There is no hall, bower, nor bench,
But water man his thirst to quench.
There be no men, but two,
Hely and Enok[4] also;
Elinglich[5] may they go
Where there dwelleth man no mo.[6]

In Cokaygne is meat and drink
Without care, thought, and swink;[7]
The meat is choice, the drink is clear,
At noon, russin,[8] and supper.
I say for sooth, boute were,[9]
There is no land on earth its peer,
Under heaven's no land, iwis,[10]
Of so great joy and bliss.
There is many a sweete sight,
All is day, there is no night.
There is neither quarrel nor strife,
There is no death, but ever life,
There is no lack of meat nor cloth,
There is no man nor woman wroth,
There is no serpent, wolf, nor fox,
Horse nor capil,[11] cow nor ox,
There is no sheep, nor swine, nor goat,
Nothing unclean, lo! God it wot.[12]
Neither harace nor stode,[13]

---

1 Equal to it. 2 Twigs, branches. 3 Pleasure. 4 Enoch and
Elijah. 5 Mournfully. 6 No other men. 7 Toil. 8 Mid-day
meal. 9 Without a doubt. 10 In truth. 11 Nag. 12 God
knows it. 13 Stud of horses or stable.

The land is full of every good.
There is no fly, flea, nor louse,
In cloth, in farm, in bed, nor house;
There is no thunder, sleet, nor hail,
Neither a vile worm nor snail,
Nor no storm, rain, or wind,
There is no man nor woman blind.
But all is sport, joy and glee,
Lucky's he who there may be.
There are rivers great and fine
Of oil, milk, honey, and wine,
Water serveth there to no thing
But to boil and to washing,
There is all manner of fruit,
All is solace and dedute.[1]

There is a right fair abbey
Both of white monks and of grey.
There be bowers and halls,
All of pastys be the walls,
Of flesh, of fish, and of rich meat,
The pleasantest that men may eat.
Flouren cakes be the shingles all
Of church, and cloister, bower, and hall.
The pins be fat puddings,
Rich meat for princes and kings.
Men may thereof eat enow

---

1 Delight.

All with right, and not with wogh.[1]
All is common to young and old,
To stout and stern, weak and bold.
There is a cloister fair and light,
Broad and long, of seemly sight.
The pillars of that cloister all
Be iturned of crystal,
With their base and capital
Of green jasper and red coral.

In the lawn there is a tree
Very pleasant for to see.
The root is ginger and galingale[2]
The scions be all sedwale,[3]
Choice maces[4] be the flower,
The rind canel[5] of sweet odour,
The fruit gillyflower of good smack,[6]
Of cubebs there is no lack;
There be roses of red ble,[7]
And lilies pleasant for to see,
That never fade day nor night,
This should be a sweet sight.
There be four wells in the abbey,

---

1 Altogether with right and not with wrongdoing.
2 A plant from the aromatic root of which a spice is prepared
3 Zedoary, a root resembling ginger. 4 Spice made of dried outer
covering of nutmeg. 5 Cinnamon. 6 Scent, taste. 7 Color.

Of triacle and of halwei,[1]
Of balm and also piement,[2]
Ever flowing to right rent.[3]
Of the streams all the mould[4]
Stones precious, and gold.
There is sapphire and uniune[5]
Carbuncle and astiune,[6]
Emerald, lugre,[7] and prassiune,[8]
Beryl, onyx, and topasiune,[9]
Amethyst and chrysolite,
Chalcedony and epetite.[10]

There be birds many and fale,[11]
Throstle, thrush, and nightingale,
Chalandre and woodwale,[12]
And other birds without tale,[13]
That cease never by their might
Merry to sing day and night.
Yet I do you more to wit:[14]
The geese iroasted on the spit
Fly to that abbey, God it wot,
And cry out "Geese, all hot, all hot!"
They bring of garlic great plenty,
The best prepared that man may see.
The leverokes that be cuth[15]
Alight down to man his mouth,
Prepared in stew-pan very well,
Stuffed with gillyflowers and canel.
There is no talk of no drink,
But take enough without swink.

---

1 Healing medicine, and balsam.   2 Mixed drink of wine, honey
and spices.   3 To good profit.   4 All the beds of the streams are
composed of, etc.   5 Pearl.   6 Unidentified precious stone.   7
Jacynth.   8 Chrysoprase.   9 Topaz.   10 Bloodstone.   11 Nu-
merous.   12 Goldfinch, or perhaps some sort of lark: woodlark.   13
Beyond count.   14 I let you know in addition.   15 The larks that
are trained.

When the monks go to mass
All the windows that be of glass
Turn into crystal bright
To give the monks more light.
When the masses be isaid,
And the books up ilaid,
The crystal turneth into glass
In the state it rather[1] was.

The young monks each day
After meat go to play.
There is no hawk nor fowl so swift
Better flying in the lift[2]
Than the monks high of mood
With their sleeves and their hood.
When the abbot seeth them flee
That he holds for much glee,
But nathless all there among
He biddeth them light to evensong.
But the monks alight not down
But fly in a randown.[3]
When the abbot him iseeth
That his monks from him fleeth,
He taketh maiden of the route,
And turneth up her white toute
And beateth the tabor with his hand,
To make his monks 'light to land.
When his monks that iseeth,
To the maid down they fleeth,
And goeth the wench all about,
And thwacketh all her white toute,
And then after their swink,
Turn meekly home to drink,
And go to their collation,
A right fair procession.

---

1 Formerly.   2 Air.   3 In a furious course.

Another abbey is thereby,
Forsooth a great fair nunnery,
Upon a river of sweet milk
Where is plenty great ot silk.
When the summer day is hot
The young nuns take a boat
And do them forth in that river
Both with oars and with stere.[1]
When they be far from the abbey
They make them naked for to play,
And leap down into the brim,
And do them slyly for to swim.

The young monks that them seeth,
They hie them up, and forth they fleeth,
And come to the nuns anon.
And each monk him taketh one,
And snellich[2] beareth forth their prey
To the mochil[3] grey abbey.
And teacheth the nuns an orison
With *jambleuc*[4] up and down.
The monk that will be staluu[5] good,
And can set aright his hood,
He shall have, without danger,[6]
Twelve wives each year:
All through right, and nought through grace,

---

1 Rudder.
2 Swiftly.   3 Great.   4 Gambols.   5 Stout. (?)   6 Punishment.

For to do himself solace.
And this monk that clepith[1] best,
Of him is hope, God it wot,
To be soon father abbot.

Whoso will that land come to
Full great penance he must do
Seven years in swine's dirt
He must wade, well ye wit,
All anon up to the chin,
So he shall that land win.

Lordlinges good and hend[2]
May ye never of world wend
For ye stand to your chance[3]
And fulfil that penance,
That ye might that land isee
And nevermore turn age.[4]
Pray we God, so mote it be.
Amen, *pour saint charité*.

13TH CENTURY.

---

1 Declared, or perhaps *clippeth*, i.e. embraces. 2 Courteous.
3 May you never leave the world till you try your fortune about
getting to that land. 4 Again.

An Anglo-Irishman's Complaint[1]

By granting charters of peace
To false English, without lease
   This land shall be much undo.
But gossipred[2] and alterage,[3]
And losing of our language
   Have mickly holp[4] thereto.

16TH CENTURY.

---

[1] See Bibliographical Notes, p. 589. The poet complains that the English settlers in Ireland are fraternizing with the Irish to the extent of adopting native customs and speaking Irish. He resents the fact that a weak government, instead of reducing to obedience these disloyal Anglo-Norman families who are "false English," appeases them with "charters of peace" and other legal concessions. The poet's sentiments find reinforcement in the preamble to the Statutes of Kilkenny (1366) which deplored the fact that "now many English of the said land, forsaking the English language, manners, mode of riding, laws and usages, live and govern themselves according to the manners, fashion and language of the Irish enemies and also have made divers marriages between themselves and the Irish enemies . . ."

[2] Standing sponsor at baptism.

[3] Fostering—an Irish custom whereby a man, to guarantee friendship or seal an agreement, would send one of his children to be brought up in the house of another man. The custom continued into the 17th century.

[4] Greatly helped.

A Modest Proposal for Preventing the Children of Ireland From Being a Burden to Their Parents or Country

BY Jonathan Swift (1667-1745)

IT IS A melancholy object to those who walk through this great town or travel in the country, when they see the streets, the roads, and cabin doors, crowded with beggars of the female sex, followed by three, four, or six children, all in rags and importuning every passenger for an alms. These mothers, instead of being able to work for their honest livelihood, are forced to employ all their time in strolling to beg sustenance for their helpless infants: who as they grow up either turn thieves for want of work, or leave their dear native country to fight for the pretender in Spain, or sell themselves to the Barbadoes.

I think it is agreed by all parties that this prodigious number of children in the arms, or on the backs, or at the heels of their mothers, and frequently of their fathers, is in the present deplorable state of the kingdom a very great additional grievance; and, therefore, whoever could find out a fair, cheap, and easy method of making these children sound, useful members of the commonwealth, would deserve so well of the public as to have his statue set up for a preserver of the nation.

But my intention is very far from being confined to provide only for the children of professed beggars; it is of a much greater extent, and shall take in the whole number of infants at a certain age who are born of parents in effect as little able to support them as those who demand our charity in the streets.

As to my own part, having turned my thoughts for many years upon this important subject, and maturely weighed the several schemes of our projectors, I have always found them grossly mistaken in their computation. It is true, a child just dropped from its dam may be supported by her milk for a solar year, with little other nourishment; at most not above the value of 2s., which the mother may certainly get, or the value in scraps, by her lawful occupation of begging; and it is exactly at one year old that I propose to provide for them in such a manner as instead of being a charge upon their parents or the parish, or wanting food and raiment for the rest of their lives, they shall on the contrary contribute to the feeding, and partly to the clothing, of many thousands.

There is likewise another great advantage in my scheme, that it will prevent those voluntary abortions, and that horrid practice of women murdering their bastard children, alas! too frequent among us! sacrificing the poor innocent babes I doubt more to avoid the expense than the shame, which would move tears and pity in the most savage and inhuman breast.

The number of souls in this kingdom being usually reckoned one million and a half, of these I calculate there may be about 200,000 couple whose wives are breeders; from which number I subtract 30,000 couple who are able to maintain their own children (although I apprehend there cannot be so many, under the present distresses of the kingdom); but this being granted, there will remain 170,000 breeders. I again subtract 50,000 for those women who miscarry, or whose children die by accident or disease within the year. There only remains 120,000 children of poor parents annually born. The question therefore is, how this number shall be reared and provided for? which, as I have already said, under the present situation of affairs, is utterly impossible by all the methods hitherto proposed. For we can neither employ them in handicraft or agriculture; we neither build houses (I mean in the country) nor cultivate land; they can very seldom pick up a livelihood by stealing, till they arrive at six years old, except where they are of towardly parts; although I confess they learn the rudiments much earlier; during which time, they can however be properly looked upon only as probationers; as I have been informed by a principal gentleman in the county of Cavan, who protested to me that he never knew above one or two instances under the age of six, even in a part of the kingdom so renowned for the quickest proficiency in that art.

I am assured by our merchants, that a boy or a girl before twelve years old is no saleable commodity; and even when they come to this age they will not yield above £3 or £3 and half a crown at most on the exchange; which cannot turn to account either to the parents or kingdom, the charge of nutriment and rags having been at least four times that value.

I shall now therefore humbly propose my own thoughts, which I hope will not be liable to the least objection.

I have been assured by a very knowing American of my acquaintance in London, that a young healthy child well nursed is at a year old a most delicious, nourishing, and wholesome food, whether stewed, roasted, baked, or boiled; and I make no doubt that it will equally serve in a fricassee or a ragout.

I do therefore humbly offer it to public consideration that of the 120,000 children already computed, 20,000 may be reserved for breed, whereof only one-fourth part to be males; which is more than we allow to sheep, black cattle, or swine; and my reason is, that these children are seldom the fruits of marriage, a circumstance not much regarded by our savages, therefore one male will be sufficient to serve four females. That the remaining 100,000 may, at a year old, be offered in sale to the persons of quality and fortune through the kingdom; always advising the mother to let them suck plentifully in the last month, so as to render them plump and fat for a good table. A child will make two dishes at an entertainment for friends; and when the family dines alone, the fore or hind quarter will make a reasonable dish, and seasoned with a little pepper or salt will be very good boiled on the fourth day, especially in winter.

I have reckoned upon a medium that a child just born will weigh 12 pounds, and in a solar year, if tolerably nursed, will increase to 28 pounds.

I grant this food will be somewhat dear, and therefore very proper for landlords, who, as they have already devoured most of the parents, seem to have the best title to the children.

Infant's flesh will be in season throughout the year, but more plentifully in March, and a little before and after: for we are told by a grave author, an eminent French physician, that fish being a prolific diet, there are more children born in Roman Catholic countries about nine months after Lent than at any other season; therefore, reckoning a year after Lent, the markets will be more glutted than usual, because the number of popish infants is at least three to one in this kingdom: and therefore it will have one other collateral advantage, by lessening the number of papists among us.

I have already computed the charge of nursing a beggar's child (in which list I reckon all cottagers, laborers, and four-fifths of the farmers) to be about 2s. per annum, rags included; and I believe no gentleman would repine to give 10s. for the carcass of a good fat child, which, as I have said, will make four dishes of excellent nutritive meat, when he has only some particular friend or his own family to dine with him. Thus the squire will learn to be a good landlord, and grow popular among the tenants; the mother will have 8s. net profit, and be fit for work till she produces another child.

Those who are more thrifty (as I must confess the times require) may flay the carcass; the skin of which artificially dressed will make admirable gloves for ladies, and summer boots for fine gentlemen.

As to our city of Dublin, shambles may be appointed for this purpose in the most convenient parts of it, and butchers we may be assured will not be wanting; although I rather recommend buying the children alive, and dressing them hot from the knife as we do roasting pigs.

A very worthy person, a true lover of his country, and whose virtues I highly esteem, was lately pleased in discoursing on this matter to offer a refinement upon my scheme. He said that many gentlemen of this kingdom, having of late destroyed their deer, he conceived that the want of venison might be well supplied by the bodies of young lads and maidens, not exceeding fourteen years of age nor under twelve; so great a number of both sexes in every country being now ready to starve for want of work and service; and these to be disposed of by their parents, if alive, or otherwise by their nearest relations. But with due deference to so excellent a friend and so deserving a patriot, I cannot be altogether in his sentiments; for as to the males, my American acquaintance assured me, from frequent experience that their flesh was generally tough and lean, like that of our school-boys by continual exercise, and their taste disagreeable; and to fatten them would not answer the charge. Then as to the females, it would, I think, with humble submission be a loss to the public, because they soon would become breeders themselves: and besides, it is not improbable that some scrupulous people might be apt to censure such a practice (although indeed very unjustly), as a little bordering upon cruelty; which, I confess, has always been with me the strongest objection against any project, how well soever intended.

But in order to justify my friend, he confessed that this expedient was put into his head by the famous Psalmanazar, a native of the island Formosa, who came from thence to London about twenty years ago: and in conversation told my friend, that in his country when any young person happened to be put to death, the executioner sold the carcass to persons of quality as a prime dainty; and that in his time the body of a plump girl of fifteen, who was crucified for an attempt to poison the emperor, was sold to his imperial majesty's prime minister of state, and other great mandarins of the court, in joints from the gibbet, at 400 crowns. Neither indeed can I deny, that if the same use were made of several plump young girls in this town, who without one single groat to their fortunes cannot stir abroad without a chair, and appear at playhouse and assemblies in foreign fineries which they never will pay for, the kingdom would not be the worse.

Some persons of a desponding spirit are in great concern about that vast number of poor people, who are aged, diseased, or maimed, and I have been desired to employ my thoughts what course may be taken to ease the nation of so grievous an encumbrance. But I am not in the least pain upon that matter, because it is very well known that they are every day dying and rotting by cold and famine, and filth and vermin, as fast as can be reasonably expected. And as to the young laborers, they are now in as hopeful a condition; they cannot get work, and consequently pine away for want of nourishment, to a degree that if at any time they are accidentally hired to common labor, they have not strength to perform it; and thus the country and themselves are happily delivered from the evils to come.

I have too long digressed, and therefore shall return to my subject. I think the advantages by the proposal which I have made are obvious and many, as well as of the highest importance.

For first, as I have already observed, it would greatly lessen the number of papists, with whom we are yearly overrun, being the principal breeders of the nation as well as our most dangerous enemies; and who stay at home on purpose to deliver the kingdom to the Pretender, hoping to take their advantage by the absence of so many good protestants, who have chosen rather to leave their country than stay at home and pay tithes against their conscience to an episcopal curate.

Secondly, The poorer tenants will have something valuable of their own, which by law may be made liable to distress and help to pay their landlord's rent, their corn and cattle being already seized, and money a thing unknown.

Thirdly, Whereas the maintenance of 100,000 children, from two years old and upward, cannot be computed at less than 10s. a-piece per annum, the nation's stock will be thereby increased £50,000 per annum, beside the profit of a new dish introduced to the tables of all gentlemen of fortune in the kingdom who have any refinement in taste. And the money will circulate among ourselves, the goods being entirely of our own growth and manufacture.

Fourthly, The constant breeders, beside the gain of 8s. sterling per annum by the sale of their children, will be rid of the charge of maintaining them after the first year.

Fifthly, This food would likewise bring great custom to taverns; where the vintners will certainly be so prudent as to procure the best receipts for dressing it to perfection, and consequently have their houses frequented by all the fine gentlemen, who justly value themselves upon their knowledge in good eating: and a skilful cook who understands how to oblige his guests, will contrive to make it as expensive as they please.

Sixthly, This would be a great inducement to marriage, which all wise nations have either encouraged by rewards or enforced by laws and penalties. It would increase the care and tenderness of mothers toward their children, when they were sure of a settlement for life to the poor babes, provided in some sort by the public, to their annual profit instead of expense. We should see an honest emulation among the married women, which of them could bring the fattest child to the market. Men would become as fond of their wives during the time of their pregnancy as they are now of their mares in foal, their cows in calf, their sows when they are ready to farrow; nor offer to beat or kick them (as is too frequent a practice) for fear of a miscarriage.

Many other advantages might be enumerated. For instance, the addition of some thousand carcasses in our exportation of barreled beef, the propagation of swine's flesh, and improvement in the art of making good bacon, so much wanted among us by the great destruction of pigs, too frequent at our table; which are no way comparable in taste or magnificence to a well-grown, fat, yearling child, which roasted whole will make a considerable figure at a lord mayor's feast or any other public entertainment. But this and many others I omit, being studious of brevity.

Supposing that 1000 families in this city would be constant

customers for infants' flesh, beside others who might have it at merry-meetings, particularly at weddings and christenings, I compute that Dublin would take off annually about 20,000 carcasses; and the rest of the kingdom (where probably they will be sold somewhat cheaper) the remaining 80,000.

I can think of no one objection that will possibly be raised against this proposal, unless it should be urged that the number of people will be thereby much lessened in the kingdom. This I freely own, and it was indeed one principal design in offering it to the world. I desire the reader will observe, that I calculate my remedy for this one individual kingdom of Ireland and for no other that ever was, is, or I think ever can be upon earth. Therefore let no man talk to me of other expedients: of taxing our absentees at 5s. a pound: of using neither clothes nor household furniture except what is of our own growth and manufacture: of utterly rejecting the materials and instruments that promote foreign luxury: of curing the expensiveness of pride, vanity, idleness, and gaming in our women: of introducing a vein of parsimony, prudence, and temperance: of learning to love our country, in the want of which we differ even from LAPLANDERS and the inhabitants of TOPINAMBOO: of quitting our animosities and factions, nor acting any longer like the Jews, who were murdering one another at the very moment their city was taken: of being a little cautious not to sell our country and conscience for nothing: of teaching landlords to have at least one degree of mercy toward their tenants: lastly, of putting a spirit of honesty, industry, and skill into our shopkeepers; who, if a resolution could now be taken to buy only our native goods, would immediately unite to cheat and exact upon us in the price, the measure, and the goodness, nor could ever yet be brought to make one fair proposal of just dealing, though often and earnestly invited to it.

Therefore I repeat, let no man talk to me of these and the like expedients, till he has at least some glimpse of hope that there will be ever some hearty and sincere attempt to put them in practice.

But as to myself, having been wearied out for many years with offering vain, idle, visionary thoughts, and at length utterly despairing of success, I fortunately fell upon this proposal; which, as it is wholly new, so it has something solid and real, of no expense and little trouble, full in our own power, and whereby we can incur no danger in disobliging ENGLAND. For this kind of commodity will not bear exportation, the flesh being of too tender a consistence to admit a long continuance in salt, although perhaps I could name a country which would be glad to eat up our whole nation without it.

After all, I am not so violently bent upon my own opinion as to reject any offer proposed by wise men, which shall be found equally innocent, cheap, easy, and effectual. But before something of that kind shall be advanced in contradiction to my scheme, and offering a better, I desire the author or authors will be pleased maturely to consider two points. First, as things now stand, how they will be able to find food and raiment for 100,000 useless mouths and backs. And secondly, there being a round million of creatures in human figure throughout this kingdom, whose whole subsistence put into a common stock would leave them in debt £2,000,000 sterling, adding those who are beggars by profession to the bulk of farmers, cottagers, and laborers, with the wives and children who are beggars in effect; I desire those politicians who dislike my overture, and may perhaps be so bold as to attempt an answer, that they will first ask the parents of these mortals, whether they would not at this day think it a great happiness to have been sold for food at a year old in the manner I prescribe, and thereby have avoided such a perpetual scene of misfortunes as they have since gone through by the oppression of landlords, the impossibility of paying rent without money or trade, the want of common sustenance, with neither house nor clothes to cover them from the inclemencies of the weather, and the most inevitable prospect of entailing the like or greater miseries upon their breed for ever.

I profess, in the sincerity of my heart, that I have not the

least personal interest in endeavoring to promote this necessary
work, having no other motive than the public good of my
country, by advancing our trade, providing for infants, re-
lieving the poor, and giving some pleasure to the rich. I have
no children by which I can propose to get a single penny; the
youngest being nine years old, and my wife past child-bearing.

Adventure in Cork[1]

BY Oliver Goldsmith (1728-1774)

MY DEAR MOTHER,

If you will sit down and calmly listen to what I say,
you shall be fully resolved in every one of those many
questions you have asked me. I went to Cork and con-
verted my horse, which you prize so much higher than Fiddleback, into cash, took my passage in a ship bound for America,
and at the same time paid the captain for my freight and all
the other expenses of my voyage. But it so happened that the
wind did not answer for three weeks; and you know, mother,
that I could not command the elements. My misfortune was
that when the wind served I happened to be with a party in
the country, and my friend the captain never inquired after me,
but set sail with as much indifference as if I had been on board.
The remainder of my time I employed in the city and its environs, viewing everything curious; and you know no one can
starve while he has money in his pocket.

Reduced, however, to my last two guineas, I began to think
of my dear mother and friends whom I had left behind me,
and so bought that generous beast Fiddleback and bade adieu
to Cork with only five shillings in my pocket. This to be sure
was a scanty allowance for man and horse towards a journey
of above an hundred miles; but I did not despair, for I knew
I must find friends on the road.

---

[1] See Bibliographical Notes, p. 589.

I recollected particularly an old and faithful acquaintance I made at college, who had often and earnestly pressed me to spend a summer with him; and he lived but eight miles from Cork. This circumstance of vicinity he would expatiate on to me with particular emphasis.—"We shall," says he, "enjoy the delights of both city and country, and you shall command my stable and my purse."

However, upon the way I met a poor woman all in tears, who told me her husband had been arrested for a debt he was not able to pay, and that his eight children must now starve, bereaved as they were of his industry, which had been their only support. I thought myself at home, being not far from my good friend's house, and therefore parted with a moiety of all my store; and pray, mother, ought I not to have given her the other half-crown, for what she got would be of little use to her?—However, I soon arrived at the mansion of my affectionate friend, guarded by the vigilance of a huge mastiff, who flew at me and would have torn me to pieces, but for the assistance of a woman whose countenance was not less grim than that of the dog; yet she with great humanity relieved me from the jaws of this Cerberus, and was prevailed on to carry up my name to her master.

Without suffering me to wait long, my old friend, who was then recovering from a severe fit of sickness, came down in his night-cap, night-gown, and slippers, and embraced me with the most cordial welcome, showed me in, and after giving me a history of his indisposition, assured me that he considered himself as peculiarly fortunate in having under his roof the man he most loved on earth, and whose stay with him must, above all things, contribute to perfect his recovery. I now repented sorely I had not given the poor woman the other half-crown, as I thought all my bills of humanity would be punctually answered by this worthy man. I revealed to him my whole soul; and freely owned that I had but one half-crown in my pocket; but that now, like a ship after weathering out the storm, I considered myself secure in a safe and hospitable harbour. He made no answer, but walked about the room, rubbing his hands as one in a deep study. This I imputed to the sympathetic feelings of a tender heart, which increased my esteem for him, and as that increased I gave the most favourable interpretation to his silence. I construed it into delicacy of sentiment, as if he dreaded to wound my pride by expressing his commiseration in words, leaving his generous conduct to speak for itself.

It now approached six o'clock in the evening, and as I had eaten no breakfast, and as my spirits were raised, my appetite for dinner grew uncommonly keen. At length the old woman came into the room, with two plates, one spoon, and a dirty cloth, which she laid upon the table. This appearance, without increasing my spirits, did not diminish my appetite. My protectress soon returned with a small bowl of sago, a small porringer of sour milk, a loaf of stale brown bread, and the heel of an old cheese all over crawling with mites. My friend apologized that his illness obliged him to live on slops, and that better fare was not in the house; observing at the same time that a milk diet was certainly the most healthful; and at eight o'clock he again recommended a regular life, declaring that for his part he would lie down with the lamb and rise with the lark. My hunger was at this time so exceedingly sharp that I wished for another slice of the loaf, but was obliged to go to bed without even that refreshment.

The Lenten entertainment I had received made me resolve to depart as soon as possible; accordingly next morning, when I spoke of going, he did not oppose my resolution; he rather commended my design, adding some very sage counsel upon the occasion. "To be sure," said he, "the longer you stay away from your mother, the more you will grieve her and your other friends; and possibly they are already afflicted at hearing of this foolish expedition you have made." Notwithstanding all this, and without any hope of softening such a sordid heart, I again renewed the tale of my distress, and asking "how he thought I could travel above an hundred miles upon one half-crown?" I begged to borrow a single guinea, which I assured him should be repaid with thanks. "And you know, Sir," said I, "it is no more than I have often done for you." To which he firmly answered, "Why, look you, Mr. Goldsmith, that is neither here nor there. I have paid you all you ever lent me, and this sickness of mine has left me bare of cash. But I have bethought myself of a conveyance for you; sell your horse and I will furnish you a much better one to ride on." I readily grasped at his proposal, and begged to see the nag; on which he led me to his bed-chamber, and from under the bed he pulled out a stout oak stick. "Here he is," said he; "take this in your hand, and it will carry you to your mother's with more safety than such a horse as you ride." I was in doubt when I got it into my hand whether I should not, in the first place, apply it to his pate; but a rap at the street-door made the wretch fly to it, and when I returned to the parlour, he introduced me, as if nothing of the kind had happened, to the gentleman who entered, as Mr. Goldsmith, his most ingenious and worthy friend, of whom he had so often heard him speak with rapture. I could scarcely compose myself; and must have betrayed indignation in my mien to the stranger, who was a counsellor at law in the neighbourhood, a man of engaging aspect and polite address.

After spending an hour, he asked my friend and me to dine with him at his house. This I declined at first, as I wished to have no further communication with my old hospitable friend; but at the solicitation of both I at last consented, determined as I was by two motives; one, that I was prejudiced in favour of the looks and manner of the counsellor; and the other that I stood in need of a comfortable dinner. And there indeed I found every thing that I could wish, abundance without profusion, and elegance without affectation. In the evening when my old friend, who had eaten very plentifully at his neighbour's table, but talked again of lying down with the lamb, made a motion to me for retiring, our generous host requested I should take a bed with him, upon which I plainly told my old friend that he might go home and take care of the horse he had given me, but that I should never re-enter his doors. He went away with a laugh, leaving me to add this to the other little things the counsellor already knew of his plausible neighbour.

And now, my dear mother, I found sufficient to reconcile me to all my follies; for here I spent three whole days. The counsellor had two sweet girls to his daughters, who played enchantingly on the harpsichord; and yet it was but a melancholy pleasure I felt the first time I heard them; for that being the first time also that either of them had touched the instrument since their mother's death, I saw the tears in silence trickle down their father's cheeks. I every day endeavoured to go away, but every day was pressed and obliged to stay. On my going the counsellor offered me his purse, with a horse and servant to convey me home; but the latter I declined, and only took a guinea to bear my necessary expenses on the road.

OLIVER GOLDSMITH.

To Mrs. Anne Goldsmith, Ballymahon.

The Shan Van Vocht[1]

Oh! the French are on the sea,
  Says the Shan Van Vocht;
The French are on the sea,
  Says the Shan Van Vocht:
Oh! the French are in the Bay,
They'll be here without delay,
And the Orange will decay,
  Says the Shan Van Vocht.
    Oh! the French are in the Bay,
    They'll be here by break of day,
    And the Orange will decay,
      Says the Shan Van Vocht.

---

[1] This ballad and the two that follow deal with the abortive invasion of Ireland by the French in 1796 and again in 1798 when the landing was supplemented by the uprising of the United Irishmen. *Shan Van Vocht* means *poor old woman* and is a name for Ireland.

And where will they have their camp?
   Says the Shan Van Vocht;
Where will they have their camp?
   Says the Shan Van Vocht;
On the Curragh of Kildare,
The boys they will be there,
With their pikes in good repair,
   Says the Shan Van Vocht.
     To the Curragh of Kildare
     The boys they will repair,
     And Lord Edward[2] will be there,
       Says the Shan Van Vocht.

Then what will the yeomen do?
   Says the Shan Van Vocht;
What will the yeomen do?
   Says the Shan Van Vocht;
What should the yeomen do
But throw off the Red and Blue,
And swear that they'll be true
   To the Shan Van Vocht?
     What should the yeomen do
     But throw off the red and blue,
     And swear that they'll be true
       To the Shan Van Vocht?

---

[2]-Lord Edward Fitzgerald, younger brother of the Duke of Leinster, a rebel leader in the uprising of 1798.

And what colour will they wear?
   Says the Shan Van Vocht;
What colour will they wear?
   Says the Shan Van Vocht;
What colour should be seen
Where our fathers' homes have been,
But our own immortal Green?
   Says the Shan Van Vocht.
What colour should be seen
     Where our father's homes have been.
     But our own immortal Green?
      Says the Shan Van Vocht.

And will Ireland then be free?
   Says the Shan Van Vocht;
Will Ireland then be free?
   Says the Shan Van Vocht;
Yes! Ireland shall be free,
From the centre to the sea;
Then hurrah for Liberty!
   Says the Shan Van Vocht.
     Yes! Ireland shall be free,
     From the centre to the sea:
     Then hurrah for Liberty!
      Says the Shan Van Vocht.

18TH CENTURY.

The Wearin' o' the Green

O Paddy dear, an' did ye hear the news that's goin' round?
The shamrock is by law forbid to grow on Irish ground!
No more Saint Patrick's Day we'll keep, his colour can't be
    seen,
For there's a cruel law agin the wearin' o' the Green!
I met wid Napper Tandy,[1] and he took me by the hand,
And he said, "How's poor ould Ireland, and how does she
    stand?"
She's the most disthressful country that iver yet was seen,
For they're hangin' men an' women there for the wearin' o' the
    Green.

And if the colour we must wear is England's cruel Red,
Let it remind us of the blood that Ireland has shed;
Then pull the shamrock from your hat, and throw it on the
    sod,
And never fear, 'twill take root there, tho' under foot 'tis trod!
When law can stop the blades of grass from growin' as they
    grow,
And when the leaves in summer-time their colour dare not
    show,
Then I will change the colour, too, I wear in my caubeen,[2]
But till that day, plase God, I'll stick to wearin' o' the Green.

---

[1] James Napper Tandy was a Protestant merchant who defended
the rights of Catholics, helped found the Society of United Irishmen,
and escaped, first to America, then to the continent before he could
be arrested for treason.
[2] Hat.

The Croppy Boy[1]

It was very early in the spring,
The birds did whistle and sweetly sing,
Changing their notes from tree to tree,
And the song they sang was Old Ireland free.

It was early in the night
The yeoman cavalry gave me a fright;
The yeoman cavalry was my downfall
And taken was I by Lord Cornwall.[2]

'Twas in the guard-house where I was laid
And in a parlor where I was tried;
My sentence passed and my courage low
When to Dungannon I was forced to go.

As I was passing by my father's door,
My brother William stood at the door;
My aged father stood at the door;
And my tender mother her hair she tore.

As I was walking up Wexford Street
My own first cousin I chanced to meet:
My own first cousin did me betray,
And for one bare guinea swore my life away.

My sister Mary heard the express,
She ran upstairs in her mourning-dress—
Five hundred guineas I will lay down,
To see my brother through Wexford town.

---

[1] A name given to the Wexford rebels of 1798 who were peasants and wore closely-cropped hair.

[2] Lord Cornwallis, viceroy and commander-in-chief in Ireland in 1798.

As I was walking up Wexford Hill,
Who could blame me to cry my fill?
I looked behind and I looked before,
But my tender mother I shall ne'er see more.

As I was mounted on the platform high,
My aged father was standing by;
My aged father did me deny,
And the name he gave me was the Croppy Boy.

It was in Dungannon this young man died,
And in Dungannon his body lies;
And you good Christians that do pass by
Just drop a tear for the Croppy Boy.

18TH CENTURY.

Thomas Moore (1779-1852)

Oh, Breathe Not His Name[1]

Oh, breathe not his name! let it sleep in the shade,
Where cold and unhonored his relics are laid;
Sad, silent, and dark be the tears that we shed,
As the night-dew that falls on the grass o'er his head.

But the night-dew that falls, though in silence it weeps,
Shall brighten with verdure the grave where he sleeps;
And the tear that we shed, though in secret it rolls,
Shall long keep his memory green in our souls.

---

[1] This lyric has generally been supposed to refer to Robert Emmet, the rebel leader of 1803.

The Harp That Once Through Tara's Halls

The harp that once through Tara's halls
    The soul of music shed,
Now hangs as mute on Tara's walls
    As if that soul were fled.
So sleeps the pride of former days,
    So glory's thrill is o'er,
And hearts that once beat high for praise
    Now feel that pulse no more!

No more to chiefs and ladies bright
    The harp of Tara swells;
The chord alone that breaks at night
    Its tale of ruin tells.
Thus Freedom now so seldom wakes,
    The only throb she gives
Is when some heart indignant breaks,
    To show that still she lives.

The Meeting of the Waters

There is not in the wide world a valley so sweet
As that vale in whose bosom the bright waters meet;
O, the last rays of feeling and life must depart,
Ere the bloom of that valley shall fade from my heart.

Yet it was not that nature had shed o'er the scene
Her purest of crystal and brightest of green;
'Twas not her soft magic of streamlet or hill,
O, no, it was something more exquisite still.

'Twas that friends, the belov'd of my bosom, were near,
Who made every dear scene of enchantment more dear,
And who felt how the best charms of nature improve,
When we see them reflected from looks that we love.

Sweet vale of Avoca! how calm could I rest
In thy bosom of shade, with the friends I love best,
Where the storms that we feel in this cold world should cease,
And our hearts, like thy waters, be mingled in peace.

The Song of Fionnuala[1]

Silent, O Moyle, be the roar of thy water,
   Break not, ye breezes, your chain of repose,
While, murmuring mournfully, Lir's lonely daughter
   Tells to the night star her tale of woes.
When shall the swan, her death note singing,
   Sleep, with wings in darkness furl'd?
When will heaven, its sweet bell ringing,
   Call my spirit from this stormy world?

---

[1] Fionnuala, the daughter of Lir, was changed into a swan along with her three brothers by a cruel step-mother. They had the power of speech and the gift of singing and for three hundred years they sang to the men of Ireland. When finally they were captured by the king of Connaught they were changed back into three old men and an old woman and died. "The Tragedy of the Children of Lir," with two other stories, is preserved in a manuscript of the 15th or 16th century entitled The Three Sorrowful Stories.

Sadly, O Moyle, to thy winter wave weeping,
    Fate bids me languish long ages away;
Yet still in her darkness doth Erin lie sleeping,
    Still doth the pure light its dawning delay.
When will that daystar, mildly springing,
    Warm our isle with peace and love?
When will heaven, its sweet bell ringing,
    Call my spirit to the fields above?

She Is Far from the Land[1]

She is far from the land where her young hero sleeps,
    And lovers are round her, sighing:
But coldly she turns from their gaze, and weeps,
    For her heart in his grave is lying.

She sings the wild song of her dear native plains,
    Every note which he loved awaking;—
Ah! little they think who delight in her strains,
    How the heart of the Minstrel is breaking.

He had lived for his love, for his country he died,
    They were all that to life had entwined him;
Nor soon shall the tears of his country be dried,
    Nor long will his love stay behind him.

Oh! make her a grave where the sun-beams rest,
    When they promise a glorious morrow;
They'll shine o'er her sleep, like a smile from the West,
    From her own loved island of sorrow.

---

[1] This lyric commemorates the love of Sarah Curran for Robert Emmet.

The Minstrel Boy

The Minstrel Boy to the war is gone,
    In the ranks of death you'll find him;
His father's sword he has girded on,
    And his wild harp slung behind him.—
"Land of song!" said the warrior-bard,
    "Though all the world betray thee,
One sword, at least, thy rights shall guard,
    One faithful harp shall praise thee!"

The Minstrel fell!—but the foeman's chain
    Could not bring his proud soul under;
The harp he loved ne'er spoke again,
    For he tore its cords asunder;
And said, "No chains shall sully thee,
    Thou soul of love and bravery!
Thy songs were made for the brave and free,
    They shall never sound in slavery!"

Dear Harp of my Country

Dear Harp of my Country! in darkness I found thee,
    The cold chain of silence had hung o'er thee long,
When proudly, my own Island Harp, I unbound thee,
    And gave all thy chords to light, freedom, and song!
The warm lay of love and the light note of gladness
    Have waken'd thy fondest, thy liveliest thrill;
But, so oft hast thou echoed the deep sigh of sadness,
    That ev'n in thy mirth it will steal from thee still.

Dear Harp of my Country! farewell to thy numbers,
   This sweet wreath of song is the last we shall twine!
Go, sleep with sunshine of Fame on thy slumbers,
   Till touch'd by some hand less unworthy than mine;
If the pulse of the patriot, soldier, or lover,
   Have throbb'd at our lay, 'tis thy glory alone;
I was *but* as the wind, passing heedlessly over,
   And all the wild sweetness I wak'd was thy own.

The Hedge School

BY William Carleton (1794-1869)

THE VILLAGE of Findramore was situated at the foot of a long
green hill, the outline of which formed a low arch, as it rose to
the eye against the horizon. This hill was studded with clumps
of beeches, and sometimes enclosed as a meadow. In the
month of July, when the grass on it was long, many an hour
have I spent in solitary enjoyment, watching the wavy motion
produced upon its pliant surface by the sunny winds, or the
flight of the cloud-shadows, like gigantic phantoms, as they
swept rapidly over it, whilst the murmur of the rocking trees,
and the glancing of their bright leaves in the sun, produced a
heartfelt pleasure, the very memory of which rises in my imagination like some fading recollection of a brighter world.

At the foot of this hill ran a clear, deep-banked river,
bounded on one side by a slip of rich, level meadow, and on the
other by a kind of common for the village geese, whose white
feathers, during the summer season lay scattered over its green
surface. It was also the play-ground for the boys of the village
school; for there ran that part of the river which, with very cor-
rect judgment, the urchins had selected as their bathing-place.
A little slope, or watering-ground in the bank, brought them to

the edge of the stream, where the bottom fell away into the
fearful depths of the whirlpool, under the hanging oak on the
other bank. Well do I remember the first time I ventured to
swim across it, and even yet do I see, in imagination, the two
bunches of water flaggons on which the inexperienced swim-
mers trusted themselves in the water.

About two hundred yards above this, the boreen,[1] which led
from the village to the main road, crossed the river, by one of
those old narrow bridges whose arches rise like round ditches
across the road—an almost impassable barrier to horse and car.
On passing the bridge, in a northern direction, you found a
range of low thatched houses on each side of the road: and if
one o'clock, the hour of dinner, drew near, you might observe
columns of blue smoke curling up from a row of chimneys,
some made of wicker creels plastered over with a rich coat of
mud; some, of old, narrow, bottomless tubs; and others, with a
greater appearance of taste, ornamented with thick, circular
ropes of straw, sewed together like bees' skeps,[2] with the peel of
a brier; and many having nothing but the open vent above. But
the smoke by no means escaped by its legitimate aperture, for
you might observe little clouds of it bursting out of the doors
and windows; the panes of the latter being mostly stopped at
other times with old hats and rags, were now left entirely open
for the purpose of giving it a free escape.

Before the doors, on right and left, was a series of dung-
hills, each with its concomitant sink of green, rotten water; and
if it happened that a stout-looking woman, with watery
eyes, and a yellow cap hung loosely upon her matted locks,
came, with a chubby urchin on one arm, and a pot of dirty
water in her hand, its unceremonious ejection in the aforesaid
sink would be apt to send you up the village with your finger and
thumb (for what purpose you would yourself perfectly understand) closely, but not knowingly, applied to your nostrils.
But, independently of this, you would be apt to have other

---

[1] A little road.
[2] Hives.

reasons for giving your horse, whose heels are by this time surrounded by a dozen of barking curs, and the same number of shouting urchins, a pretty sharp touch of the spurs, as well as for complaining bitterly of the odour of the atmosphere. It is no landscape without figures; and you might notice, if you are, as I suppose you to be, a man of observation, in every sink as you pass along, a "slip-of-a-pig," stretched in the middle of the mud, the very *beau ideal* of luxury, giving occasionally a long, luxuriant grunt, highly expressive of his enjoyment; or, perhaps, an old farrower, lying in indolent repose, with half a dozen young ones jostling each other for their draught, and punching her belly with their little snouts, reckless of the fumes they are creating; whilst the loud crow of the cock, as he confidently flaps his wings on his own dunghill, gives the warning note for the hour of dinner.

As you advance, you will also perceive several faces thrust out of the doors, and rather than miss a sight of you, a grotesque visage peeping by a short cut through the paneless windows—or a tattered female flying to snatch up her urchin that has been tumbling itself, heels up, in the dust of the road, lest "the gintleman's horse might ride over it"; and if you happen to look behind, you may observe a shaggy-headed youth in tattered frize,[1] with one hand thrust indolently in his breast, standing at the door in conversation with the inmates, a broad grin of sarcastic ridicule on his face, in the act of breaking a joke or two upon yourself, or your horse; or, perhaps, your jaw may be saluted with a lump of clay, just hard enough not to fall asunder as it flies, cast by some ragged gorsoon[2] from behind a hedge, who squats himself in a ridge of corn to avoid detection.

Seated upon a hob at the door, you may observe a toil-worn man, without coat or waistcoat; his red, muscular, sunburnt shoulder peering through the remnant of a shirt, mending his

---

[1] I.e. frieze—a kind of coarse woollen cloth, with a nap, usually on one side only. NED

[2] A boy; from the French garçon.

shoes with a piece of twisted flax, called a *lingel*, or, perhaps, sewing two footless stockings (or *martyeens*) to his coat, as a substitute for sleeves.

In the gardens, which are usually fringed with nettles, you will see a solitary labourer, working with that carelessness and apathy that characterise an Irishman when he labours for *himself*—leaning upon his spade to look after you, and glad of any excuse to be idle.

The houses, however, are not all such as I have described—far from it. You see here and there, between the more humble cabins, a stout, comfortable-looking farm-house, with ornamental thatching and well-glazed windows; adjoining to which is a hay-yard, with five or six large stacks of corn, well-trimmed and roped, and a fine, yellow, weather-beaten old hay-rick, half cut—not taking into account twelve or thirteen circular strata of stones, that mark out the foundations on which others has been raised. Neither is the rich smell of oaten or wheaten bread, which the good wife is baking on the griddle, unpleasant to your nostrils; nor would the bubbling of a large pot, in which you might see, should you chance to enter, a prodigious square of fat, yellow, and almost transparent bacon tumbling about, to be an unpleasant object; truly, as it hangs over a large fire, with well-swept hearthstone, it is in good keeping with the white settle and chairs, and the dresser with noggins, wooden trenchers, and pewter dishes, perfectly clean, and as well polished as a French courtier.

As you leave the village, you have, to the left, a view of the hill which I have already described, and to the right a level expanse of fertile country, bounded by a good view of respectable mountains, peering decently into the sky; and in a line that forms an acute angle from the point of the road where you ride, is a delightful valley, in the bottom of which shines a pretty lake; and a little beyond, on the slope of a green hill, rises a splendid house, surrounded by a park, well-wooded and stocked with deer. You have now topped the little hill above the village, and a straight line of level road, a mile long, goes forward to a country town, which lies immediately behind that white church with its spire cutting into the sky, before you. You descend on the other side, and, having advanced a few perches, look to the left, where you see a long, thatched chapel, only distinguished from a dwelling-house by its want of chimneys, and a small stone cross that stands on the top of the eastern gable; behind it is a graveyard; and beside it a snug public-house, well white-washed; then, to the right, you observe a door apparently in the side of a clay bank, which rises considerably above the pavement of the road. What! you ask yourself, can this be a human habitation?—but ere you have time to answer the question, a confused buzz of voices from within reaches your ear, and the appearance of a little "gorsoon," with a red, close-cropped head and Milesian[1] face, having in his hand a short, white stick, or the thigh-bone of a horse, which you at once recognise as "the pass" of a village school, gives you the full information. He has an ink-horn, covered with leather, dangling at the button-hole (for he has long since played away the buttons) of his frize jacket—his mouth is circumscribed with a streak of ink—his pen is stuck knowingly behind his ear—his shins are dotted over with fire-blisters, black, red, and blue—on each heel a kibe—his "leather crackers," *videlicet*—breeches, shrunk up upon him, and only reaching as far down as the caps of his knees. Having spied you, he places his hand over his brows, to throw back the dazzling light of the sun, and peers at you from under it, till he breaks out into a laugh, exclaiming, half to himself, half to you,

"You a gintleman!—no, nor one of your breed never was, you procthorin' thief, you!"

You are now immediately opposite the door of the seminary, when half a dozen of those seated next it notice you.

"Oh, sir, here's a gintleman on a horse!—masther, sir, here's a gintleman on a horse, wid boots and spurs on him, that's looking in at us."

---

[1] The Irish were fond of describing themselves as Milesians, i.e., the descendants of the sons of Mil, legendary conquerors of Ireland.

"Silence!" exclaims the master; "back from the door; boys rehearse; every one of you rehearse, I say, you Bœotians, till the gintleman goes past!"

"I want to go out, if you plase, sir."

"No, you don't, Phelim."

"I do, indeed, sir."

"What!—is it afther conthradictin' me you'd be? Don't you see the porter's' out, and you can't go."

"Well, 'tis Mat Meehan has it, sir: and he's out this half-hour, sir; I can't stay in, sir—iphfff—iphffff!"

"You want to be idling your time looking at the gintleman, Phelim."

"No, indeed, sir—iphffff!"

"Phelim, I know you of ould—go to your sate. I tell you, Phelim, you were born for the encouragement of the hemp manufacture, and you'll die promoting it."

In the meantime, the master puts his head out of the door, his body stooped to a "half bend"—a phrase, and the exact curve which it forms, I leave for the present to your own sagacity—and surveys you until you pass. That is an Irish hedge-school, and the personage who follows you with his eye, a hedge-schoolmaster.

James Clarence Mangan (1803-1849)

A Vision of Connaught in the Thirteenth Century

I walked entranced
  Through a land of Morn;
The sun, with wondrous excess of light,
  Shone down and glanced
  Over seas of corn

And lustrous gardens aleft and right
    Even in the clime
        Of resplendent Spain,
Beams no such sun upon such a land;
    But it was the time,
      'Twas in the reign,
Of Cáhal Mór of the Wine-red Hand.[1]

    Anon stood nigh
      By my side a man
Of princely aspect and port sublime.
    Him queried I—
        "O, my Lord and Khan,
What clime is this, and what golden time?"
    When he—"The clime
      Is a clime to praise,
The clime is Erin's, the green and bland;
    And it is the time,
      These be the days,
Of Cáhal Mór of the Wine-red Hand!"

    Then saw I thrones,
      And circling fires,
And a Dome rose near me, as by a spell,
    Whence flowed the tones
      Of silver lyres,

---

[1] Cathal of the Red Hand was the illegitimate son of Turlogh Mor O'Conor, King of Connaught. When Turlogh's wife by magic turned one of Cathal's hands red, he fled and took service as a farm hand. When Turlogh died Cathal made his identity known by exhibiting his red hand and established a claim to the throne. There were other claimants however and Cathal did not become king until 1202. In 1224 he abdicated in favor of his son and with his bard, Morrogh O'Daly, entered the abbey of Grey Friars of Knockmoy which he had founded in 1189. He instituted tithes, built magnificent abbeys and was apparently a favorite with the poets and chroniclers.

And many voices in wreathèd swell;
 And their thrilling chime
  Fell on mine ears
As the heavenly hymn of an angel-band—
 "It is now the time,
  These be the years,
Of Cáhal Mór of the Wine-red Hand!"

 I sought the hall,
  And, behold!—a change
From light to darkness, from joy to woe!
 King, nobles, all,
  Looked aghast and strange;
The minstrel-group sat in dumbest show!
 Had some great crime
  Wrought this dread amaze,
This terror? None seemed to understand
 'Twas then the time
  We were in the days,
Of Cáhal Mór of the Wine-red Hand.

 I again walked forth;
  But lo! the sky
Showed fleckt with blood, and an alien sun
 Glared from the north,
  And there stood on high,
Amid his shorn beams, a skeleton!
 It was by the stream
  Of the castled Maine,
One Autumn eve, in the Teuton's land,
 That I dreamed this dream
  Of the time and reign
Of Cáhal Mór of the Wine-red Hand!

To My Native Land

AWAKE! arise! shake off thy dreams!
    Thou art not what thou wert of yore:
Of all those rich, those dazzling beams,
    That once illum'd thine aspect o'er
Show me a solitary one
Whose glory is not quenched and gone.

The harp remaineth where it fell,
    With mouldering frame and broken chord;
Around the song there hangs no spell—
    No laurel wreath entwines the sword;
And startlingly the footstep falls
Along thy dim and dreary halls.

When other men in future years,
    In wonder ask, how this could be?
Then answer only by thy tears,
    That ruin fell on thine and thee;
Because thyself wouldst have it so—
Because thou welcomedst the blow!

To stamp dishonour on thy brow
    Was not within the power of earth;
And art thou agonised, when now
    The hour that lost thee all thy worth
And turned thee to the thing thou art,
Rushes upon thy bleeding heart?

Weep, weep, degraded one—the deed,
  The desperate deed was all thine own:
Thou madest more than maniac speed
  To hurl thine honours from their throne.
Thine honours fell, and when they fell
The nations rang thy funeral knell.

Well may thy sons be seared in soul,
  Their groans be deep by night and day;
Till day and night forget to roll,
  Their noblest hopes shall morn decay—
Their freshest flowers shall die by blight—
Their brightest sun shall set at night.

The stranger, as he treads thy sod,
  And views thy universal wreck,
May execrate the foot that trod
  Triumphant on a prostrate neck;
But what is that to thee? Thy woes
May hope in vain for pause or close.

Awake! arise! shake off thy dreams!
  'Tis idle all to talk of power,
And fame and glory—these are themes
  Befitting ill so dark an hour;
'Till miracles be wrought for thee,
Nor fame nor glory shalt thou see.

Thou art forsaken by the earth,
  Which makes a byword of thy name;
Nations, and thrones, and powers whose birth
  As yet is not, shall rise to fame,
Shall flourish and may fail—but thou
Shalt linger as thou lingerest now.

And till all earthly power shall wane,
    And Time's grey pillar, groaning, fall;
Thus shall it be, and still in vain
    Thou shalt essay to burst the thrall
Which binds, in fetters forged by fate,
The wreck and ruin of what once was great.

The Hunt

BY Charles Lever (1806-1872)

. . . Mr. Blake and his family, though estranged from my
uncle for several years past, had been always most kind and
good-natured to me; and although I could not, with propriety,
have cultivated any close intimacy with them, I had every
reason to suppose that they entertained towards me nothing
but sentiments of good-will. The head of the family was a
Galway squire of the oldest and most genuine stock, a great
sportsman, a negligent farmer, and most careless father; he
looked upon a fox as an infinitely more precious part of the
creation than a French governess, and thought that riding well
with hounds was a far better gift than all the learning of a
Porson.[1] His daughters were after his own heart,—the best-
tempered, least-educated, most high-spirited, gay, dashing,
ugly girls in the county, ready to ride over a four-foot paling
without a saddle, and to dance the "Wind that shakes the
barley" for four consecutive hours, against all the officers that
their hard fate, and the Horse Guards, ever condemned to
Galway.

The mamma was only remarkable for her liking for whist,
and her invariable good fortune thereat,—a circumstance the
world were agreed in ascribing less to the blind goddess than
her own natural endowments.

---

[1] Richard Porson (1759-1808), an English scholar.

Lastly, the heir of the house was a stripling of about my own age, whose accomplishments were limited to selling spavined and broken-winded horses to the infantry officers, playing a safe game at billiards, and acting as jackal-general to his sisters at balls, providing them with a sufficiency of partners, and making a strong fight for a place at the supper-table for his mother. These fraternal and filial traits, more honored at home than abroad, had made Mr. Matthew Blake a rather well-known individual in the neighborhood where he lived.

Though Mr. Blake's property was ample, and strange to say for his county, unencumbered, the whole air and appearance of his house and grounds betrayed anything rather than a sufficiency of means. The gate lodge was a miserable mud-hovel with a thatched and falling roof; the gate itself, a wooden contrivance, one half of which was boarded and the other railed; the avenue was covered with weeds, and deep with ruts; and the clumps of young plantation, which had been planted and fenced with care, were now open to the cattle, and either totally uprooted or denuded of their bark and dying. The lawn, a handsome one of some forty acres, had been devoted to an exercise-ground for training horses, and was cut up by their feet beyond all semblance of its original destination; and the house itself, a large and venerable structure of above a century old, displayed every variety of contrivance, as well as the usual one of glass, to exclude the weather. The hall-door hung by a single hinge, and required three persons each morning and evening to open and shut it; the remainder of the day it lay pensively open; the steps which led to it were broken and falling; and the whole aspect of things without was ruinous in the extreme. Within, matters were somewhat better, for though the furniture was old, and none of it clean, yet an appearance of comfort was evident; and the large grate, blazing with its pile of red-hot turf, the deep-cushioned chairs, the old black mahogany dinner-table, and the soft carpet, albeit deep with dust, were not to be despised on a winter's evening, after a hard day's run with the "Blazers." Here it was, however, that Mr. Philip Blake had dispensed his hospitalities for above fifty years, and his father before him; and here, with a retinue of servants as *gauches* and ill-ordered as all about them, was he accustomed to invite all that the county possessed of rank and wealth, among which the officers quartered in his neighborhood were never neglected, the Miss Blakes having as decided a taste for the army as any young ladies of the west of Ireland; and while the Galway squire, with his cords and tops, was detailing the latest news from Ballinasloe in one corner, the dandy from St. James's Street might be seen displaying more arts of seductive flattery in another than his most accurate *insouciance* would permit him to practise in the elegant salons of London or Paris, and the same man who would have "cut his brother," for a solecism of dress or equipage, in Bond Street, was now to be seen quietly domesticated, eating family dinners, rolling silk for the young ladies, going down the middle in a country dance, and even descending to the indignity of long whist at "tenpenny" points, with only the miserable consolation that the company were not honest.

It was upon a clear frosty morning, when a bright blue sky and a sharp but bracing air seem to exercise upon the feelings a sense no less pleasurable than the balmiest breeze and warmest sun of summer, that I whipped my leader short round, and entered the precincts of "Gurt-na-Morra." As I proceeded along the avenue, I was struck by the slight traces of repairs here and there evident,—a gate or two that formerly had been parallel to the horizon had been raised to the perpendicular; some ineffectual efforts at paint were also perceptible upon the palings; and, in short, everything seemed to have undergone a kind of attempt at improvement.

When I reached the door, instead of being surrounded, as of old, by a tribe of menials frieze-coated, bare-headed, and bare-legged, my presence was announced by a tremendous ringing of bells from the hands of an old functionary in a very formidable livery, who peeped at me through the hall-window, and whom, with the greatest difficulty, I recognized as my quondam acquaintance, the butler. His wig alone would have graced a king's counsel; and the high collar of his coat, and the stiff pillory of his cravat denoted an eternal adieu to so humble a vocation as drawing a cork. Before I had time for any conjecture as to the altered circumstances about, the activity of my friend at the bell had surrounded me with "four others worse than himself," at least they were exactly similarly attired; and probably from the novelty of their costume, and the restraints of so unusual a thing as dress, were as perfectly unable to assist themselves or others as the Court of Aldermen would be were they to rig out in plate armor of the fourteenth century. How much longer I might have gone on conjecturing the reasons for the masquerade around, I cannot say; but my servant, an Irish disciple of my uncle's, whispered in my ear, "It's a redbreeches day, Master Charles,—they'll have the hoith of company in the house." From the phrase, it needed little explanation to inform me that it was one of those occasions on which Mr. Blake attired all the hangers-on of his house in livery, and that great preparations were in progress for a more than usually splendid reception.

In the next moment I was ushered into the breakfast-room, where a party of above a dozen persons were most gayly enjoying all the good cheer for which the house had a well-deserved repute. After the usual shaking of hands and hearty greetings were over, I was introduced in all form to Sir George Dashwood, a tall and singularly handsome man of about fifty, with an undress military frock and ribbon. His reception of me was somewhat strange; for as they mentioned my relationship to Godfrey O'Malley, he smiled slightly, and whispered something to Mr. Blake, who replied, "Oh, no, no; not the least. A mere boy; and besides—" What he added I lost, for at that moment Nora Blake was presenting me to Miss Dashwood.

If the sweetest blue eyes that every beamed beneath a forehead of snowy whiteness, over which dark brown and waving hair fell less in curls than masses of locky richness, could only have known what wild work they were making of my poor heart, Miss Dashwood, I trust, would have looked at her teacup or her muffin rather than at me, as she actually did on that fatal morning. If I were to judge from her costume, she had

only just arrived, and the morning air had left upon her cheek
a bloom that contributed greatly to the effect of her lovely
countenance. Although very young, her form had all the round-
ness of womanhood; while her gay and sprightly manner indicated all the *sans géne* which only very young girls possess, and
which, when tempered with perfect good taste, and accompanied by beauty and no small share of talent, forms an irresistible power of attraction.

Beside her sat a tall, handsome man of about five-and-thirty
or perhaps forty years of age, with a most soldierly air, who as I
was presented to him scarcely turned his head, and gave me
a half-nod of very unequivocal coldness. There are moments
in life in which the heart is, as it were, laid bare to any chance
or casual impression with a wondrous sensibility of pleasure
or its opposite. This to me was one of those; and as I turned
from the lovely girl, who had received me with a marked
courtesy, to the cold air and repelling *hauteur* of the dark-
browed captain, the blood rushed throbbing to my forehead;
and as I walked to my place at the table, I eagerly sought his
eye, to return him a look of defiance and disdain, proud and
contemptuous as his own. Captain Hammersley, however,
never took further notice of me, but continued to recount, for
the amusement of those about him, several excellent stories of
his military career, which, I confess, were heard with every test
of delight by all save me. One thing galled me particularly,—
and how easy is it, when you have begun by disliking a person,
to supply food for your antipathy,—all his allusions to his
military life were coupled with half-hinted and ill-concealed
sneers at civilians of every kind, as though every man not a
soldier were absolutely unfit for common intercourse with the
world, still more for any favorable reception in ladies' society.

The young ladies of the family were a well-chosen auditory,
for their admiration of the army extended from the Life Guards
to the Veteran Battalion, the Sappers and Miners included; and
as Miss Dashwood was the daughter of a soldier, she of course
coincided in many of, if not all, his opinions. I turned towards
my neighbor, a Clare gentleman, and tried to engage him in

conversation, but he was breathlessly attending to the captain. On my left sat Matthew Blake, whose eyes were firmly riveted upon the same person, and who heard his marvels with an interest scarcely inferior to that of his sisters. Annoyed and in ill-temper, I ate my breakfast in silence, and resolved that the first moment I could obtain a hearing from Mr. Blake I would open my negotiation, and take my leave at once of Gurt-na-Morra.

We all assembled in a large room, called by courtesy the library, when breakfast was over; and then it was that Mr. Blake, taking me aside, whispered, "Charley, it's right I should inform you that Sir George Dashwood there is the Commander of the Forces, and is come down here at this moment to—" What for, or how it should concern me, I was not to learn; for at that critical instant my informant's attention was called off by Captain Hammersley asking if the hounds were to hunt that day.

"My friend Charley here is the best authority upon that matter," said Mr. Blake, turning towards me.

"They are to try the Priest's meadows," said I, with an air of some importance; "but if your guests desire a day's sport, I'll send word over to Brackely to bring the dogs over here, and we are sure to find a fox in your cover."

"Oh, then, by all means," said the captain, turning towards Mr. Blake, and addressing himself to him,—"by all means; and Miss Dashwood, I'm sure, would like to see the hounds throw off."

Whatever chagrin the first part of his speech caused me, the latter set my heart a-throbbing; and I hastened from the room to despatch a messenger to the huntsman to come over to Gurt-na-Morra, and also another to O'Malley Castle to bring my best horse and my riding equipments as quickly as possible.

"Matthew, who is this captain?" said I, as young Blake met me in the hall.

"Oh, he is the aide-de-camp of General Dashwood. A nice fellow, is n't he?"

"I don't know what you may think," said I, "but I take

him for the most impertinent, impudent, supercilious—"

The rest of my civil speech was cut short by the appearance of the very individual in question, who, with his hands in his pockets and a cigar in his mouth, sauntered forth down the steps, taking no more notice of Matthew Blake and myself than the two fox-terriers that followed at his heels.

However anxious I might be to open negotiations on the subject of my mission, for the present the thing was impossible; for I found that Sir George Dashwood was closeted closely with Mr. Blake, and resolved to wait till evening, when chance might afford me the opportunity I desired.

As the ladies had retired to dress for the hunt, and as I felt no peculiar desire to ally myself with the unsocial captain, I accompanied Matthew to the stable to look after the cattle, and make preparations for the coming sport.

"There's Captain Hammersley's mare," said Matthew, as he pointed out a highly bred but powerful English hunter. "She came last night; for as he expected some sport, he sent his horses from Dublin on purpose. The others will be here to-day."

"What is his regiment?" said I, with an appearance of carelessness, but in reality feeling curious to know if the captain was a cavalry or infantry officer.

"The —th Light Dragoons."

"You never saw him ride?" said I.

"Never; but his groom there says he leads the way in his own country."

"And where may that be?"

"In Leicestershire, no less," said Matthew.

"Does he know Galway?"

"Never was in it before. It's only this minute he asked Moses Daly if the ox-fences were high here."

"Ox-fences! Then he does not know what a wall is?"

"Devil a bit; but we'll teach him."

"That we will," said I, with as bitter a resolution to impart the instruction as ever schoolmaster did to whip Latin grammar into one of the great unbreeched.

"But I had better send the horses down to the Mill," said Matthew; "we'll draw that cover first."

So saying, he turned towards the stable, while I sauntered alone towards the road by which I expected the huntsman. I had not walked half a mile before I heard the yelping of the dogs, and a little farther on I saw old Brackely coming along at a brisk trot, cutting the hounds on each side, and calling after the stragglers.

"Did you see my horse on the road, Brackely?" said I.

"I did, Misther Charles; and troth, I'm sorry to see him. Sure yerself knows better than to take out the Badger, the best steeple-chaser in Ireland, in such a country as this,— nothing but awkward stone-fences, and not a foot of sure ground in the whole of it."

"I know it well, Brackely; but I have my reasons for it."

"Well, may be you have; what cover will your honor try first?"

"They talk of the Mill," said I; "but I'd much rather try Morran-a-Gowl."

"Morran-a-Gowl! Do you want to break your neck entirely?"

"No, Brackely, not mine."

"Whose, then, alannah?"

"An English captain's, the devil fly away with him! He's come down here to-day, and from all I can see is a most impudent fellow; so, Brackely—"

"I understand. Well, leave it to me; and though I don't like the only deer-park wall on the hill, we'll try it this morning with the blessing. I'll take him down by Woodford, over the Devil's Mouth,—it's eighteen foot wide this minute with the late rains,—into the four callows; then over the stone walls, down to Dangan; then take a short cast up the hill, blow him a bit, and give him the park wall at the top. You must come in then fresh, and give him the whole run home over Sleibhmich. The Badger knows it all, and takes the road always in a fly,—a mighty distressing thing for the horse that follows, more particularly if he does not understand a stony country. Well, if he lives through this, give him the sunk fence and the stone wall

at Mr. Blake's clover-field, for the hounds will run into the
fox about there; and though we never ride that leap since Mr.
Malone broke his neck at it, last October, yet upon an occasion
like this, and for the honor of Galway—"

"To be sure, Brackely; and here's a guinea for you, and now
trot on towards the house. They must not see us together, or
they might suspect something. But, Brackely," said I, calling
out after him, "if he rides at all fair, what's to be done?"

"Troth, then, myself does n't know. There is nothing so bad
west of Athlone. Have ye a great spite again him?"

"I have," said I, fiercely.

"Could ye coax a fight out of him?"

"That's true," said I; "and now ride on as fast as you can."

Brackely's last words imparted a lightness to my heart and
my step, and I strode along a very different man from what I
had left the house half an hour previously.

Although we had not the advantages of a southerly wind
and cloudy sky, the day towards noon became strongly over-
cast, and promised to afford us good scenting weather; and as
we assembled at the meet, mutual congratulations were ex-
changed upon the improved appearance of the day. Young
Blake had provided Miss Dashwood with a quiet and well-
trained horse, and his sisters were all mounted as usual upon
their own animals, giving to our turnout quite a gay and lively
aspect. I myself came to cover upon a hackney, having sent
Badger with a groom, and longed ardently for the moment
when, casting the skin of my great-coat and overalls, I should
appear before the world in my well-appointed "cords and tops."
Captain Hammersley had not as yet made his appearance, and
many conjectures were afloat as to whether "he might have
missed the road, or changed his mind," or "forgot all about it,"
as Miss Dashwood hinted.

"Who, pray, pitched upon this cover?" said Caroline Blake,
as she looked with a practised eye over the country on either
side.

"There is no chance of a fox late in the day at the Mill,"
said the huntsman, inventing a lie for the occasion.

"Then of course you never intend us to see much of the sport; for after you break cover, you are entirely lost to us."

"I thought you always followed the hounds," said Miss Dashwood, timidly.

"Oh, to be sure we do, in any common country, but here it is out of the question; the fences are too large for any one, and if I am not mistaken, these gentlemen will not ride far over this. There, look yonder, where the river is rushing down the hill: that stream, widening as it advances, crosses the cover nearly midway,—well, they must clear that; and then you may see these walls of large loose stones nearly five feet in height. This is the usual course the fox takes, unless he heads towards the hills and goes towards Dangan, and then there's an end of it; for the deer-park wall is usually a pull up to every one except perhaps, to our friend Charley yonder, who has tried his fortune against drowning more than once there."

"Look, here he comes," said Matthew Blake, "and looking splendidly too,—a little too much in flesh perhaps, if anything."

"Captain Hammersley!" said the four Miss Blakes, in a breath. "Where is he?"

"No; it's the Badger I'm speaking of," said Matthew, laughing, and pointing with his finger towards a corner of the field where my servant was leisurely throwing down a wall about two feet high to let him pass.

"Oh, how handsome! What a charger for a dragoon!" said Miss Dashwood.

Any other mode of praising my steed would have been much more acceptable. The word "dragoon" was a thorn in my tenderest part that rankled and lacerated at every stir. In a moment I was in the saddle, and scarcely seated when at once all the *mauvais honte* of boyhood left me, and I felt every inch a man. I often look back to that moment of my life, and comparing it with similar ones, cannot help acknowledging how purely is the self-possession which so often wins success the result of some slight and trivial association. My confidence in my horsemanship suggested moral courage of a very different kind; and I felt that Charles O'Malley curveting upon a thorough-bred, and the same man ambling upon a shelty, were two and very dissimilar individuals.

"No chance of the captain," said Matthew, who had returned from a reconnaissance upon the road; "and after all it's a pity, for the day is getting quite favorable."

While the young ladies formed pickets to look out for the gallant militaire, I seized the opportunity of prosecuting my acquaintance with Miss Dashwood, and even in the few and passing observations that fell from her, learned how very different an order of being she was from all I had hitherto seen of country belles. A mixture of courtesy with naïveté; a wish to please, with a certain feminine gentleness, that always flatters a man, and still more a boy that fain would be one,—gained momentarily more and more upon me, and put me also on my mettle to prove to my fair companion that I was not altogether a mere uncultivated and unthinking creature, like the remainder of those about me.

"Here he is at last," said Helen Blake, as she cantered across a field waving her handkerchief as a signal to the captain, who was now seen approaching at a brisk trot.

As he came along, a small fence intervened; he pressed his horse a little, and as he kissed hands to the fair Helen, cleared it in a bound, and was in an instant in the midst of us.

"He sits his horse like a man, Misther Charles," said the old huntsman; "troth, we must give him the worst bit of it."

Captain Hammersley was, despite all the critical acumen with which I canvassed him, the very beau-ideal of a gentleman rider; indeed, although a very heavy man, his powerful English thorough-bred, showing not less bone than blood, took away all semblance of overweight; his saddle was well fitting and well placed, as also was his large and broad-reined snaffle; his own costume of black coat, leathers, and tops was in perfect keeping, and even to his heavy-handled hunting-whip I could find nothing to cavil at. As he rode up he paid his respects to the ladies in his usual free and easy manner, expressed some surprise, but no regret, at hearing that he was late, and never deigning any notice of Matthew or myself, took his place beside

Miss Dashwood, with whom he conversed in a low undertone.

"There they go!" said Matthew, as five or six dogs, with their heads up, ran yelping along a furrow, then stopped, howled again, and once more set off together. In an instant all was commotion in the little valley below us. The huntsman, with his hand to his mouth, was calling off the stragglers, and the whipper-in followed up the leading dogs with the rest of the pack. "They've found! They're away!" said Matthew; and as he spoke a yell burst from the valley, and in an instant the whole pack were off at full speed. Rather more intent that moment upon showing off my horsemanship than anything else, I dashed spurs into Badger's sides, and turned him towards a rasping ditch before me; over we went, hurling down behind us a rotten bank of clay and small stones, showing how little safety there had been in topping instead of clearing it at a bound. Before I was well-seated again the captain was beside me. "Now for it, then," said I; and away we went. What might be the nature of his feelings I cannot pretend to state, but my own were a strange *mélange* of wild, boyish enthusiasm, revenge, and recklessness. For my own neck I cared little,— nothing; and as I led the way by half a length, I muttered to myself, "Let him follow me fairly this day, and I ask no more."

The dogs had got somewhat the start of us; and as they were in full cry, and going fast, we were a little behind. A thought therefore struck me that, by appearing to take a short cut upon the hounds, I should come down upon the river where its breadth was greatest, and thus, at one *coup*, might try my friend's mettle and his horse's performance at the same time. On we went, our speed increasing, till the roar of the river we were now approaching was plainly audible. I looked half around, and now perceived the captain was standing in his stirrups, as if to obtain a view of what was before him; otherwise his countenance was calm and unmoved, and not a muscle betrayed that he was not cantering on a parade. I fixed myself firmly in my seat, shook my horse a little together, and with a shout whose import every Galway hunter well knows rushed him at the river. I saw the water dashing among the large stones; I heard it splash; I felt a bound like the *ricochet* of a shot, and we were over, but so narrowly that the bank had yielded beneath his hind legs, and it needed a bold effort of the noble animal to regain his footing. Scarcely was he once more firm, when Hammersley flew by me, taking the lead, and sitting quietly in his saddle, as if racing. I know of little in my after-life like the agony of that moment; for although I was far, very far, from wishing real ill to him, yet I would gladly have broken my leg or my arm if he could not have been able to follow me. And now, there he was, actually a length and a half in advance! and worse than all, Miss Dashwood must have witnessed the whole, and doubtless his leap over the river was better and bolder than mine. One consolation yet remained, and while I whispered it to myself I felt comforted again. "His is an English mare. They understand these leaps; but what can he make of a Galway wall?" The question was soon to be solved. Before us, about three fields, were the hounds still in full cry; a large stone-wall lay between, and to it we both directed our course together. "Ha!" thought I, "he is floored at last," as I perceived that the captain held his course rather more in hand, and suffered me to lead. "Now, then, for it!" So saying, I rode at the largest part I could find, well knowing that Badger's powers were here in their element. One spring, one plunge, and away we were galloping along at the other side. Not so the captain; his horse had refused the fence, and he was now taking a circuit of the field for another trial of it.

"Pounded, by Jove!" said I, as I turned round in my saddle to observe him. Once more she came at it, and once more balked, rearing up, at the same time, almost so as to fall backward.

My triumph was complete; and I again was about to follow the hounds, when, throwing a look back, I saw Hammersley clearing the wall in a most splendid manner, and taking a stretch of at least thirteen feet beyond it. Once more he was on my flanks, and the contest renewed. Whatever might be the sentiments of the riders (mine I confess to), between the horses it now became a tremendous struggle. The English mare, though evidently superior in stride and strength, was slightly overweighted, and had not, besides, that cat-like activity an Irish horse possesses; so that the advantages and disadvantages on either side were about equalized. For about half an hour now the pace was awful. We rode side by side, taking our leaps at exactly the same instant, and not four feet apart. The hounds were still considerably in advance, and were heading towards the Shannon, when suddenly the fox doubled, took the hillside, and made for Dangan. "Now, then, comes the trial of strength," I said, half aloud, as I threw my eye up a steep and rugged mountain, covered with wild furze and tall heath, around the crest of which ran, in a zigzag direction, a broken and dilapidated wall, once the enclosure of a deer park. This wall, which varied from four to six feet in height, was of solid masonry, and would, in the most favorable ground, have been a bold leap. Here, at the summit of a mountain, with not a yard of footing, it was absolutely desperation.

By the time that we reached the foot of the hill, the fox, followed closely by the hounds, had passed through a breach in the wall; while Matthew Blake, with the huntsmen and whipper-in, was riding along in search of a gap to lead the horses through. Before I put spurs to Badger to face the hill, I turned one look towards Hammersley. There was a slight curl, half-smile, half-sneer, upon his lip that actually maddened me, and had a precipice yawned beneath my feet, I should have dashed at it after that. The ascent was so steep that I was obliged to take the hill in a slanting direction; and even thus, the loose footing rendered it dangerous in the extreme.

At length I reached the crest, where the wall, more than five feet in height, stood frowning above and seeming to defy me. I turned my horse full round, so that his very chest almost touched the stones, and with a bold cut of the whip and a loud halloo, the gallant animal rose, as if rearing, pawed for an instant to regain his balance, and then, with a frightful struggle, fell backwards, and rolled from top to bottom of the hill, carrying me along with him; the last object that crossed my sight, as I lay bruised and motionless, being the captain as he took the wall in a flying leap, and disappeared at the other side. After a few scrambling efforts to rise, Badger regained his legs and stood beside me; but such was the shock and concussion of my fall that all the objects around seemed wavering and floating before me, while showers of bright sparks fell in myriads before my eyes. I tried to rise, but fell back helpless. Cold perspiration broke over my forehead, and I fainted. From that moment I can remember nothing, till I felt myself galloping along at full speed upon a level table-land, with the hounds about three fields in advance, Hammersley riding foremost, and taking all his leaps coolly as ever. As I swayed to either side upon my saddle, from weakness, I was lost to all thought or recollection, save a flickering memory of some plan of vengeance, which still urged me forward. The chase had now lasted above an hour, and both hounds and horses began to feel the pace at which they were going. As for me, I rode mechanically; I neither knew nor cared for the dangers before me. My eye rested on but one object; my whole being was concentrated upon one vague and undefined sense of revenge. At this instant the huntsman came alongside of me.

"Are you hurted, Misther Charles? Did you fall? Your cheek is all blood, and your coat is torn in two; and, Mother o' God! his boot is ground to powder; he does not hear me! Oh, pull up! pull up, for the love of the Virgin! There's the clover-field and the sunk fence before you, and you'll be killed on the spot!"

"Where?" cried I, with the cry of a madman. "Where's the clover-field; where's the sunk fence? Ha! I see it; I see it now."

So saying, I dashed the rowels into my horse's flanks, and in an instant was beyond the reach of the poor fellow's remonstrances. Another moment I was beside the captain. He turned round as I came up; the same smile was upon his mouth; I could have struck him. About three hundred yards before us lay the sunk fence; its breadth was about twenty feet, and a wall of close brickwork formed its face. Over this the hounds were now clambering; some succeeded in crossing, but by far the greater number fell back, howling, into the ditch.

I turned towards Hammersley. He was standing high in his stirrups, and as he looked towards the yawning fence, down which the dogs were tumbling in masses, I thought (perhaps it was but a thought) that his cheek was paler. I looked again; he was pulling at his horse. Ha! it was true then; he would not face it. I turned round in my saddle, looked him full in the face, and as I pointed with my whip to the leap, called out in a voice hoarse with passion, "Come on!" I saw no more. All objects were lost to me from that moment. When next my senses cleared, I was standing amidst the dogs, where they had just killed. Badger stood blown and trembling beside me, his head drooping and his flanks gored with spur-marks. I looked about, but all consciousness of the past had fled; the concussion of my fall had shaken my intellect, and I was like one but half-awake. One glimpse, short and fleeting, of what was taking place shot through my brain, as old Brackely whispered to me, "By my soul, ye did for the captain there." I turned a vague look upon him, and my eyes fell upon the figure of a man that lay stretched and bleeding upon a door before me. His pale face was crossed with a purple stream of blood that trickled from a wound beside his eyebrow; his arms lay motionless and heavily at either side. I knew him not. A loud report of a pistol aroused me from my stupor; I looked back. I saw a crowd that broke suddenly asunder and fled right and left. I heard a heavy crash upon the ground; I pointed with my finger, for I could not utter a word.

"It is the English mare, yer honor; she was a beauty this morning, but she's broke her shoulder-bone and both her legs, and it was best to put her out of pain."

Samuel Ferguson (1810-1886)

The Abdication of Fergus Mac Roy

Once, ere God was crucified,
I was King o'er Uladh[1] wide:
King, by law of choice and birth,
O'er the fairest realm of Earth.

I was head of Rury's race;
Emain was my dwelling-place;
Right and Might were mine; nor less
Stature, strength, and comeliness.

Neither lacked I love's delight,
Nor the glorious meeds of fight.
All on earth was mine could bring
Life's enjoyment to a king.

Much I loved the jocund chase,
Much the horse and chariot race:
Much I loved the deep carouse,
Quaffing in the Red Branch House.

But, in Council call'd to meet,
Loved I not the judgment seat;
And the suitors' questions hard
Won but scantly my regard.

Rather would I, all alone,
Care and state behind me thrown,
Walk the dew through showery gleams
O'er the meads, or by the streams,

---

[1] Ulster.

Chanting, as the thoughts might rise,
Unimagined melodies;
While with sweetly-pungent smart
Secret happy tears would start.

Such was I, when in the dance,
Nessa did bestow a glance,
And my soul that moment took
Captive in a single look.

I am but an empty shade,
Far from life and passion laid;
Yet does sweet remembrance thrill
All my shadowy being still.

Nessa had been Fathna's spouse,
Fathna of the Royal house,
And a beauteous boy had borne **him**:
Fourteen summers did adorn him:

Yea; thou deem'st it marvellous,
That a widow's glance should thus
Turn from lure of maidens' eyes
All a young king's fantasies.

Yet if thou hadst known but **half**
Of the joyance of her laugh,
Of the measures of her walk,
Of the music of her talk,

Of the witch'ry of her wit,
Even when smarting under it,—
Half the sense, the charm, the grace,
Thou hadst worshipp'd in my place.

And, besides, the thoughts I wove
Into songs of war and love,
She alone of all the rest
Felt them with a perfect zest.

"Lady, in thy smiles to live
Tell me but the boon to give,
Yea, I lay in gift complete
Crown and sceptre at thy feet."

"Not so great the boon I crave:
Hear the wish my soul would have";
And she glanc'd a loving eye
On the stripling standing by:—

"Conor is of age to learn;
Wisdom is a king's concern;
Conor is of royal race,
Yet may sit in Fathna's place.

"Therefore, king, if thou wouldst prove
That I have indeed thy love,
On the judgment seat permit
Conor by thy side to sit,

"That by use the youth may draw
Needful knowledge of the Law."
I with answer was not slow,
"Be thou mine, and be it so."

I am but a shape of air,
Far removed from love's repair;
Yet, were mine a living frame
Once again I'd say the same.

Thus, a prosperous wooing sped,
Took I Nessa to my bed,
While in council and debate
Conor daily by me sate.

Modest was his mien in sooth,
Beautiful the studious youth,
Questioning with earnest gaze
All the reasons and the ways

In the which, and why because,
Kings administer the Laws.
Silent so with looks intent
Sat he till the year was spent.

But the strifes the suitors raised
Bred me daily more distaste,
Every faculty and passion
Sunk in sweet intoxication.

Till upon a day in court
Rose a plea of weightier sort:
Tangled as a briary thicket
Were the rights and wrongs intricate

Which the litigants disputed,
Challenged, mooted, and confuted;
Till, when all the plea was ended,
Naught at all I comprehended.

Scorning an affected show
Of the thing I did not know,
Yet my own defect to hide,
I said "Boy-judge, thou decide."

Conor, with unalter'd mien,
In a clear sweet voice serene,
Took in hand the tangled skein
And began to make it plain.

As a sheep-dog sorts his cattle,
As a king arrays his battle,
So, the facts on either side
He did marshal and divide.

Every branching side-dispute
Traced he downward to the root
Of the strife's main stem, and there
Laid the ground of difference bare.

Then to scope ot either cause
Set the compass of the laws,
This adopting, that rejecting,—
Reasons to a head collecting,—

As a charging cohort goes
Through and over scatter'd foes,
So, from point to point, he brought
Onward still the weight of thought

Through all error and confusion,
Till he set the clear conclusion
Standing like a king alone,
All things adverse overthrown,

And gave judgment clear and sound:—
Praises fill'd the hall around;
Yea, the man that lost the cause
Hardly could withhold applause.

By the wondering crowd surrounded
I sat shamefaced and confounded.
Envious ire awhile oppress'd me
Till the nobler thought possess'd me;

And I rose, and on my feet
Standing by the judgment-seat,
Took the circlet from my head,
Laid it on the bench, and said,

"Men of Uladh, I resign
That which is not rightly mine,
That a worthier than I
May your judge's place supply.

"Lo, it is no easy thing
For a man to be a king
Judging well, as should behove
One who claims a people's love.

"Uladh's judgment-seat to fill
I have neither wit nor will.
One is here may justly claim
Both the function and the name.

"Conor is of royal blood;
Fair he is; I trust him good;
Wise he is we all may say
Who have heard his words to-day.

"Take him therefore in my room,
Letting me the place assume—
Office but with life to end—
Of his councillor and friend."

So young Conor gain'd the crown;
So I laid the kingship down;
Laying with it as it went
All I knew of discontent.

The Burial of King Cormac[1]

"Crom Cruach[2] and his sub-gods twelve,"
Said Cormac, "are but carven treene;
The axe that made them, haft or helve,
Had worthier of our worship been.

"But He who made the tree to grow,
And hid in earth the iron-stone,
And made the man with mind to know
The axe's use, is God alone."

Anon to priests of Crom was brought—
Where, girded in their service dread,
They minister'd on red Moy Slaught—
Word of the words King Cormac said.

They loosed their curse against the king;
They cursed him in his flesh and bones;
And daily in their mystic ring
They turn'd the maledictive stones,

Till, where at meat the monarch sate,
Amid the revel and the wine,
He choked upon the food he ate,
At Sletty, southward of the Boyne.

---

[1] Cormac Mac Art, who reigned in the third century A.D. is one of the most famous of Irish kings.

[2] God of Winter and patron of agriculture, who stood on Mag Slecht (Moy Slaught) in County Cavan and was worshiped at Samhain, the Celtic New Year.

High vaunted then the priestly throng,
  And far and wide they noised abroad
With trump and loud liturgic song
  The praise of their avenging God.

But ere the voice was wholly spent
  That priest and prince should still obey,
To awed attendants o'er him bent
  Great Cormac gather'd breath to say,—

"Spread not the beds of Brugh for me
  When restless death-bed's use is done:
But bury me at Rossnaree
  And face me to the rising sun.

"For all the kings who lie in Brugh
  Put trust in gods of wood and stone;
And 'twas at Ross that first I knew
  One, Unseen, who is God alone.

"His glory lightens from the east;
  His message soon shall reach our shore;
And idol-god, and cursing priest
  Shall plague us from Moy Slaught no more."

Dead Cormac on his bier they laid:—
  "He reign'd a king for forty years,
And shame it were," his captains said,
  "He lay not with his royal peers.

"His grandsire, Hundred-Battle,[1] sleeps
  Serene in Brugh: and, all around,
Dead kings in stone sepulchral keeps
  Protect the sacred burial ground.

[1] Cormac was the grandson of Conn of the Hundred Battles, also called Conn the Hundred Fighter.

"What though a dying man should rave
   Of changes o'er the eastern sea?
In Brugh of Boyne shall be his grave,
   And not in noteless Rossnaree."

Then northward forth they bore the bier,
   And down from Sletty side they drew,
With horsemen and with charioteer,
   To cross the fords of Boyne to Brugh.

There came a breath of finer air
   That touch'd the Boyne with ruffling wings,
It stirr'd him in his sedgy lair
   And in his mossy moorland springs.

And as the burial train came down
   With dirge and savage dolorous shows,
Across their pathway, broad and brown
   The deep, full-hearted river rose;

From bank to bank through all his fords,
   'Neath blackening squalls he swell'd and boil'd;
And thrice the wondering gentile lords
   Essay'd to cross, and thrice recoil'd.

Then forth stepp'd grey-hair'd warriors four:
   They said, "Through angrier floods than these,
On link'd shields once our king we bore
   From Dread-Spear and the hosts of Deece.

"And long as loyal will holds good,
   And limbs respond with helpful thews,
Nor flood, nor fiend within the flood,
   Shall bar him of his burial dues."

With slanted necks they stoop'd to lift;
  They heaved him up to neck and chin;
And, pair and pair, with footsteps swift,
  Lock'd arm and shoulder, bore him in.

'Twas brave to see them leave the shore;
  To mark the deep'ning surges rise,
And fall subdued in foam before
  The tension of their striding thighs.

'Twas brave, when now a spear-cast out,
  Breast-high the battling surges ran;
For weight was great, and limbs were stout,
  And loyal man put trust in man.

But ere they reach'd the middle deep,
  Nor steadying weight of clay they bore,
Nor strain of sinewy limbs could keep
  Their feet beneath the swerving four.

And now they slide, and now they swim,
  And now, amid the blackening squall,
Grey locks afloat, with clutching grim,
  They plunge around the floating pall.

While, as a youth with practised spear
  Through justling crowds bears off the ring,
Boyne from their shoulders caught the bier
  And proudly bore away the king.

At morning, on the grassy marge
  Of Rossnaree, the corpse was found,
And shepherds at their early charge
  Entomb'd it in the peaceful ground.

A tranquil spot: a hopeful sound
   Comes from the ever youthful stream,
And still on daisied mead and mound
   The dawn delays with tenderer beam.

Round Cormac Spring renews her buds:
   In march perpetual by his side,
Down come the earth-fresh April floods,
   And up the sea-fresh salmon glide:

And life and time rejoicing run
   From age to age their wonted way;
But still he waits the risen Sun,
   For still 'tis only dawning Day.

The Wedding of the Clans

BY Aubrey De Vere (1814-1902)

I go to knit two clans together;
   Our clan and this clan unseen of yore:—
Our clan fears nought! but I go, whither?
   This day I go from my mother's door.

Thou redbreast sing'st the old song over,
   Though many a time thou hast sung it before;
They never sent thee to some strange new lover:—
   I sing a new song by my mother's door.

I stepp'd from my little room down by the ladder,
   The ladder that never so shook before;
I was sad last night; to-day I am sadder,
   Because I go from my mother's door.

The last snow melts upon bush and bramble;
   The gold bars shine on the forest's floor;
Shake not, thou leaf! it is I must tremble
   Because I go from my mother's door.

From a Spanish sailor a dagger I bought me;
   I trail'd a rose-three our grey bawn[1] o'er;
The creed and my letters our bard taught me;
   My days were sweet by my mother's door.

My little white goat that with raised feet huggest
   The oak stock, thy horns in the ivies frore,[2]
Could I wrestle like thee—how the wreaths thou tuggest!—
   I never would move from my mother's door.

Oh weep no longer, my nurse and mother!
   My foster-sister, weep not so sore!
You cannot come with me, Ir, my brother—
   Along I go from my mother's door.

Farewell, my wolf-hound, that slew Mac Owing
   As he caught me and far through the thickets bore:
My heifer, Alb, in the green vale lowing,
   My cygnet's nest upon Lorna's shore!

He has kill'd ten chiefs, this chief that plights me;
   His hand is like that of the giant Balor:[3]
But I fear his kiss; and his beard affrights me,
   And the great stone dragon above his door.

---

[1] Meadow.
[2] Frozen, frosty. NED
[3] A Celtic god famous because of his poisonous eye.

Had I daughters nine with me they should tarry;
 They should sing old songs; they should dance at my door;
They should grind at the quern;—no need to marry;
 Oh when will this marriage-day be o'er?

Had I buried, like Moirin, three mates already
 I might say, "Three husbands! then why not four?"
But my hand is cold and my foot unsteady
 Because I never was married before!

The Fairies

by William Allingham (1824-1889)

Up the airy mountain,
 Down the rushy glen,
We daren't go a-hunting
 For fear of little men;
Wee folk, good folk,
 Trooping all together;
Green jacket, red cap,
 And white owl's feather!

Down along the rocky shore
 Some make their home—
They live on crispy pancakes
 Of yellow tide-foam;
Some in the reeds
 Of the black mountain lake.
With frogs for their watch-dogs,
 All night awake.

High on the hill-top
    The old King sits;
He is now so old and gray
    He's nigh lost his wits.
With a bridge of white mist,
    Columbkill he crosses,
On his stately journeys
    From Slieveleague to Rosses;
Or going up with music
    On cold starry nights,
To sup with the Queen
    Of the gay Northern Lights.

They stole little Bridget
    For seven years long;
When she came down again
    Her friends were all gone.
They took her lightly back,
    Between the night and morrow,
They thought that she was fast asleep
    But she was dead with sorrow.
They have kept her ever since
    Deep within the lake,
On a bed of flag-leaves,
    Watching till she wakes.

By the craggy hill-side,
    Through the mosses bare,
They have planted thorn-trees
    For pleasure here and there.
Is any man so daring
    As dig one up in spite,
He shall find their sharpest thorns
    In his bed at night.

Up the airy mountain,
    Down the rushy glen,
We daren't go a-hunting
    For fear of little men;
Wee folk, good folk,
    Trooping all together;
Green jacket, red cap,
    And white owl's feather!

Aghadoe

BY John Todhunter (1839-1916)

There's a glade in Aghadoe, Aghadoe, Aghadoe,
There's a green and silent glade in Aghadoe,
    Where we met, my Love and I, Love's fair planet in the sky,
O'er that sweet and silent glade in Aghadoe.

There's a glen in Aghadoe, Aghadoe, Aghadoe,
There's a deep and secret glen in Aghadoe,
    Where I hid him from the eyes of the red-coats and their
        spies
That year the trouble came to Aghadoe!

Oh! my curse on one black heart in Aghadoe, Aghadoe,
On Shaun Dhuv, my mother's son in Aghadoe,
    When your throat fries in hell's drouth salt the flame be in
        your mouth,
For the treachery you did in Aghadoe!

For they tracked me to that glen in Aghadoe, Aghadoe,
When the price was on his head in Aghadoe;
    O'er the mountain through the wood, as I stole to him with
        food,
When in hiding lone he lay in Aghadoe.

But they never took him living in Aghadoe, Aghadoe;
With the bullets in his heart in Aghadoe,
　　There he lay, the head—my breast keeps the warmth where
　　　　once 'twould rest—
Gone, to win the traitor's gold from Aghadoe!

I walked to Mallow Town from Aghadoe, Aghadoe,
Brought his head from the gaol's gate to Aghadoe,
　　Then I covered him with fern, and I piled on him the
　　　　cairn,
Like an Irish king he sleeps in Aghadoe.

Oh, to creep into that cairn in Aghadoe, Aghadoe!
There to rest upon his breast in Aghadoe!
　　Sure your dog for you could die with no truer heart than I—
Your own love cold on your cairn in Aghadoe.

The Peeler[1] and the Goat

　　A Bansha Peeler wint won night
　　On duty and pathrollin' O,
　　An' met a goat upon the road,
　　And tuck her for a sthroller O.
　　Wud bay'net fixed he sallied forth,
　　An' caught her by the wizzen O,
　　An' then he swore a mighty oath,
　　"I'll send you off to prison O."

---

[1] Policeman, so called after Sir Robert Peel, Chief Secretary for
Ireland, later Prime Minister of England, who was largely responsible
for establishing an Irish police force.

"Oh, mercy, sir!" the goat replied,
"Pray let me tell my story O!
I am no rogue, no Ribbonman,[1]
No Croppy, Whig, or Tory O;
I'm guilty not of any crime
Of petty or high thraison O,
I'm sadly wanted at this time,
For this is the milkin' saison O."

"It is in vain for to complain
Or give your tongue such bridle O,
You're absent from your dwellin' place,
Disorderly and idle O.
Your hoary locks will not prevail,
Nor your sublime oration O,
You'll be thransported by Peel's Act,
Upon my information O."

"No penal law did I transgress
By deeds or combination O.
I have no certain place to rest,
No home or habitation O.
But Bansha is my dwelling-place,
Where I was bred and born O.
Descended from an honest race,
That's all the trade I've learned O."

"I will chastise your insolince
And violent behaviour O;
Well bound to Cashel you'll be sint,
Where you will gain no favor O.
The magistrates will all consint
To sign your condemnation O;
From there to Cork you will be sint
For speedy thransportation O."

---

[1] Member of a secret revolutionary society opposing the English
government and Orangeism.

"This parish an' this neighborhood
Are paiceable and thranquil O;
There's no disturbance here, thank God!
An' long may it continue so,
I don't regard your oath a pin,
Or sign for my committal O,
My jury will be gintlemin
And grant me my acquittal O."

"The consequince be what it will,
A peeler's power I'll let you know,
I'll handcuff you, at all events,
And march you off to Bridewell O.
An' sure, you rogue, you can't deny
Before the judge or jury O,
Intimidation with your horns,
An' threatening me with fury O."

"I make no doubt but you are dhrunk,
Wud whiskey, rum, or brandy O,
Or you wouldn't have such gallant spunk
To be so bould or manly O.
You readily would let me pass
If I had money handy O,
To thrate you to a potheen[1] glass—
Oh! it's then I'd be the dandy O."

---

[1] Illegally distilled whiskey.

The Nameless Dun[1]

BY William Larminie (1850-1900)

WHO were the builders? Question not the silence
That settles on the lake for evermore,
Save when the sea-bird screams and to the islands
The echo answers from the steep-cliffed shore.

O half-remaining ruin, in the lore
Of human life a gap shall all deplore
Beholding thee; since thou art like the dead
Found slain, no token to reveal the why,
The name, the story. Some one murder'd
We know, we guess; and gazing upon thee,
And, filled by thy long silence of reply,
We guess some garnered sheaf of tragedy;—
Of tribe or nation slain so utterly
That even their ghosts are dead, and on their grave
Springeth no bloom of legend in its wildness;
And age by age weak washing round the islands
No faintest sign of story lisps the wave.

---

[1] A *dun* was a fortified dwelling.

The Murrigan

BY George Moore (1852-1933)

One day in my walks in the high wood I spied a man standing on a boulder in the midst of the river, seemingly undecided whether he should jump to the next one; and knowing the pool to be deep between the boulders I tried to dissuade him. There's no chance of drowning, he cried to me, but if I miss my step I'll be up to my belt. I called out that to cross the river he would be trespassing on private rights, but he did not heed my warning. He jumped again; and, laying hold of a protruding root, began to climb the bank, telling me as he made his way up that the master (the gentleman in whose house I was staying) would have nothing to say against the gathering of a few ferns along the river's bank. A fern-gatherer, I said, and followed him asking questions, not so much for the answers he gave as for the pleasure it was to listen to his low, musical voice, a tenor voice, in keeping, it seemed to me, with his pale, almost affectionate eyes, shining like jewels in a pointed oval face; a young man who had just passed out of his first youth, an Irish peasant, but far from the typical, I said, when I left him to his search and continued my walk through the beech wood, not able to forget his spare chestnut beard, his moustache and his comely, well-knit figure. These, so it seemed to me, I had seen before and many times, but where I had seen them I could not remember, and it was not till after long soul searching it occurred to me that I had seen him in pictures. Yes, I murmured to myself, he is the Jesus that has come down to us from the fifteenth century, imagined first perhaps by Fra Angelico, and repeated ever since by many thousands of painters, inclining more and more to the feminine and epicene type, becoming a woman in Holman Hunt's picture, The Light of the World, Miss Christina Rossetti, with a blonde beard and moustache. But, I continued, my fern-gatherer does not reproduce the fond

emptiness of Jesus's face; he is with it all a man; and there can
be no doubt that I am doing him an injustice by associating
him with Holman Hunt's version of Christina Rossetti in a
blonde beard. My fern-gatherer is a man and altogether himself
in the life he has chosen for himself. A romantic figure, I added,
one which does honour to the town of Westport.

He had already captured my imagination by dinnertime,
and at the first pause in the conversation, when the girls'
narratives of the day's doings had ceased, I related our meeting,
and learnt that legends had already begun to collect about him.
His name? I asked anxiously, feeling I should be disappointed
if his name were among those that one wearies of in Ireland
—Higgins, Walsh, O'Connor, Murphy. That it might not be
Murphy I prayed inly. Alec Trusselby! It would be strange,
indeed, I exclaimed, if legends had not begun to collect about
a name like that, and begged that all that was known about him
should be told to me at once. Everybody was willing to tell,
and the biographical scraps uttered from different ends and
sides of the dinner-table were in keeping with his name.

I learnt from one member of the family that Alec had been
to America and had suffered from sunstroke, from another that
he lived in the woods all the summer-time, bringing back beech
and oak ferns to Westport and getting for them a fair share of
money; and from another that his voice and manner were so
winning that it was difficult not to be his customer, and as every
customer became a patron, Alec had no cause for complaint.
Even if he had he is not the kind of man that would complain,
a girl suddenly interjected, and turning to her I asked: How is
that? She replied that he was a very shy man who would remain
silent for long intervals to break into speech suddenly like a
bird. This seemed to me a good description, but I had not seen
enough of Alec at that time to be able to vouch for its accuracy.
A girl told me the report was that Alec had built himself a
summer dwelling in a great tree, and I answered that what she
said did not surprise me. Lying in his bed under the boughs, I
said, he caught his style from the moody blackbird who fills
the wood at dawn with his exalted lay; more likely still from the

meditative thrush. But how does Alec live through the winter?
I asked, and it was delightful to hear that in the winter he related stories about the firesides in the cottages, and that no one
refused Alec bed and board if he could help it; Alec's company
was sought for by everybody; and a suspicion was abroad that
to treat him ill was to bring ill luck upon oneself. Gathering
ferns in the summer and telling stories in the winter, I repeated,
becoming possessed in a moment of an absorbing interest in
Alec Trusselby. Is he an Irish speaker? I asked, and heard that
he was one of the best in the county of Mayo. But, a girl
cried across the table, mind, if he suspects you of laughing at
him he will run away at once, and don't tell him you're a
Protestant, he might refuse to go into the woods with you.
With a heretic? I added.

A custard pudding interrupted the conversation about Alec,
but as soon as everybody had been helped it returned to him,
and I learnt that the gentle winning personality that had awakened fellow-feeling in me was only one side of Alec Trusselby;
there was another, and one well known to the Westport police
—staunch friends of his, always ready to take his part when
Alec's less reputable associates mocked him in the street after
drinking his money away in the public-house, their joke being
to try to grab the Murrigan, not an easy thing to do, for it
never left his hand, and where the Murrigan was concerned
Alec was resolute and strong. The Murrigan? I interjected.
He calls his blackthorn the Murrigan, one of the girls answered,
but we don't know what the word means, whether it's an Irish
word or a word invented by himself. I wonder if the police
could tell me? I said. Now why should the police be bothering
their heads with what Alec means when he calls his stick the
Murrigan? my friend, the girl's father, blurted out; and he
laughed the short, quick, intelligent laugh whereby I remember
him. Haven't they enough to do to keep him out of jail? And he
told a story how, returning home late one night, he had come
upon Trusselby and the police—the sergeant and the constable engaged in trying to persuade Alec to return to his
lodging You see, Alec, you're free to follow them if you like:

the constable has let go your arm, the sergeant was saying. But
if you take my advice you'll be taking yourself and the Murrigan
home like the quiet, good man that you are, the divil a better.
If they insult you again we'll let yourself and the Murrigan at
them, but this time we'll be asking you to let them pass on, for
to break their skulls with the Murrigan would be conferring
too much honour upon them. You see, said mine host, we have
all a kindly feeling for Trusselby, myself as well as the police;
to keep him out of jail takes us all our time, and we haven't that
much over to be ferreting out the meaning of all the talk that
goes on between himself and his stick as he walks the roads.
But he's not half-witted? I asked, looking round the dinner-
table, preferring a general to an individual opinion, and the
company was agreed that Alec could not be held to be a loon.
And his stories? I asked; but none at the table had felt sufficient curiosity to ask him to tell one. I'd give a great deal, I
said, to hear Trusselby tell a story, and was warned not to offer
him a big sum of money, but to wait an occasion to win his
confidence. If you offer him a sovereign to tell you a story
you'll frighten him; he'll begin to suspect some evil and you'll
get nothing out of him. But I may not meet Trusselby again,
and if I did, to the end of my visit is not a long time to win his
confidence—I shall be leaving in a few days. You can stay as
long as you like, my host and hostess interjected, we would like
to see you friends with Trusselby before you leave.

   The next day one of the girls rushed into the room in which
I was writing: Trusselby is coming down the hill, she said, and
I bolted out after him. You sell ferns, don't you? I asked; he
answered that he did, and I asked him to get me some. He said
he would and passed on, and I returned to the house disappointed. But luck was with me, and two evenings later, returning
home after dining with a friend, I met Trusselby at the river-
side, whirling the Murrigan and apparently in a convivial mood.
Well, Alec, I said, have you come upon the royal or the hart's
tongue in your walks? You're the gentleman I met the other
day up at the old mill, aren't you? he asked. I answered that I
was, and we walked on together, myself making conversation,

afraid every moment that Trusselby would say: I must be
wishing you goodnight, sir, or I'll be locked out. But it was
unlikely that Trusselby had a latchkey, it was more probable
that he contemplated spending the night out, which would
be no great hardship, for the night was warm and still, and
were it not that a bench is a hard bed, the most home-loving
and respectable man in Westport might have liked to have
lain out of doors, sooner or later to be hushed to sleep by the
almost inaudible sound of water rippling past and the soft
cawing of sleepy rooks. A night it was that would keep anybody
out of his bed till midnight at least, except, perhaps, a dry old
curmudgeon. A breathless night, full of stars, and perchance
stories, I said to myself, and then aloud to Alec: Yes, we met
up at the old mill, but you didn't find the ferns you were looking for? Is it the royal you're after? Alec asked, and I answered
that that was what I had in mind, and having listened to
Trusselby for some time on the rarity of the fern, I broke in
with the remark that I'd never seen a finer blackthorn than the
one he was carrying.

He had come upon it in a brake, he said, in a thicket that
often served him as a bedroom in a summer's night when his
quest for ferns had led him far from Westport. And it was one
morning at sunrise that I spied her; she was no thicker that
morning than one of my fingers, and I said to myself: In about
three years' time that stem will be the finest in Ireland if the
top be cut at once so that it may be throwing out little knots
and spikes. The knots begin almost at the top, sir, and at every
knot there is three spikes. You would be lost if you started
counting them, just as you might be if you were to start on the
stars in the skies. It was the blessing of God that I saw the
Murrigan that morning, for a year later it would have been too
late to cut the top. I was only in time, and there it stayed for
its three years sprouting, with three spikes coming out on
every knot. You can see them, sir, all the way up. Faith, there
isn't half-an-inch of the stick without its three spikes. But if
somebody had gone into the brake and seen the stick before
you? I asked. I had to risk that, sir, for it takes three full years

for the stick to furnish, and often I didn't like going to the brake for fear a person might spy me and be wondering what I was after and perhaps be coming in behind me and find out the stick; but sure I had the luck all the time and nobody came. In three years to the day, your honour, I was down in the dingle cutting my stick, my heart filled with joy so furnished was it. Mind you, sir, the seasoning of a blackthorn isn't understood by every man, for when you've cut your stick you must season it, and the place I was living in then had a fine old chimney with a flue inside of it on which you could rest a stick, and there the Murrigan rested seasoning. After six good months I took it down and gave it a rub with an oil rag, and I'll tell you, mister, it was good for sore eyes to see the way it was coming up. Take a look at it yourself now and tell me, is there a bit of Spanish mahogany in the country is its equal for colour. To this I agreed, and asked: Is that the reason you call it the Murrigan? Well, it isn't, your honour. Do you see, Murrigan means "great queen" in the Irish, and my stick here is the queen of the fair this many a day. The stick knows it too, for if I'm not at the fair off goes the Murrigan without me; I look round in the morning, but not a stick can I see, so I say: The Murrigan's gone, and she'll be breaking the head of some poor chap out of sheer light-heartedness and divilment. That's the way it does be, sir, for after she's gone there's somebody has a cracked head somewhere. No one knows who breaks it, barring the Murrigan, and she tells nobody, but just flies back unbeknownst to anybody, and finds her old place in the corner just as any creature would. And there I find her, waiting for me. Have a look at the Murrigan, sir, for you'll never see another like her. She's as beautifully ornamented as the Brooch of Tara itself. So the Murrigan goes to the fair by herself? She does so, your honour, and she flies round the heads of the people, urging them on the way the old Murrigan used to do when Brian Boru was in it, waking up the spirit of fight in them. The Murrigan whirls like an eagle over the heads of the people, prodding them here and poking them there, and putting them at each other. When I'm there, and the Murrigan with me, I feel my hand rise up and my head is that elated I don't know whether it's me or the Murrigan is doing the deeds, and I don't know if the stars that are in my head aren't thicker and twice as thick than they are in the sky. All I can see is the Murrigan about me and she whirling like a bird, but never leaving me five fingers; a faithful thing the Murrigan, bless her soul, and she saved my life many a time, good luck to her!

Trusselby kissed his blackthorn and we leaned our backs against the parapet of the bridge, looking up into the sky, the town asleep, nothing to be heard about us but the ripple of the river. Trusselby seemed to have forgotten me, and I wondered of what he could be thinking, of some battle long ago, I thought, in which doubtless the Murrigan played a great part, and seeing a smile playing over his bland, almost holy face, I said: There used to be great fighting long ago? It was about fighting I was thinking, your honour, a great fair at Castlebar, when there were more two-year-olds than three-year-olds about. To check the story that was on his lips with a question would have been fatal, so I held my peace, hoping to learn whether the fair was lacking in three-year-old bullocks or three-year-old colts and fillies. He began again after a pause. You see, sir, in the old times when your ancestors were in it, God rest their souls, in the days of your grandfather, there was an O'Brien sold a heifer to a Fitzgerald for a two-year-old, but the heifer itself was a three-year-old; and the next fair day there was a fight between Fitzgerald and O'Brien; and at the next fair the Fitzgerald brothers and the O'Brien brothers were fighting; and the fair day after that the cousins were in the fight, and after the cousins the friends came in on one side and the other, until it was a dangerous thing to hold any fair in the country at all, so great was the fighting; after whacking with all the blackthorns in the country over all the skulls in the country for more than fifty years the war finished, and it was only at the heel of the hunt that I strolled in one fair day to Castlebar. There was a man there, and somebody made a cake of his skull with a tap of a stick. Nobody knew who did it. He said it was the policeman, and he took out a summons against the policeman. Well, I was a witness in the case, your honour, and I couldn't see an innocent man condemned even if he was a peeler itself. When I came before the magistrate he asked if I was standing by at the time. I was, your Worship, says I; and he says: Was it the policeman broke the man's head? and I said: It was not, your Worship; the policeman didn't hit the man that tap. A tap, you call it, said the man, Michael Joyce was his name, and he lifted up the bloody bandage that was upon his brow. 'Tis more than a tap, your Worship, says I, it's a clout; but tap or clout, it wasn't the policeman gave it to him. You're on your oath, Alec Trusselby, he said. And I said: Before God! and I gave a swear that it wasn't the policeman. Now what do you think but the magistrate was looking into Joyce's face, and he saw three little weeney holes around his eye, and he took notice of them three little holes, and when I picked up the Murrigan and was going out of the box he said: Let me have a look at your stick, Trusselby, so I gave it to him, and he said: Wasn't it you gave the man the tap? And I said: It was so, your Worship. Tell me, says he, why did you strike that blow? So I ups and I told him the story of the two-year-olds and the three-year-olds. Which was he, said the magistrate, was he a two-year-old or a three-year-old? Your Worship, says I, he was like myself, he was a two-year-old. And why did you assault and batter the man? Well, you see, your Worship, says I, there was only a few of us in that fair. We was outnumbered altogether by the three-year-olds, and Joyce yonder was saying he'd like well to see the man who'd tread on the tail of his coat, and seeing that there would be a fight in which we might be worsted I just gave him a tap to make him quiet like, and to keep him out of harm's way.

So that's the story of the Murrigan? It is, your honour, I've told you the whole of it. A wonderful stick she is; look at her; every knob with three little spikes like the blessed shamrock that St. Patrick picked so that he would be able to explain the Holy Trinity to the pagans. A beautiful stick, I said, and a very interesting story. You know many stories, Alec, and can tell them better than any man now living. It's puffing me up with pride and goster you'd be, your honour, and after reminding him that he had promised to bring me some beech and oak ferns we parted, myself regretting that my shyness had prevented me from asking Alec to tell me a story.

The Rising of the Moon

BY Lady Gregory (1852-1932)

PERSONS: Sergeant.
                Policeman X.
                Policeman B.
                A Ragged Man.

Scene: Side of a quay in a seaport town. Some posts and chains. A large barrel. Enter three policemen. Moonlight.

(Sergeant, who is older than the others, crosses the stage to right and looks down steps. The others put down a paste-pot and unroll a bundle of placards.)

POLICEMAN B: I think this would be a good place to put up a notice. *(He points to barrel.)*

POLICEMAN X: Better ask him. *(Calls to Sergt.)* Will this be a good place for a placard?
(No answer.)

POLICEMAN B: Will we put up a notice here on the barrel?
(No answer.)

SERGEANT: There's a flight of steps here that leads to the water. This is a place that should be minded well. If he got down here, his friends might have a boat to meet him; they might send it in here from outside.

POLICEMAN B: Would the barrel be a good place to put a notice up?

SERGEANT: It might; you can put it there.
(They paste the notice up.)

SERGEANT: *(Reading it.)* Dark hair—dark eyes, smooth face, height five feet five—there's not much to take hold of in that—It's a pity I had no chance of seeing him before he broke out of gaol. They say he's a wonder, that it's he makes all the plans for the whole organization. There isn't another man in Ireland would have broken gaol the way he did. He must have some friends among the gaolers.

POLICEMAN B: A hundred pounds is little enough for the Government to offer for him. You may be sure any man in the force that takes him will get promotion.

SERGEANT: I'll mind this place myself. I wouldn't wonder at all if he came this way. He might come slipping along there *(points to side of quay)*, and his friends might be waiting for him there *(points down steps)*, and once he got away it's little chance we'd have of finding him; it's maybe under a load of kelp he'd be in a fishing boat, and not one to help a married man that wants it to the reward.

POLICEMAN X: And if we get him itself, nothing but abuse on our heads for it from the people, and maybe from our own relations.

SERGEANT: Well, we have to do our duty in the force. Haven't we the whole country depending on us to keep law and order? It's those that are down would be up and those that are up would be down, if it wasn't for us. Well, hurry on, you have plenty of other places to placard yet, and come back here then to me. You can take the lantern. Don't be too long now. It's very lonesome here with nothing but the moon.

POLICEMAN B: It's a pity we can't stop with you. The Government should have brought more police into the town, with *him* in gaol, and at assize time too. Well, good luck to your watch.

(They go out.)

SERGEANT: *(Walks up and down once or twice and looks at placard.)* A hundred pounds and promotion sure. There must be a great deal of spending in a hundred pounds. It's a pity some honest man not to be the better of that.

(A ragged man appears at left and tries to slip past. Sergeant suddenly turns.)

SERGEANT: Where are you going?

MAN: I'm a poor ballad-singer, your honour. I thought to sell some of these *(holds out bundle of ballads)* to the sailors. *(He goes on.)*

SERGEANT: Stop! Didn't I tell you to stop? You can't go on there.

MAN: Oh, very well. It's a hard thing to be poor. All the world's against the poor!

SERGEANT: Who are you?

MAN: You'd be as wise as myself if I told you, but I don't mind. I'm one Jimmy Walsh, a ballad-singer.

SERGEANT: Jimmy Walsh? I don't know that name.

MAN: Ah, sure, they know it well enough in Ennis. Were you ever in Ennis, sergeant?

SERGEANT: What brought you here?

MAN: Sure, it's to the assizes I came, thinking I might make a few shillings here or there. It's in the one train with the judges I came.

SERGEANT: Well, if you came so far, you may as well go farther, for you'll walk out of this.

MAN: I will, I will; I'll just go on where I was going.
(Goes towards steps.)

SERGEANT: Come back from those steps; no one has leave to pass down them to-night.

MAN: I'll just sit on the top of the steps till I see will some sailor buy a ballad off me that would give me my supper. They do be late going back to the ship. It's often I saw them in Cork carried down the quay in a hand-cart.

SERGEANT: Move on, I tell you. I won't have any one lingering about the quay to-night.

MAN: Well, I'll go. It's the poor have the hard life! Maybe yourself might like one, sergeant. Here's a good sheet now. *(Turns one over.)* "Content and a pipe"—that's not much. "The Peeler and the goat"—you wouldn't like that. "Johnny Hart"—that's a lovely song.

SERGEANT: Move on.

MAN: Ah, wait till you hear it.   *(Sings:)*

There was a rich farmer's daughter lived near the town of Ross;

She courted a Highland soldier, his name was Johnny Hart;

Says the mother to her daughter, "I'll go distracted mad

If you marry that Highland soldier dressed up in Highland plaid."

SERGEANT: Stop that noise.

(Man wraps up his ballads and shuffles towards the steps.)

SERGEANT: Where are you going?

MAN: Sure you told me to be going, and I am going.

SERGEANT: Don't be a fool. I didn't tell you to go that way; I told you to go back to the town.

MAN: Back to the town, is it?

SERGEANT: *(Taking him by the shoulder and shoving him before him.)*   Here, I'll show you the way. Be off with you. What are you stopping for?

MAN: *(Who has been keeping his eye on the notice, points to it.)*   I think I know what you're waiting for, sergeant.

SERGEANT: What's that to you?

MAN: And I know well the man you're waiting for—I know him well—I'll be going.

(He shuffles on.)

SERGEANT: You know him? Come back here. What sort is he?

MAN: Come back is it, sergeant? Do you want to have me killed?

SERGEANT: Why do you say that?

MAN: Never mind. I'm going. I wouldn't be in your shoes if the reward was ten times as much.   *(Goes on off stage to left.)*   Not if it was ten times as much.

SERGEANT: *(Rushing after him.)*   Come back here, come back.   *(Drags him back.)*   What sort is he? Where did you see him?

MAN: I saw him in my own place, in the County Clare. I tell you you wouldn't like to be looking at him. You'd be afraid

to be in the one place with him. There isn't a weapon he
doesn't know the use of, and as to strength, his muscles
are as hard as that board (*slaps barrel*).

SERGEANT: Is he as bad as that?

MAN: He is then.

SERGEANT: Do you tell me so?

MAN: There was a poor man in our place, a sergeant from
Ballyvaughan.—It was with a lump of stone he did it.

SERGEANT: I never heard of that.

MAN: And you wouldn't, sergeant. It's not everything that
happens gets into the papers. And there was a policeman in
plain clothes, too . . . It is in Limerick he was. . . . It was
after the time of the attack on the police barrack at Kilmal-
lock. . . . Moonlight . . . just like this . . . waterside. . . .
Nothing was known for certain.

SERGEANT: Do you say so? It's a terrible county to belong to.

MAN: That's so, indeed! You might be standing there, looking out that way, thinking you saw him coming up this side
of the quay (*points*), and he might be coming up this other
side (*points*), and he'd be on you before you knew where you
were.

SERGEANT: It's a whole troop of police they ought to put here
to stop a man like that.

MAN: But if you'd like me to stop with you, I could be looking down this side. I could be sitting up here on this barrel.

SERGEANT: And you know him well, too?

MAN: I'd know him a mile off, sergeant.

SERGEANT: But you wouldn't want to share the reward?

MAN: Is it a poor man like me, that has to be going the roads
and singing in fairs, to have the name on him that he took
a reward? But you don't want me. I'll be safer in the town.

SERGEANT: Well, you can stop.

MAN: (*Getting up on barrel.*) All right, sergeant. I wonder,
now, you're not tired out, sergeant, walking up and down
the way you are.

SERGEANT: If I'm tired I'm used to it.

MAN: You might have hard work before you to-night yet. Take it easy while you can. There's plenty of room up here on the barrel, and you see farther when you're higher up.

SERGEANT: Maybe so. (*Gets up beside him on barrel, facing right. They sit back to back, looking different ways.*) You made me feel a bit queer with the way you talked.

MAN: Give me a match, sergeant (*he gives it and man lights pipe*); take a draw yourself? It'll quiet you. Wait now till I give you a light, but you needn't turn round. Don't take your eye off the quay for the life of you.

SERGEANT: Never fear, I won't. (*Lights pipe. They both smoke.*) Indeed it's a hard thing to be in the force, out at night and no thanks for it, for all the danger we're in. And it's little we get but abuse from the people, and no choice but to obey our orders, and never asked when a man is sent into danger, if you are a married man with a family.

MAN: (*Sings*)—

As through the hills I walked to view the hills and shamrock plain,

I stood awhile where nature smiles to view the rocks and streams,

On a matron fair I fixed my eyes beneath a fertile vale,

As she sang her song it was on the wrong of poor old Granuaile.

SERGEANT: Stop that; that's no song to be singing in these times.

MAN: Ah, sergeant, I was only singing to keep my heart up. It sinks when I think of him. To think of us two sitting here, and he creeping up the quay, maybe, to get to us.

SERGEANT: Are you keeping a good lookout?

MAN: I am; and for no reward too. Amn't I the foolish man? But when I saw a man in trouble, I never could help trying to get him out of it. What's that? Did something hit me? (*Rubs his heart.*)

SERGEANT: (*Patting him on the shoulder.*) You will get your reward in heaven.

MAN: I know that, I know that, sergeant, but life is precious.

SERGEANT: Well, you can sing if it gives you more courage.

MAN: *(Sings)*—

Her head was bare, her hands and feet with iron bands were
bound,

Her pensive strain and plaintive wail mingles with the evening gale,

And the song she sang with mournful air, I am old
Granuaile.

Her lips so sweet that monarchs kissed . . .

SERGEANT: That's not it. . . . "Her gown she wore was stained
with gore." . . . That's it—you missed that.

MAN: You're right, sergeant, so it is; I missed it. *(Repeats
line.)* But to think of a man like you knowing a song like
that.

SERGEANT: There's many a thing a man might know and
might not have any wish for.

MAN: Now, I daresay, sergeant, in your youth, you used
to be sitting up on a wall, the way you are sitting up on this
barrel now, and the other lads beside you, and you singing
"Granuaile"? . . .

SERGEANT: I did then.

MAN: And the "Shan Bhean Bhocht"? . . .

SERGEANT: I did then.

MAN: And the "Green on the Cape?"

SERGEANT: That was one of them.

MAN: And maybe the man you are watching for to-night used
to be sitting on the wall, when he was young, and singing
those same songs. . . . It's a queer world. . . .

SERGEANT: Whisht! . . . I think I see something coming. . . .
It's only a dog.

MAN: And isn't it a queer world? . . . Maybe it's one of the
boys you used to be singing with that time you will be
arresting to-day or to-morrow, and sending into the dock. . . .

SERGEANT: That's true indeed.

MAN: And maybe one night, after you had been singing, if

the other boys had told you some plan they had, some plan
to free the country, you might have joined with them . . . and
maybe it is you might be in trouble now.

SERGEANT: Well, who knows but I might? I had a great spirit
in those days.

MAN: It's a queer world, sergeant, and it's little any mother
knows when she sees her child creeping on the floor what
might happen to it before it has gone through its life, or who
will be who in the end.

SERGEANT: That's a queer thought now, and a true thought.
Wait now till I think it out. . . . If it wasn't for the sense I
have, and for my wife and family, and for me joining the
force the time I did, it might be myself now would be after
breaking gaol and hiding in the dark, and it might be him
that's hiding in the dark and that got out of gaol would be
sitting up where I am on this barrel. . . . And it might be
myself would be creeping up trying to make my escape from
himself, and it might be himself would be keeping the law,
and myself would be breaking it, and myself would be trying
maybe to put a bullet in his head, or to take up a lump of a
stone the way you said he did . . . no, that myself did. . . .
Oh! (*Gasps. After a pause.*)   What's that?   (*Grasps man's
arm.*)

MAN: (*Jumps off barrel and listens, looking out over water.*)
It's nothing, sergeant.

SERGEANT: I thought it might be a boat. I had a notion there
might be friends of his coming about the quays with a boat.

MAN: Sergeant, I am thinking it was with the people you
were, and not with the law you were, when you were a young
man.

SERGEANT: Well, if I was foolish then, that time's gone.

MAN: Maybe, sergeant, it comes into your head sometimes,
in spite of your belt and your tunic, that it might have been
as well for you to have followed Granuaile.

SERGEANT: It's no business of yours what I think.

MAN: Maybe, sergeant, you'll be on the side of the country
yet.

SERGEANT: *(Gets off barrel.)* Don't talk to me like that. I have my duties and I know them. *(Looks round.)* That was a boat; I hear the oars.

(Goes to the steps and looks down.)

MAN: *(Sings)*—

O, then, tell me, Shawn O'Farrell,
　Where the gathering is to be.
In the old spot by the river
　Right well known to you and me!

SERGEANT: Stop that! Stop that, I tell you!

MAN: *(Sings louder)*—

One word more, for signal token,
　Whistle up the marching tune,
With your pike upon your shoulder,
　At the Rising of the Moon.

SERGEANT: If you don't stop that, I'll arrest you.

(A whistle from below answers, repeating the air.)

SERGEANT: That's a signal. *(Stands between him and steps.)* You must not pass this way. . . . Step farther back. . . . Who are you? You are no ballad-singer.

MAN: You needn't ask who I am; that placard will tell you. *(Points to placard.)*

SERGEANT: You are the man I am looking for.

MAN: *(Takes off hat and wig. Sergeant seizes them.)* I am. There's a hundred pounds on my head. There is a friend of mine below in a boat. He knows a safe place to bring me to.

SERGEANT: *(Looking still at hat and wig.)* It's a pity! It's a pity. You deceived me. You deceived me well.

MAN: I am a friend of Granuaile. There is a hundred pounds on my head.

SERGEANT: It's a pity, it's a pity!

MAN: Will you let me pass, or must I make you let me?

SERGEANT: I am in the force. I will not let you pass.

MAN: I thought to do it with my tongue. *(Puts hand in breast.)* What is that?

(Voice of Policeman X outside:) Here, this is where we left him.

SERGEANT: It's my comrades coming.

MAN: You won't betray me . . . the friend of Granuaile.
   (Slips behind barrel.)

(Voice of Policeman B:)   That was the last of the placards.

POLICEMAN X: *(As they come in.)*   If he makes his escape
   it won't be unknown he'll make it.
   (Sergeant puts hat and wig behind his back.)

POLICEMAN B: Did any one come this way?

SERGEANT: *(After a pause.)*   No one.

POLICEMAN B: No one at all?

SERGEANT: No one at all.

POLICEMAN B: We had no orders to go back to the station;
   we can stop along with you.

SERGEANT: I don't want you. There is nothing for you to do
   here.

POLICEMAN B: You bade us to come back here and keep
   watch with you.

SERGEANT: I'd sooner be alone. Would any man come this
   way and you making all that talk? It is better the place to be
   quiet.

POLICEMAN B: Well, we'll leave you the lantern anyhow.
   (Hands it to him.)

SERGEANT: I don't want it. Bring it with you.

POLICEMAN B: You might want it. There are clouds coming
   up and you have the darkness of the night before you yet.
   I'll leave it over here on the barrel.   *(Goes to barrel.)*

SERGEANT: Bring it with you I tell you. No more talk.

POLICEMAN B: Well, I thought it might be a comfort to you.
   I often think when I have it in my hand and can be flashing
   it about into every dark corner *(doing so)* that it's the same
   as being beside the fire at home, and the bits of bogwood
   blazing up now and again.
   (Flashes it about, now on the barrel, now on Sergeant.)

SERGEANT: *(Furious.)*   Be off the two of you, yourselves and
   your lantern!
   *(They go out. Man comes from behind barrel. He and Ser-
   geant stand looking at one another.)*

SERGEANT: What are you waiting for?

MAN: For my hat, of course, and my wig. You wouldn't wish
me to get my death of cold?

(Sergeant gives them.)

MAN: *(Going towards steps.)*   Well, good-night, comrade,
and thank you. You did me a good turn to-night, and I'm
obliged to you. Maybe I'll be able to do as much for you
when the small rise up and the big fall down . . . when we
all change places at the Rising *(waves his hand and disap-
pears)* of the Moon.

SERGEANT: *(Turning his back to audience and reading placard.)*   A hundred pounds reward! A hundred pounds!
(Turns towards audience.)   I wonder, now, am I as great
a fool as I think I am?

                              Curtain.

The Grave of Rury[1]

BY T. W. Rolleston (1857-1920)

Clear as air, the western waters.
Evermore their sweet, unchanging song
Murmur in their stony channels
Round O'Conor's sepulchre in Cong.

Crownless, hopeless, here he lingered;
Year on year went by him like a dream,
While the far-off roar of conquest
Murmured faintly like the singing stream.

---

[1] Rory O'Conor was the last High King of Ireland because in sub-
mitting to Henry II in 1171 he acknowledged the fact that Ireland
was no longer independent. He spent the closing years of his life in
the monastery of St. Fechin at Cong, County Mayo. He had no
successor.

Here he died, and here they tombed him,
Men of Fechin, chanting round his grave.
Did they know, ah! did they know it,
What they buried by the babbling wave?

Now above the sleep of Rury
Holy things and great have passed away;
Stone by stone the stately Abbey
Falls and fades in passionless decay.

Darkly grows the quiet ivy,
Pale the broken arches glimmer through;
Dark upon the cloister-garden
Dreams the shadow of the ancient yew.

Through the roofless aisles the verdure
Flows, the meadow-sweet and fox-glove bloom.
Earth, the mother and consoler,
Winds soft arms about the lonely tomb.

Peace and holy gloom possess him,
Last of Gaelic monarchs of the Gael,
Slumbering by the young, eternal
River-voices of the western vale.

Poisson D'Avril

BY E. Œ. Somerville (1859-1949)
AND Martin Ross (1862-1915)

THE atmosphere of the waiting-room set at naught at a single
glance the theory that there can be no smoke without fire. The
station-master, when remonstrated with, stated, as an incon-
trovertible fact, that any chimney in the world would smoke
in a south-easterly wind, and further, said there wasn't a poker,

and that if you poked the fire the grate would fall out. He was, however, sympathetic, and went on his knees before the smouldering mound of slack, endeavouring to charm it to a smile by subtle proddings with the handle of the ticket punch. Finally, he took me to his own kitchen fire and talked politics and salmon fishing, the former with judicious attention to my presumed point of view, and careful suppression of his own, the latter with no less tactful regard for my admission that for three days I had not caught a fish, while the steam rose from my wet boots, in witness of the ten miles of rain through which an outside car had carried me.

Before the train was signalled I realized for the hundredth time the magnificent superiority of the Irish mind to the trammels of officialdom, and the inveterate supremacy in Ireland of the personal element.

"You might get a foot-warmer at Carrig Junction," said a species of lay porter in a knitted jersey, ramming my suit-case upside down under the seat. "Sometimes they're in it, and more times they're not."

The train dragged itself rheumatically from the station, and a cold spring rain—the time was the middle of a most inclement April—smote it in flank as it came into the open. I pulled up both windows and began to smoke; there is, at least, a semblance of warmth in a thoroughly vitiated atmosphere.

It is my wife's habit to assert that I do not read her letters, and being now on my way to join her and my family in Gloucestershire, it seemed a sound thing to study again her latest letter of instructions.

"I am starting to-day, as Alice wrote to say we must be there two days before the wedding, so as to have a rehearsal for the pages. Their dresses have come, and they look too delicious in them—"

(I here omit profuse particulars not pertinent to this tale)—

"It is sickening for you to have had such bad sport. If the worst comes to the worst couldn't you buy one?—"

I smote my hand upon my knee. I had forgotten the infernal salmon! What a score for Philippa! If these *contretemps*

would only teach her that I was not to be relied upon, they
would have their uses, but experience is wasted upon her; I
have no objection to being called an idiot, but, that being so,
I ought to be allowed the privileges and exemptions proper to
idiots. Philippa had, no doubt, written to Alice Hervey, and
assured her that Sinclair would be only too delighted to bring
her a salmon, and Alice Hervey, who was rich enough to find
much enjoyment in saving money, would reckon upon it, to
its final fin in mayonnaise.

Plunged in morose meditations, I progressed through a
country parcelled out by shaky and crooked walls into a patch-
wood of hazel scrub and rocky fields, veiled in rain. About
every six miles there was a station, wet and windswept; at one
the sole occurrence was the presentation of a newspaper to the
guard by the station-master; at the next the guard read aloud
some choice excerpts from the same to the porter. The Personal
Element was potent on this branch of the Munster and Connaught Railway. Routine, abhorrent to all artistic minds, was
sheathed in conversation; even the engine-driver, a functionary
ordinarily as aloof as the Mikado, alleviated his enforced isola-
tion by sociable shrieks to every level crossing, while the long
row of public-houses that formed, as far as I could judge, the
town of Carrig, received a special and, as it seemed, humorous
salutation.

The time-table decreed that we were to spend ten minutes
at Carrig Junction; it was fifteen before the crowd of market
people on the platform had been assimilated; finally, the window of a neighbouring carriage was flung open, and a wrathful
English voice asked how much longer the train was going to
wait. The station-master, who was at the moment engrossed
in conversation with the guard and a man who was carrying
a long parcel wrapped in newspaper, looked round, and said
gravely:

"Well now, that's a mystery!"

The man with the parcel turned away, and convulsively
studied a poster. The guard put his hand over his mouth.

The voice, still more wrathfully, demanded the earliest hour at which its owner could get to Belfast.

"Ye'll be asking me next when I take me breakfast," replied the station-master, without haste or palpable annoyance.

The window went up again with a bang, the man with the parcel dug the guard in the ribs with his elbow, and the parcel slipped from under his arm and fell on the platform.

"Oh my! oh my! Me fish!" exclaimed the man, solicitously picking up a remarkably good-looking salmon that had slipped from its wrapping of newspaper.

Inspiration came to me, and I, in my turn, opened my window and summoned the station-master.

Would his friend sell me the salmon? The station-master entered upon the mission with ardour, but without success.

No; the gentleman was only just after running down to the town for it in the delay, but why wouldn't I run down and get one for myself? There was half a dozen more of them below at Coffey's, selling cheap; there would be time enough, the mail wasn't signalled yet.

I jumped from the carriage and doubled out of the station at top speed, followed by an assurance from the guard that he would not forget me.

Congratulating myself on the ascendancy of the personal element, I sped through the soapy limestone mud towards the public-houses. En route I met a heated man carrying yet another salmon, who, without preamble, informed me that there were three or four more good fish in it, and that he was after running down from the train himself.

"Ye have whips o' time!" he called after me. "It's the first house that's not a public-house. Ye'll see boots in the window —she'll give them for tenpence a pound if ye're stiff with her!"

I ran past the public-houses.

"Tenpence a pound!" I exclaimed inwardly, "at this time of year! That's good enough."

Here I perceived the house with boots in the window, and dived into its dark doorway.

A cobbler was at work behind a low counter. He mumbled something about herself, through lengths of waxed thread that hung across his mouth, a fat woman appeared at an inner door, and at that moment I heard, appallingly near, the whistle of the incoming mail. The fat woman grasped the situation in an instant, and with what appeared but one movement, snatched a large fish from the floor of the room behind her and flung a newspaper round it.

"Eight pound weight!" she said swiftly. "Ten shillings!"

A convulsive effort of mental arithmetic assured me that this was more than tenpence a pound, but it was not the moment for stiffness. I shoved a half-sovereign into her fishy hand, clasped my salmon in my arms, and ran.

Needless to say it was uphill, and at the steepest gradient another whistle stabbed me like a spur; above the station roof successive and advancing puffs of steam warned me that the worst had probably happened, but still I ran. When I gained the platform my train was already clear of it, but the personal element held good. Every soul in the station, or so it seemed to me, lifted up his voice and yelled. The station-master put his fingers in his mouth and sent after the departing train an unearthly whistle, with a high trajectory and a serrated edge. It took effect; the train slackened, I plunged from the platform and followed it up the rails, and every window in both trains blossomed with the heads of deeply interested spectators. The guard met me on the line, very apologetic and primed with an explanation that the gentleman going for the boat train wouldn't let him wait any longer, while from our rear came an exultant cry from the station-master.

"Ye *told* him ye wouldn't forget him!"

"There's a few countrywomen in your carriage, sir," said the guard, ignoring the taunt, as he shoved me and my salmon up the side of the train, "but they'll be getting out in a couple of stations. There wasn't another seat in the train for them!"

My sensational return to my carriage was viewed with the utmost sympathy by no less than seven shawled and cloaked countrywomen. In order to make room for me one of them seated herself on the floor with her basket in her lap, another, on the seat opposite to me, squeezed herself under the central elbow flap that had been turned up to make room. The aromas of wet cloaks, turf smoke, and salt fish formed a potent blend. I was excessively hot, and the eyes of the seven women were fastened upon me with intense and unwearying interest.

"Move west a small piece, Mary Jack, if you please," said a voluminous matron in the corner, "I declare we're as throng as three in a bed this minute!"

"Why then, Julia Casey, there's little throubling yourself," grumbled the woman under the flap. "Look at the way meself is! I wonder is it to be putting humps on themselves the gentry has them things down on top o' them! I'd sooner be carrying a basket of turnips on me back than to be scrooged this way!"

The woman on the floor at my feet rolled up at me a glance of compassionate amusement at this rustic ignorance, and tactfully changed the conversation by supposing that it was at Coffey's I got the salmon.

I said it was.

There was a silence, during which it was obvious that one question burnt in every heart.

"I'll go bail she axed him tinpence!" said the woman under the flap, as one who touches the limits of absurdity.

"It's a beautiful fish!" I said defiantly. "Eight pounds weight. I gave her ten shillings for it."

What is described in newspapers as "sensation in court" greeted this confession.

"Look!" said the woman under the flap, darting her head out of the hood of her cloak, like a tortoise, "'tis what it is, ye haven't as much roguery in your heart as 'd make ye a match for her!"

"Divil blow the ha'penny Eliza Coffey paid for that fish!" burst out the fat woman in the corner. "Thim lads o' her's had a creel full o' thim snatched this morning before it was making day!"

"How would the gentleman be a match for her!" shouted the woman on the floor through a long-drawn whistle that told of a coming station. "Sure a Turk itself wouldn't be a match for her! That one has a tongue that'd clip a hedge!"

At the station they clambered out laboriously, and with groaning. I handed down to them their monster baskets, laden, apparently, with ingots of lead; they told me in return that I was a fine grauver man, and it was a pity there weren't more like me; they wished, finally, that my journey might well thrive with me, and passed from my ken, bequeathing to me, after the agreeable manner of their kind, a certain comfortable mental sleekness that reason cannot immediately dispel. They also left me in possession of the fact that I was about to present the irreproachable Alice Hervey with a contraband salmon.

The afternoon passed cheerlessly into evening, and my journey did not conspicuously thrive with me. Somewhere in the dripping twilight I changed trains, and again later on, and at each change the salmon moulted some more of its damp raiment of newspaper, and I debated seriously the idea of interring it, regardless of consequences, in my portmanteau. A lamp was banged into the roof of my carriage, half an inch of orange flame, poised in a large glass globe, like a gold fish, and of about as much use as an illuminant. Here also was handed in the dinner basket that I had wired for, and its contents, arid though they were, enabled me to achieve at least some measure of mechanical distension, followed by a dreary lethargy that was not far from drowsiness.

At the next station we paused long; nothing whatever occurred, and the rain drummed patiently upon the roof. Two nuns and some schoolgirls were in the carriage next door, and their voices came plaintively and in snatches through the partition; after a long period of apparent collapse, during which I closed my eyes to evade the cold gaze of the salmon through the netting, a voice in the next carriage said resourcefully:

"Oh, girls, I'll tell you what we'll do! We'll say the Rosary!"

"Oh, that will be lovely!" said another voice; "well, who'll give it out? Theresa Condon, you'll give it out."

Theresa Condon gave it out, in a not unmelodious monotone, interspersed with the responses, always in a lower cadence; the words were indistinguishable, but the rise and fall of the western voices was lulling as the hum of bees. I fell asleep.

I awoke in total darkness; the train was motionless, and complete and profound silence reigned. We were at a station, that much I discerned by the light of the dim lamp at the far end of a platform glistening with wet. I struck a match and ascertained that it was eleven o'clock, precisely the hour at which I was to board the mail train. I jumped out and ran down the platform; there was no one in the train; there was no one even on the engine, which was forlornly hissing to itself in the silence. There was not a human being anywhere. Every door was closed, and all was dark. The name-board of the station was faintly visible; with a lighted match I went along it letter by letter. It seemed as if the whole alphabet were in it, and by the time I had got to the end I had forgotten the beginning. One fact I had, however, mastered, that it was not the junction at which I was to catch the mail.

I was undoubtedly awake, but for a moment I was inclined to entertain the idea that there had been an accident, and that I had entered upon existence in another world. Once more I assailed the station house and the appurtenances thereof, the ticket office, the waiting-room, finally, and at some distance, the goods store, outside which the single lamp of the station commented feebly on the drizzle and the darkness. As I approached it a crack of light under the door became perceptible, and a voice was suddenly uplifted within.

"Your best now agin that! Throw down your jack!"

I opened the door with pardonable violence, and found the guard, the station-master, the driver, and the stoker, seated on barrels round a packing-case, on which they were playing a game of cards.

To have too egregiously the best of a situation is not, to a generous mind, a source of strength. In the perfection of their overthrow I permitted the driver and stoker to wither from their places, and to fade away into the outer darkness without any suitable send-off; with the guard and the station-master I dealt more faithfully, but the pleasure of throwing water on

drowned rats is not a lasting one. I accepted the statements that
they thought there wasn't a Christian in the train, that a few
minutes here or there wouldn't signify, that they would have
me at the junction in twenty minutes, and it was often the mail
was late.

Fired by this hope I hurried back to my carriage, preceded
at an emulous gallop by the officials. The guard thrust in with
me the lantern from the card table, and fled to his van.

"Mind the Goods, Tim!" shouted the station-master, as he
slammed my door, "she might be coming any time now!"

The answer travelled magnificently back from the engine.

"Let her come! She'll meet her match!" A war-whoop upon
the steam whistle fittingly closed the speech, and the train
sprang into action.

We had about fifteen miles to go, and we banged and
bucketed over it in what was, I should imagine, record time.
The carriage felt as if it were galloping on four wooden legs,
my teeth chattered in my head, and the salmon slowly churned
its way forth from its newspaper, and moved along the netting
with dreadful stealth.

All was of no avail.

"Well," said the guard, as I stepped forth on to the deserted
platform of Loughranny, "that owld Limited Mail's th' un-
punctualest thrain in Ireland! If you're a minute late she's
gone from you, and maybe if you were early you might be half
an hour waiting for her!"

On the whole the guard was a gentleman. He said he would
show me the best hotel in the town, though he feared I would
be hard set to get a bed anywhere because of the "Feis" (a Feis,
I should explain, is a festival, devoted to competitions in Irish
songs and dances). He shouldered my portmanteau, he even
grappled successfully with the salmon, and, as we traversed the
empty streets, he explained to me how easily I could catch the
morning boat from Rosslare, and how it was, as a matter of
fact, quite the act of providence that my original scheme had
been frustrated.

All was dark at the uninviting portals of the hotel favoured by the guard. For a full five minutes we waited at them, ringing hard: I suggested that we should try elsewhere.

"He'll come," said the guard, with the confidence of the Pied Piper of Hamelin, retaining an implacable thumb upon the button of the electric bell. "He'll come. Sure it rings in his room!"

The victim came, half awake, half dressed, and with an inch of dripping candle in his fingers. There was not a bed there, he said, nor in the town neither.

I said I would sit in the dining-room till the time for the early train.

"Sure there's five beds in the dining-room," replied the boots, "and there's mostly two in every bed."

His voice was firm, but there was a wavering look in his eye.

"What about the billiard-room, Mike?" said the guard, in wooing tones.

"Ah, God bless you! we have a mattress on the table this minute!" answered the boots, wearily, "and the fellow that got the First Prize for Reels asleep on top of it!"

"Well, and can't ye put the palliasse on the floor under it, ye omadhawn?" said the guard, dumping my luggage and the salmon in the hall, "sure there's no snugger place in the house! I must run away home now, before Herself thinks I'm dead altogether!"

His retreating footsteps went lightly away down the empty street.

"Annything don't throuble *him!*" said the boots bitterly.

As for me, nothing save the Personal Element stood between me and destitution.

It was in the dark of the early morning that I woke again to life and its troubles. A voice, dropping, as it were, over the edge of some smothering over-world, had awakened me. It was the voice of the First Prize for Reels, descending through a pocket of the billiard-table.

"I beg your pardon, sir, are ye going on the 5 to Cork?"

I grunted a negative.

"Well, if ye were, ye'd be late," said the voice.

I received this useful information in indignant silence, and endeavoured to wrap myself again in the vanishing skirts of a dream.

"I'm going on the 6:30 meself," proceeded the voice, "and it's unknown to me how I'll put on me boots. Me feet is swelled the size o' three-pound loaves with the dint of the little dancing-shoes I had on me in the competition last night. Me feet's delicate that way, and I'm a great epicure about me boots."

I snored aggressively, but the dream was gone. So, for all practical purposes was the night.

The First Prize for Reels arose, presenting an astonishing spectacle of grass-green breeches, a white shirt, and pearl-grey stockings, and accomplished a toilet that consisted of removing these and putting on ordinary garments, completed by the apparently excruciating act of getting into his boots. At any other hour of the day I might have been sorry for him. He then removed himself and his belongings to the hall, and there entered upon a resounding conversation with the boots, while I crawled forth from my lair to renew the strife with circumstances and to endeavour to compose a telegram to Alice Hervey of explanation and apology that should cost less than seven and six-pence. There was also the salmon to be dealt with.

Here the boots intervened, opportunely, with a cup of tea, and the intelligence that he had already done up the salmon in straw bottle-covers and brown paper, and that I could travel Europe with it if I liked. He further informed me that he would run up to the station with the luggage now, and that maybe I wouldn't mind carrying the fish myself; it was on the table in the hall.

My train went at 6:15. The boots had secured for me one of many empty carriages, and lingered conversationally till the train started; he regretted politely my bad night at the hotel, and assured me that only for Jimmy Durkan having a little drink taken—Jimmy Durkan was the First Prize for Reels—he would have turned him off the billiard-table for my benefit. He finally confided to me that Mr. Durkan was engaged to his sister, and was a rising baker in the town of Limerick; "indeed," he said, "any girl might be glad to get him. He dances like whalebone, and he makes grand bread!"

Here the train started.

It was late that night when, stiff, dirty, with tired eyes blinking in the dazzle of electric lights, I was conducted by the Herveys' beautiful footman into the Herveys' baronial hall, and was told by the Herveys' imperial butler that dinner was over, and the gentlemen had just gone into the drawing-room. I was in the act of hastily declining to join them there, when a voice cried:

"Here he is!"

And Philippa, rustling and radiant, came forth into the hall, followed in shimmers of satin, and flutterings of lace, by Alice Hervey, by the bride elect, and by the usual festive rout of exhilarated relatives, male and female, whose mission it is to keep things lively before a wedding.

"Is this a wedding present for me, Uncle Sinclair?" cried the bride elect, through a deluge of questions and commiserations, and snatched from under my arm the brown paper parcel that had remained there from force of direful habit.

"I advise you not to open it!" I exclaimed; "it's a salmon!"

The bride elect, with a shriek of disgust, and without an instant of hesitation, hurled it at her nearest neighbour, the head bridesmaid. The head bridesmaid, with an answering shriek, sprang to one side, and the parcel that I had cherished with a mother's care across two countries and a stormy Channel fell, with a crash, on the flagged floor.

Why did it crash?

"A salmon!" screamed Philippa, gazing at the parcel, round which a pool was already forming, "why, that's whisky! Can't you smell it?"

The footman here respectfully interposed, and kneeling down, cautiously extracted from folds of brown paper a straw bottle-cover full of broken glass and dripping with whisky.

"I'm afraid the other things are rather spoiled, sir," he said seriously, and drew forth, successively, a very large pair of high-low shoes, two long grey worsted stockings, and a pair of grass-green breeches.

They brought the house down, in a manner doubtless familiar to them when they shared the triumphs of Mr. Jimmy Durkan, but they left Alice Hervey distinctly cold.

"You know, darling," she said to Philippa afterwards, "I don't think it was very clever of dear Sinclair to take the wrong parcel. I *had* counted on that salmon "

From the Preface to
John Bull's Other Island

BY George Bernard Shaw (1856-1950)

WHAT IS AN IRISHMAN?

When I say that I am an Irishman I mean that I was born in Ireland, and that my native language is the English of Swift and not the unspeakable jargon of the mid-XIX century London newspapers. My extraction is the extraction of most Englishmen: that is, I have no trace in me of the commercially imported North Spanish strain which passes for aboriginal Irish: I am a genuine typical Irishman of the Danish, Norman, Cromwellian, and (of course) Scotch invasions. I am violently and arrogantly Protestant by family tradition; but let no English Government therefore count on my allegiance: I am English enough to be an inveterate Republican and Home Ruler. It is true that one of my grandfathers was an Orangeman; but then his sister was an abbess; and his uncle, I am proud to say, was hanged as a rebel. When I look round me on the hybrid cosmopolitans, slum poisoned or square pampered, who call themselves Englishmen today, and see them bullied by the Irish Protestant garrison as no Bengalee now lets himself be bullied by an Englishman; when I see the Irishman everywhere standing clearheaded, sane, hardily callous to the boyish sentimentalities, susceptibilities, and credulities that make the Englishman the dupe of every charlatan and the idolater of every numskull, I perceive that Ireland is the only spot on earth which still produces the ideal Englishman of history. Blackguard, bully, drunkard, liar, foulmouth, flatterer, beggar, backbiter, venal functionary, corrupt judge, envious friend, vindictive opponent, unparalleled political traitor: all these your Irishman may easily be, just as he may be a gentleman (a species extinct in England, and nobody a penny the worse); but he is never quite the hysterical, nonsense-crammed, fact-proof, truth-terrified, unballasted sport of all the bogey panics and all the silly enthusiasms that now calls itself "God's Englishman." England cannot do without its Irish and its Scots today, because it cannot do without at least a little sanity.

THE PROTESTANT GARRISON

The more Protestant an Irishman is—the more English he is, if it flatters you to have it put that way, the more intolerable he finds it to be ruled by English instead of Irish folly. A "loyal" Irishman is an abhorrent phenomenon, because it is an unnatural one. No doubt English rule is vigorously exploited in the interests of the property, power, and promotion of the Irish classes as against the Irish masses. Our delicacy is part of a keen sense of reality which makes us a very practical, and even, on occasion, a very coarse people. The Irish soldier takes the King's shilling and drinks the King's health; and the Irish squire takes the title deeds of the English settlement and rises uncovered to the strains of the English national anthem. But do not mistake this cupboard loyalty for anything deeper. It gains a broad base from the normal attachment of every reasonable man to the established government as long as it is bearable; for we all, after a certain age, prefer peace to revolution and order to chaos, other things being equal. Such considerations produce loyal Irishmen as they produce loyal Poles and Fins, loyal Hindoos, loyal Filipinos, and faithful slaves. But there is nothing more in it than that. If there is an entire lack of gall in the feeling of the Irish gentry towards the English, it is because the Englishman is always gaping admiringly at the Irishman as at some clever child prodigy. He overrates him with a generosity born of a traditional conviction of his own superiority in the deeper aspects of human character. As the Irish gentleman, tracing his pedigree to the conquest or one of the invasions, is equally convinced that if this superiority really exists, he is the genuine true blue heir to it, and as he is easily able to hold his own in all the superficial social accomplishments, he finds English society agreeable, and English houses very comfortable, Irish establishments being generally straitened by an attempt to keep a park and a stable on an income which would not justify an Englishman in venturing upon a wholly detached villa.

OUR TEMPERAMENTS CONTRASTED

But however pleasant the relations between the Protestant garrison and the English gentry may be, they are always essentially of the nature of an *entente cordiale* between foreigners. Personally I like Englishmen much better than Irishmen (no doubt because they make more of me) just as many Englishmen like Frenchmen better than Englishmen, and never go on board a Peninsular and Oriental steamer when one of the ships of the Messageries Maritimes is available. But I never think of an Englishman as my countryman. I should as soon think of applying that term to a German. And the Englishman has the same feeling. When a Frenchman fails to make the distinction, we both feel a certain disparagement involved in the misapprehension. Macaulay, seeing that the Irish had in Swift an author worth stealing, tried to annex him by contending that he must be classed as an Englishman because he was not an aboriginal Celt. He might as well have refused the name of Briton to Addison because he did not stain himself blue and attach scythes to the poles of his sedan chair. In spite of all such trifling with facts, the actual distinction between the idolatrous Englishman and the fact-facing Irishman, of the same extraction though they be, remains to explode those two hollowest of fictions, the Irish and English "races." There is no Irish race any more than there is an English race or a Yankee race. There is an Irish climate, which will stamp an immigrant more deeply and durably in two years, apparently, than the English climate will in two hundred. It is reinforced by an artificial economic climate which does some of the work attributed to the natural geographic one; but the geographic climate is eternal and irresistible, making a mankind and a womankind that Kent, Middlesex, and East Anglia cannot produce and do not want to imitate.

How can I sketch the broad lines of the contrast as they strike me? Roughly I should say that the Englishman is wholly at the mercy of his imagination, having no sense of reality to check it. The Irishman, with a far subtler and more fastidious imagination, has one eye always on things as they are. If you compare Moore's visionary Minstrel Boy with Mr Rudyard Kipling's quasi-realistic Soldiers Three, you may yawn over Moore or gush over him, but you will not suspect him of having had any illusions about the contemporary British private; whilst as to Mr Kipling, you will see that he has not, and unless he settles in Ireland for a few years will always remain constitutionally and congenitally incapable of having, the faintest inkling of the reality which he idolizes as Tommy Atkins. Perhaps you have never thought of illustrating the contrast between English and Irish by Moore and Mr Kipling, or even by Parnell and Gladstone. Sir Boyle Roche and Shakespear may seem more to your point. Let me find you a more dramatic instance. Think of the famous meeting between the

Duke of Wellington, that intensely Irish Irishman, and Nelson, that intensely English Englishman. Wellington's contemptuous disgust at Nelson's theatricality as a professed hero, patriot, and rhapsode, a theatricality which in an Irishman would have been an insufferably vulgar affectation, was quite natural and inevitable. Wellington's formula for that kind of thing was a well-known Irish one: "Sir: dont be a damned fool." It is the formula of all Irishmen for all Englishmen to this day. It is the formula of Larry Doyle for Tom Broadbent in my play, in spite of Doyle's affection for Tom. Nelson's genius, instead of producing intellectual keenness and scrupulousness, produced mere delirium. He was drunk with glory, exalted by his fervent faith in the sound British patriotism of the Almighty, nerved by the vulgarest anti-foreign prejudice, and apparently unchastened by any reflections on the fact that he had never had to fight a technically capable and properly equipped enemy except on land, where he had never been successful. Compare Wellington, who had to fight Napoleon's armies, Napoleon's marshals, and finally Napoleon himself, without one moment of illusion as to the human material he had to command, without one gush of the "Kiss me, Hardy" emotion which enabled Nelson to idolize his crews and his staff, without forgetting even in his dreams that the normal British officer of that time was an incapable amateur (as he still is) and the normal British soldier a never-do-well (he is now a depressed and respectable young man). No wonder Wellington became an accomplished comedian in the art of anti-climax, scandalizing the unfortunate Croker, responding to the demand for glorious sentiments by the most disenchanting touches of realism, and, generally, pricking the English windbag at its most explosive crises of distention. Nelson, intensely nervous and theatrical, made an enormous fuss about victories so cheap that he would have deserved shooting if he had lost them, and, not content with lavishing splendid fighting on helpless adversaries like the heroic De Brueys or Villeneuve (who had not even the illusion of heroism when he went like a lamb to the slaughter), got himself killed by his passion for exposing himself to death in that sublime defiance of it which was perhaps the supreme tribute of the exquisite coward to the King of Terrors (for, believe me, you cannot be a hero without being a coward: supersense cuts both ways), the result being a tremendous effect on the gallery. Wellington, most capable of captains, was neither a hero nor a patriot: perhaps not even a coward; and had it not been for the Nelsonic anecdotes invented for him—"Up guards, and at em" and so forth—and the fact that the antagonist with whom he finally closed was such a master of theatrical effect that Wellington could not fight him without getting into his limelight, nor overthrow him (most unfortunately for us all) without drawing the eyes of the whole world to the catastrophe, the Iron Duke would have been almost forgotten by this time. Now that contrast is English against Irish all over, and is the more delicious because the real Irishman in it is the Englishman of tradition, whilst the real Englishman is the traditional theatrical foreigner.

The value of the illustration lies in the fact that Nelson and Wellington were both in the highest degree efficient, and both in the highest degree incompatible with one another on any other footing than one of independence. The government of Nelson by Wellington or of Wellington by Nelson is felt at once to be a dishonorable outrage to the governed and a finally impossible task for the governor.

I daresay some Englishman will now try to steal Wellington as Macaulay tried to steal Swift. And he may plead with some truth that though it seems impossible that any other country than England could produce a hero so utterly devoid of common sense, intellectual delicacy, and international chivalry as Nelson, it may be contended that Wellington was rather an eighteenth century aristocratic type, than a specifically Irish type. George IV and Byron, contrasted with Gladstone, seem Irish in respect of a certain humorous blackguardism, and a power of appreciating art and sentiment without being duped by them into mistaking romantic figments for realities. But faithlessness and the need for carrying off the worthlessness and impotence that accompany it, produce in all nations a gay, sceptical, amusing, blaspheming, witty fashion which suits the flexibility of the Irish mind very well; and the contrast between this fashion and the energetic infatuations that have enabled intellectually ridiculous men, without wit or humor, to go on crusades and make successful revolutions, must not be confused with the contrast between the English and Irish idiosyncrasies. The Irishman makes a distinction which the Englishman is too lazy intellectually (the intellectual laziness and slovenliness of the English is almost beyond belief) to make. The Englishman, impressed with the dissoluteness of the faithless wits of the Restoration and the Regency, and with the victories of the wilful zealots of the patriotic, religious, and revolutionary wars, jumps to the conclusion that wilfulness is the main thing. In this he is right. But he overdoes his jump so far as to conclude also that stupidity and wrong-headedness are better guarantees of efficiency and trustworthiness than intellectual vivacity, which he mistrusts as a common symptom of worthlessness, vice, and instability. Now in this he is most dangerously wrong. Whether the Irishman grasps the truth as firmly as the Englishman may be open to question; but he is certainly comparatively free from the error. That affectionate and admiring love of sentimental stupidity for its own sake, both in men and women, which shines so steadily through the novels of Thackeray, would hardly be possible in the works of an Irish novelist. Even Dickens, though too vital a genius and too severely educated in the school of shabby-genteel poverty to have any doubt of the national danger of fatheadedness in high places, evidently assumes rather too hastily the superiority of Mr Meagles to Sir John Chester and Harold Skimpole. On the other hand, it takes an Irishman years of residence in England to learn to respect and like a blockhead. An Englishman will not respect nor like anyone else. Every English statesman has to maintain his popularity by pretending to be ruder, more ignorant, more sentimental, more superstitious, more stupid than any man who has lived behind the scenes of public life for ten minutes can possibly be. Nobody dares to publish really intimate memoirs of him or really private letters of his until his whole generation has passed away, and his party can no longer be compromised by the discovery that the platitudinizing twaddler and hypocritical opportunist was really a man of some perception as well as of strong constitution, peg-away industry, personal ambition, and party keenness.

ENGLISH STUPIDITY EXCUSED

I do not claim it as a natural superiority in the Irish nation that it dislikes and mistrusts fools, and expects its political leaders to be clever and humbug-proof. It may be that if our resources included the armed force and virtually unlimited money which push the political and military figureheads of England through bungled enterprises to a muddled success, and create an illusion of some miraculous and divine innate English quality that enables a general to become a conqueror with abilities that would not suffice to save a cabman from having his license marked, and a member of parliament to become Prime Minister with the outlook on life of a sporting country solicitor educated by a private governess, we should lapse into gross intellectual sottishness, and prefer leaders who encouraged our vulgarities by sharing them, and flattered us by associating them with purchased successes, to our betters. But as it is, we cannot afford that sort of encouragement and flattery in Ireland. The odds against which our leaders have to fight would be too heavy for the fourth-rate Englishman whose leadership consists for the most part in marking time ostentatiously until they are violently shoved, and then stumbling blindly forward (or backward) wherever the shove sends them. We cannot crush England as a Pickford's van might crush a perambulator. We are the perambulator and England the Pickford. We must study her and our real weaknesses and real strength; we must practise upon her slow conscience and her

quick terrors; we must deal in ideas and political principles
since we cannot deal in bayonets; we must outwit, outwork,
outstay her; we must embarrass, bully, even conspire and
assassinate when nothing else will move her, if we are not all
to be driven deeper and deeper into the shame and misery of
our servitude. Our leaders must be not only determined
enough, but clever enough to do this. We have no illusions as
to the existence of any mysterious Irish pluck, Irish honesty,
Irish bias on the part of Providence, or sterling Irish solidity of
character, that will enable an Irish blockhead to hold his own
against England. Blockheads are of no use to us: we were compelled to follow a supercilious, unpopular, tongue-tied, aristocratic Protestant Parnell, although there was no lack among
us of fluent imbeciles, with majestic presences and oceans of
dignity and sentiment, to promote into his place could they
have done his work for us. It is obviously convenient that Mr
Redmond should be a better speaker and rhetorician than
Parnell; but if he began to use his powers to make himself
agreeable instead of making himself reckoned with by the
enemy; if he set to work to manufacture and support English
shams and hypocrisies instead of exposing and denouncing
them; if he constituted himself the permanent apologist of
doing nothing, and, when the people insisted on his doing
something, only roused himself to discover how to pretend
to do it without really changing anything, he would lose his
leadership as certainly as an English politician would, by the
same course, attain a permanent place on the front bench. In
short, our circumstances place a premium on political ability
whilst the circumstances of England discount it; and the
quality of the supply naturally follows the demand. If you
miss in my writings that hero-worship of dotards and duffers
which is planting England with statues of disastrous statesmen
and absurd generals, the explanation is simply that I am an
Irishman and you an Englishman.

IRISH PROTESTANTISM REALLY PROTESTANT

When I repeat that I am an Irish Protestant, I come to
a part of the relation between England and Ireland that you

will never understand unless I insist on explaining it to you with that Irish insistence on intellectual clarity to which my English critics are so intensely recalcitrant.

First, let me tell you that in Ireland Protestantism is really Protestant. It is true that there is an Irish Protestant Church (disestablished some 35 years ago) in spite of the fact that a Protestant Church is, fundamentally, a contradiction in terms. But this means only that the Protestants use the word Church to denote their secular organization, without troubling themselves about the metaphysical sense of Christ's famous pun, "Upon this rock I will build my church." The Church of England, which is a reformed Anglican Catholic Anti-Protestant Church, is quite another affair. An Anglican is acutely conscious that he is not a Wesleyan; and many Anglican clergymen do not hesitate to teach that all Methodists incur damnation. In Ireland all that the member of the Irish Protestant Church knows is that he is not a Roman Catholic. The decorations of even the "lowest" English Church seem to him to be extravagantly Ritualistic and Popish. I myself entered the Irish Church by baptism, a ceremony performed by my uncle in "his own church." But I was sent, with many boys of my own denomination, to a Wesleyan school where the Wesleyan catechism was taught without the least protest on the part of the parents, although there was so little presumption in favor of any boy there being a Wesleyan that if all the Church boys had been withdrawn at any moment, the school would have become bankrupt. And this was by no means analogous to the case of those working class members of the Church of England in London, who send their daughters to Roman Catholic schools rather than to the public elementary schools. They do so for the definite reason that the nuns teach girls good manners and sweetness of speech, which have no place in the County Council curriculum. But in Ireland the Church parent sends his son to a Wesleyan school (if it is convenient and socially eligible) because he is indifferent to the form of Protestantism, provided it is Protestantism. There is also in Ireland a characteristically Protestant refusal to take ceremonies and even sacraments very seriously

except by way of strenuous objection to them when they are
conducted with candles or incense. For example, I was never
confirmed, although the ceremony was specially needed in my
case as the failure of my appointed godfather to appear at my
baptism had led to his responsibilities being assumed on the
spot, at my uncle's order, by the sexton. And my case was a
very common one, even among people quite untouched by
modern scepticisms. Apart from the weekly churchgoing,
which holds its own as a respectable habit, the initiations are
perfunctory, the omissions regarded as negligible. The distinction between churchman and dissenter, which in England is a
class distinction, a political distinction, and even occasionally
a religious distinction, does not exist. Nobody is surprised in
Ireland to find that the squire who is the local pillar of the
formerly established Church is also a Plymouth Brother, and,
except on certain special or fashionable occasions, attends the
Methodist meeting-house. The parson has no priestly character and no priestly influence: the High Church curate of
course exists and has his vogue among religious epicures of
the other sex; but the general attitude of his congregation
towards him is that of Dr Clifford. The clause in the Apostles'
creed professing belief in a Catholic Church is a standing puz-
zle to Protestant children; and when they grow up they dis-
miss it from their minds more often than they solve it, because
they really are not Catholics but Protestants to the extremest
practicable degree of individualism. It is true that they talk of
church and chapel with all the Anglican contempt for chapel;
but in Ireland the chapel means the Roman Catholic church,
for which the Irish Protestant reserves all the class rancor, the
political hostility, the religious bigotry, and the bad blood
generally that in England separates the Establishment from
the nonconforming Protestant organizations. When a vulgar
Irish Protestant speaks of a "Papist" he feels exactly as a vulgar
Anglican vicar does when he speaks of a Dissenter. And when
the vicar is Anglican enough to call himself a Catholic priest,
wear a cassock, and bless his flock with two fingers, he becomes
horrifically incomprehensible to the Irish Protestant Church-

man, who, on his part, puzzles the Anglican by regarding a Methodist as tolerantly as an Irishman who likes grog regards an Irishman who prefers punch.

A FUNDAMENTAL ANOMALY

Now nothing can be more anomalous, and at bottom impossible, than a Conservative Protestant party standing for the established order against a revolutionary Catholic party. The Protestant is theoretically an anarchist as far as anarchism is practicable in human society: that is, he is an individualist, a freethinker, a self-helper, a Whig, a Liberal, a mistruster and vilifier of the State, a rebel. The Catholic is theoretically a Collectivist, a self-abnegator, a Tory, a Conservative, a supporter of Church and State one and undivisible, an obeyer. This would be a statement of fact as well as of theory if men were Protestants and Catholics by temperament and adult choice instead of by family tradition. The peasant who supposed that Wordsworth's son would carry on the business now the old gentleman was gone was not a whit more foolish than we who laugh at his ignorance of the nature of poetry whilst we take it as a matter of course that a son should "carry on" his father's religion. Hence, owing to our family system, the Catholic Churches are recruited daily at the font by temperamental Protestants, and the Protestant organizations by temperamental Catholics, with consequences most disconcerting to those who expect history to be deducible from the religious professions of the men who make it.

Still, though the Roman Catholic Church may occasionally catch such Tartars as Luther and Voltaire, or the Protestant organizations as Newman and Manning, the general run of mankind takes its impress from the atmosphere in which it is brought up. In Ireland the Roman Catholic peasant cannot escape the religious atmosphere of his Church. Except when he breaks out like a naughty child he is docile; he is reverent; he is content to regard knowledge as something not his business; he is a child before his Church, and accepts it as the highest authority in science and philosophy. He speaks of himself as a son of the Church, calling his priest father instead of brother or Mister. To rebel politically, he must break away from parish tutelage and follow a Protestant leader on national questions. His Church naturally fosters his submissiveness. The British Government and the Vatican may differ very vehemently as to whose subject the Irishman is to be; but they are quite agreed as to the propriety of his being a subject. Of the two, the British Government allows him more liberty, giving him as complete a democratic control of local government as his means will enable him to use, and a voice in the election of a formidable minority in the House of Commons, besides allowing him to read and learn what he likes—except when it makes a tufthunting onslaught on a seditious newspaper. But if he dared to claim a voice in the selection of his parish priest, or a representative at the Vatican, he would be denounced from the altar as an almost inconceivable blasphemer; and his educational opportunities are so restricted by his Church that he is heavily handicapped in every walk of life that requires any literacy. It is the aim of his priest to make him and keep him a submissive Conservative; and nothing but gross economic oppression and religious persecution could have produced the strange phenomenon of a revolutionary movement not only tolerated by the Clericals, but, up to a certain point, even encouraged by them. If there is such a thing as political science, with natural laws like any other science, it is certain that only the most violent external force could effect and maintain this unnatural combination of political revolution with Papal reaction, and of hardy individualism and independence with despotism and subjugation.

That violent external force is the clumsy thumb of English rule. If you would be good enough, ladies and gentlemen of England, to take your thumb away and leave us free to do something else than bite it, the unnaturally combined elements in Irish politics would fly asunder and recombine according to their proper nature with results entirely satisfactory to real Protestantism.

THE NATURE OF POLITICAL HATRED

Just reconsider the Home Rule question in the light of that very English characteristic of the Irish people, their political hatred of priests. Do not be distracted by the shriek of indignant denial from the Catholic papers and from those who have witnessed the charming relations between the Irish peasantry and their spiritual fathers. I am perfectly aware that the Irish love their priests as devotedly as the French loved them before the Revolution or as the Italians loved them before they imprisoned the Pope in the Vatican. They love their landlords too: many an Irish gentleman has found in his nurse a foster-mother more interested in him than his actual mother. They love the English, as every Englishman who travels in Ireland can testify. Please do not suppose that I speak satirically: the world is full of authentic examples of the concurrence of human kindliness with political rancor. Slaves and schoolboys often love their masters; Napoleon and his soldiers made desperate efforts to save from drowning the Russian soldiers under whom they had broken the ice with their cannon; even the relations between nonconformist peasants and country parsons in England are not invariably unkindly; in the southern States of America planters are often traditionally fond of negroes and kind to them, with substantial returns in humble affection; soldiers and sailors often admire and cheer their officers sincerely and heartily; nowhere is actual personal intercourse found compatible for long with the intolerable friction of hatred and malice. But people who persist in pleading these amiabilities as political factors must be summarily bundled out of the room when questions of State are to be discussed. Just as an Irishman may have English friends whom he may prefer to any Irishman of his acquaintance, and be kind, hospitable, and serviceable in his intercourse with Englishmen, whilst being perfectly prepared to make the Shannon run red with English blood if Irish freedom could be obtained at that price; so an Irish Catholic may like his priest as a man and revere him as a confessor and spiritual pastor whilst being implacably determined to seize the first opportunity of throwing off his yoke. This is political hatred: the only hatred that civilization allows to be mortal hatred.

THE REVOLT AGAINST THE PRIEST

Realize, then, that the popular party in Ireland is seething with rebellion against the tyranny of the Church. Imagine the feelings of an English farmer if the parson refused to marry him for less than £20, and if he had virtually no other way of getting married! Imagine the Church Rates revived in the form of an unofficial Income Tax scientifically adjusted to your taxable capacity by an intimate knowledge of your affairs verified in the confessional! Imagine being one of a peasantry reputed the poorest in the world, under the thumb of a priesthood reputed the richest in the world! Imagine a Catholic middle class continually defeated in the struggle of professional, official, and fashionable life by the superior education of its Protestant competitors, and yet forbidden by its priests to resort to the only efficient universities in the country! Imagine trying to get a modern education in a seminary of priests, where every modern book worth reading is on the index, and the earth is still regarded, not perhaps as absolutely flat, yet as being far from so spherical as Protestants allege! Imagine being forbidden to read this preface because it proclaims your own grievance! And imagine being bound to submit to all this because the popular side must hold together at all costs in the face of the Protestant enemy! That is, roughly, the predicament of Roman Catholic Ireland.

PROTESTANT LOYALTY: A FORECAST

Now let us have a look at Protestant Ireland. I have already said that a "loyal" Irishman is an abhorrent phenomenon, because he is an unnatural one. In Ireland it is not "loyalty" to drink the English king's health and stand uncovered to the English national anthem: it is simply exploitation of English rule in the interests of the property, power, and promotion of the Irish classes as against the Irish masses. From any other point of view it is cowardice and dishonor. I have known a Protestant go to Dublin Castle to be sworn in as a special constable, quite resolved to take the baton and break the heads of a patriotic faction just then upsetting the peace of the town, yet back out at the last moment because he could not bring himself to swallow the oath of allegiance tendered with the baton. There is no such thing as genuine loyalty in Ireland. There is a separation of the Irish people into two hostile camps: one Protestant, gentlemanly, and oligarchical; the other Roman Catholic, popular, and democratic. The oligarchy governs Ireland as a bureaucracy deriving authority from the king of England. It cannot cast him off without casting off its own ascendancy. Therefore it naturally exploits him sedulously, drinking his health, waving his flag, playing his anthem, and using the foolish word "traitor" freely in its cups. But let the English Government make a step towards the democratic party, and the Protestant garrison revolts at once, not with tears and prayers and anguish of soul and years of trembling reluctance, as the parliamentarians of the XVII century revolted against Charles I, but with acrid promptitude and strident threatenings. When England finally abandons the garrison by yielding to the demand for Home Rule, the Protestants will not go under, nor will they waste much time in sulking over their betrayal, and comparing their fate with that of Gordon left by Gladstone to perish on the spears of heathen fanatics. They cannot afford to retire into an Irish Faubourg St Germain. They will take an energetic part in the national government, which will be sorely in need of parliamentary and official forces independent of Rome. They will get not only the Protestant votes, but the votes of Catholics in that spirit of toleration which is everywhere extended to heresies that happen to be politically serviceable to the orthodox. They will not relax their determination to hold every inch of the government of Ireland that they can grasp; but as that government will then be a national Irish government instead of as now an English

government, their determination will make them the vanguard
of Irish Nationalism and Democracy as against Romanism and
Sacerdotalism, leaving English Unionists grieved and shocked
at their discovery of the true value of an Irish Protestant's
loyalty.

But there will be no open break in the tradition of the
party. The Protestants will still be the party of Union, which
will then mean, not the Repeal of Home Rule, but the maintenance of the Federal Union of English-speaking common-
wealths, now theatrically called the Empire. They will pull
down the Union Jack without the smallest scruple; but they
know the value of the Channel Fleet, and will cling closer than
brothers to that and any other Imperial asset that can be exploited for the protection of Ireland against foreign aggression
or the sharing of expenses with the British taxpayer. They
know that the Irish coast is for the English invasion-scare-
monger the heel of Achilles, and that they can use this to make
him pay for the boot.

PROTESTANT PUGNACITY

If any Englishman feels incredulous as to this view of
Protestantism as an essentially Nationalist force in Ireland,
let him ask himself which leader he, if he were an Irishman,
would rather have back from the grave to fight England: the
Catholic Daniel O'Connell or the Protestant Parnell. O'Connell organized the Nationalist movement only to draw its teeth,
to break its determination, and to declare that Repeal of the
Union was not worth the shedding of a drop of blood. He died
in the bosom of his Church, not in the bosom of his country.
The Protestant leaders, from Lord Edward Fitzgerald to Parnell, have never divided their devotion. If any Englishman
thinks that they would have been more sparing of blood than
the English themselves are, if only so cheap a fluid could have
purchased the honor of Ireland, he greatly mistakes the Irish
Protestant temper. The notion that Ireland is the only country
in the world not worth shedding a drop of blood for is not a

Protestant one, and certainly not countenanced by English practice. It was hardly reasonable to ask Parnell to shed blood *quant. suff.* in Egypt to put an end to the misgovernment of the Khedive and replace him by Lord Cromer for the sake of the English bondholders, and then to expect him to become a Tolstoyan or an O'Connellite in regard to his own country. With a wholly Protestant Ireland at his back he might have bullied England into conceding Home Rule; for the insensibility of the English governing classes to philosophical, moral, social considerations—in short, to any considerations which require a little intellectual exertion and sympathetic alertness—is tempered, as we Irish well know, by an absurd susceptibility to intimidation.

For let me halt a moment here to impress on you, O English reader, that no fact has been more deeply stamped into us than that we can do nothing with an English Government unless we frighten it, any more than you can yourself. When power and riches are thrown haphazard into children's cradles as they are in England, you get a governing class without industry, character, courage, or real experience; and under such circumstances reforms are produced only by catastrophes followed by panics in which "something must be done." Thus it costs a cholera epidemic to achieve a Public Health Act, a Crimean War to reform the Civil Service, and a gunpowder plot to disestablish the Irish Church. It was by the light, not of reason, but of the moon, that the need for paying serious attention to the Irish land question was seen in England. It cost the American War of Independence and the Irish Volunteer movement to obtain the Irish parliament of 1782, the constitution of which far overshot the nationalist mark of today in the matter of independence.

It is vain to plead that this is human nature and not class weakness. The Japanese have proved that it is possible to conduct social and political changes intelligently and providentially instead of drifting along helplessly until public disasters compel a terrified and inconsiderate rearrangement. Innumera-

ble experiments in local government have shewn that when
men are neither too poor to be honest nor too rich to understand and share the needs of the people—as in New Zealand,
for example—they can govern much more providently than
our little circle of aristocrats and plutocrats.

THE JUST ENGLISHMAN

English Unionists, when asked what they have to say in
defence of their rule of subject peoples, often reply that the
Englishman is just, leaving us divided between our derision
of so monstrously inhuman a pretension, and our impatience
with so gross a confusion of the mutually exclusive functions
of judge and legislator. For there is only one condition on
which a man can do justice between two litigants, and that is
that he shall have no interest in common with either of them,
whereas it is only by having every interest in common with
both of them that he can govern them tolerably. The indispensable preliminary to Democracy is the representation of
every interest: the indispensable preliminary to justice is the
elimination of every interest. When we want an arbitrator
or an umpire, we turn to a stranger: when we want a government, a stranger is the one person we will not endure. The
Englishman in India, for example, stands, a very statue of justice, between two natives. He says, in effect, "I am impartial
in your religious disputes because I believe in neither of your
religions. I am impartial in your conflicts of custom and sentiment because your customs and sentiments are different from,
and abysmally inferior to, my own. Finally, I am impartial
as to your interests because they are both equally opposed to
mine, which is to keep you both equally powerless against me
in order that I may extract money from you to pay salaries and
pensions to myself and my fellow Englishmen as judges and
rulers over you. In return for which you get the inestimable
benefit of a government that does absolute justice as between
Indian and Indian, being wholly preoccupied with the maintenance of absolute injustice as between India and England."

It will be observed that no Englishman, without making himself ridiculous, could pretend to be perfectly just or disinterested in English affairs, or would tolerate a proposal to establish the Indian or Irish system in Great Britain. Yet if the justice of the Englishman is sufficient to ensure the welfare of India or Ireland, it ought to suffice equally for England. But the English are wise enough to refuse to trust to English justice themselves, preferring democracy. They can hardly blame the Irish for taking the same view.

In short, dear English reader, the Irish Protestant stands outside that English Mutual Admiration Society which you call the Union or the Empire. You may buy a common and not ineffective variety of Irish Protestant by delegating your powers to him, and in effect making him the oppressor and you his sorely bullied and bothered catspaw and military maintainer; but if you offer him nothing for his loyalty except the natural superiority of the English character, you will—well, try the experiment, and see what will happen! You would have a ten-times better chance with the Roman Catholic; for he has been saturated from his youth up with the Imperial idea of foreign rule by a spiritually superior international power, and is trained to submission and abnegation of his private judgment. A Roman Catholic garrison would take its orders from England and let her rule Ireland if England were Roman Catholic. The Protestant garrison simply seizes on the English power; uses it for its own purposes; and occasionally orders the English Government to remove an Irish secretary who has dared to apply English ideas to the affairs of the garrison. Whereupon the English Government abjectly removes him, and implores him, as a gentleman and a loyal Englishman, not to reproach it in the face of the Nationalist enemy.

Such incidents naturally do not shake the sturdy conviction of the Irish Protestant that he is more than a match for any English Government in determination and intelligence. Here, no doubt, he flatters himself; for his advantage is not really an advantage of character, but of comparative directness of interest, concentration of force on one narrow issue, simplicity of aim, with freedom from the scruples and responsibilities of world-politics. The business is Irish business, not English; and he is Irish. And his object, which is simply to secure the dominance of his own caste and creed behind the power of England, is simpler and clearer than the confused aims of English Cabinets struggling ineptly with the burdens of empire, and biassed by the pressure of capital anywhere rather than in Ireland. He has no responsibility, no interest, no status outside his own country and his own movement, which means that he has no conscience in dealing with England; whereas England, having a very uneasy conscience, and many hindering and hampering responsibilities and interests in dealing with him, gets bullied and driven by him, and finally learns sympathy with Nationalist aims by her experience of the tyranny of the Orange party.

IRISH CATHOLICISM FORECAST

Let us suppose that the establishment of a national government were to annihilate the oligarchic party by absorbing the Protestant garrison and making it a Protestant National Guard. The Roman Catholic laity, now a cipher, would organize itself; and a revolt against Rome and against the priesthood would ensue. The Roman Catholic Church would become the official Irish Church. The Irish parliament would insist on a voice in the promotion of churchmen; fees and contributions would be regulated; blackmail would be resisted; sweating in conventual factories and workshops would be stopped; and the ban would be taken off the universities. In a word, the Roman Catholic Church, against which Dublin Castle is powerless, would meet the one force on earth that can cope with it victoriously. That force is Democracy, a thing far more Catholic than itself. Until that force is let loose against it, the Protestant garrison can do nothing to the priesthood except consolidate it and drive the people to rally round it in defence of their altars against the foreigner and the heretic. Where it *is* let loose, the Catholic laity will make as short work of sacerdotal tyranny in Ireland as it has done in France and Italy. And in doing so it will be forced to face the old problem of the relations of Church and State. A Roman Catholic party must submit to Rome: an anti-clerical Catholic party must of necessity become an Irish Catholic party. The Holy Roman Empire, like the other Em-pires, has no future except as a Federation of national Catholic Churches; for Christianity can no more escape Democracy than Democracy can escape Socialism. It is noteworthy in this connection that the Anglican Catholics have played and are playing a notable part in the Socialist movement in England in opposition to the individualist Secularists of the urban pro-letariat; but they are quit of the preliminary dead lift that awaits the Irish Catholic. Their Church has thrown off the yoke of Rome, and is safely and permanently Anglicized. But the Catholic Church in Ireland is still Roman. Home Rule will herald the day when the Vatican will go the way of Dublin Castle, and the island of the saints assume the headship of her own Church. It may seem incredible that long after the last Orangeman shall lay down his chalk for ever, the familiar scrawl on every blank wall in the north of Ireland "To hell with the Pope!" may reappear in the south, traced by the hands of Catholics who shall have forgotten the traditional counter legend, "To hell with King William!" (of glorious, pious, and immortal memory); but it may happen so. "The island of the saints" is no idle phrase. Religious genius is one of our na-tional products; and Ireland is no bad rock to build a Church on. Holy and beautiful is the soul of Catholic Ireland: her prayers are lovelier than the teeth and claws of Protestantism, but not so effective in dealing with the English.

ENGLISH VOLTAIREANISM

Let me familiarize the situation by shewing how closely it reproduces the English situation in its essentials. In Eng-land, as in France, the struggle between the priesthood and the laity has produced a vast body of Voltaireans. But the essential identity of the French and English movements has been obscured by the ignorance of the ordinary Englishman, who, instead of knowing the distinctive tenets of his church or sect, vaguely believes them to be the eternal truth as opposed to the damnable error of all the other denominations. He thinks of Voltaire as a French "infidel," instead of as the champion of the laity against the official theocracy of the State Church. The Nonconformist leaders of our Free Churches are all Voltaireans. The warcry of the Passive Resisters is Voltaire's warcry, "Ecrasez l'infâme." No account need be taken of the technical difference between Voltaire's "infâme" and Dr Clifford's. One was the unreformed Roman Church of France: the other is the reformed Anglican Church; but in both cases the attack has been on a priestly tyranny and a professional monopoly. Voltaire convinced the Genevan ministers that he was the philosophic champion of their Protestant, Individualistic, Democratic Deism against the State Church of Roman Catholic France; and his heroic energy and beneficence as a philanthropist, which now only makes the list of achievements on his monument at Ferney the most impressive epitaph in Europe, then made the most earnest of the Lutheran ministers glad to claim a common inspiration with him. Unfortunately Voltaire had an irrepressible sense of humor. He joked about Habakkuk; and jokes about Habakkuk smelt too strongly of brimstone to be tolerated by Protestants to whom the Bible was not a literature but a fetish and a talisman. And so Voltaire, in spite of the church he "erected to God," became in England the bogey-atheist of three generations of English ignoramuses, instead of the legitimate successor of Martin Luther and John Knox.

Nowadays, however, Voltaire's jokes are either forgotten or else fall flat on a world which no longer venerates Habakkuk; and his true position is becoming apparent. The fact that Voltaire was a Roman Catholic layman, educated at a Jesuit college, is the conclusive reply to the shallow people who imagine that Ireland delivered up to the Irish democracy—

that is, to the Catholic laity—would be delivered up to the tyranny of the priesthood.

SUPPOSE!

Suppose, now, that the conquest of France by Henry V of England had endured, and that France in the XVIII century had been governed by an English viceroy through a Huguenot bureaucracy and a judicial bench appointed on the understanding that loyalty for them meant loyalty to England, and patriotism a willingness to die in defence of the English conquest and of the English Church, would not Voltaire in that case have been the meanest of traitors and self-seekers if he had played the game of England by joining in its campaign against his own and his country's Church? The energy he threw into the defence of Calas and Sirven would have been thrown into the defence of the Frenchmen whom the English would have called "rebels"; and he would have been forced to identify the cause of freedom and democracy with the cause of "l'infâme." The French revolution would have been a revolution against England and English rule instead of against aristocracy and ecclesiasticism; and all the intellectual and spiritual forces in France, from Turgot to De Tocqueville, would have been burnt up in mere anti-Anglicism and nationalist dithyrambs instead of contributing to political science and broadening the thought of the world.

What would have happened in France is what has happened in Ireland; and that is why it is only the small-minded Irish, incapable of conceiving what religious freedom means to a country, who do not loathe English rule. For in Ireland England is nothing but the Pope's policeman. She imagines she is holding the Vatican cardinals at bay when she is really strangling the Voltaires, the Foxes and Penns, the Cliffords, Hortons, Campbells, Walters, and Silvester Hornes, who are to be found among the Roman Catholic laity as plentifully as among the Anglican Catholic laity in England. She gets nothing out of Ireland but infinite trouble, infinite con-

fusion and hindrance in her own legislation, a hatred that cir-
culates through the whole world and poisons it against her, a
reproach that makes her professions of sympathy with Finland
and Macedonia ridiculous and hypocritical, whilst the priest
takes all the spoils, in money, in power, in pride, and in popularity.

IRELAND'S REAL GRIEVANCE

But it is not the spoils that matter. It is the waste, the sterili-
zation, the perversion of fruitful brain power into flatulent
protest against unnecessary evil, the use of our very entrails to
tie our own hands and seal our own lips in the name of our
honor and patriotism. As far as money or comfort is concerned,
the average Irishman has a more tolerable life—especially now
that the population is so scanty—than the average Englishman.
It is true that in Ireland the poor man is robbed and starved
and oppressed under judicial forms which confer the imposing
title of justice on a crude system of bludgeoning and perjury.
But so is the Englishman. The Englishman, more docile, less
dangerous, too lazy intellectually to use such political and
legal power as lies within his reach, suffers more and makes less
fuss about it than the Irishman. But at least he has nobody to
blame but himself and his fellow countrymen. He does not
doubt that if an effective majority of the English people made
up their minds to alter the Constitution, as the majority of
the Irish people have made up their minds to obtain Home
Rule, they could alter it without having to fight an overwhelm-
ingly powerful and rich neighboring nation, and fight, too,
with ropes round their necks. He can attack any institution in
his country without betraying it to foreign vengeance and
foreign oppression. True, his landlord may turn him out of his
cottage if he goes to a Methodist chapel instead of to the parish
church. His customers may stop their orders if he votes Liberal
instead of Conservative. English ladies and gentlemen who
would perish sooner than shoot a fox do these things without
the smallest sense of indecency and dishonor. But they cannot

muzzle his intellectual leaders. The English philosopher, the English author, the English orator can attack every abuse and expose every superstition without strengthening the hands of any common enemy. In Ireland every such attack, every such exposure, is a service to England and a stab to Ireland. If you expose the tyranny and rapacity of the Church, it is an argument in favor of Protestant ascendency. If you denounce the nepotism and jobbery of the new local authorities, you are demonstrating the unfitness of the Irish to govern themselves, and the superiority of the old oligarchical grand juries.

And there is the same pressure on the other side. The Protestant must stand by the garrison at all costs: the Unionist must wink at every bureaucratic abuse, connive at every tyranny, magnify every official blockhead, because their exposure would be a victory for the Nationalist enemy. Every Irishman is in Lancelot's position: his honor rooted in dishonor stands; and faith unfaithful keeps him falsely true.

THE CURSE OF NATIONALISM

It is hardly possible for an Englishman to understand all that this implies. A conquered nation is like a man with cancer: he can think of nothing else, and is forced to place himself, to the exclusion of all better company, in the hands of quacks who profess to treat or cure cancer. The windbags of the two rival platforms are the most insufferable of all windbags. It requires neither knowledge, character, conscience, diligence in public affairs, nor any virtue, private or communal, to thump the Nationalist or Orange tub: nay, it puts a premium on the rancor or callousness that has given rise to the proverb that if you put an Irishman on a spit you can always get another Irishman to baste him. Jingo oratory in England is sickening enough to serious people: indeed one evening's mafficking in London produced a determined call for the police. Well, in Ireland all political oratory is Jingo oratory; and all political demonstrations are maffickings. English rule is such an intolerable

abomination that no other subject can reach the people.
Nationalism stands between Ireland and the light of the world.
Nobody in Ireland of any intelligence likes Nationalism any
more than a man with a broken arm likes having it set. A
healthy nation is as unconscious of its nationality as a healthy
man of his bones. But if you break a nation's nationality it
will think of nothing else but getting it set again. It will listen
to no reformer, to no philosopher, to no preacher, until the
demand of the Nationalist is granted. It will attend to no
business, however vital, except the business of unification and
liberation.

That is why everything is in abeyance in Ireland pending
the achievement of Home Rule. The great movements of the
human spirit which sweep in waves over Europe are stopped
on the Irish coast by the English guns of the Pigeon House
Fort. Only a quaint little offshoot of English pre-Raphaelitism
called the Gaelic movement has got a footing by using Nationalism as a stalking-horse, and popularizing itself as an attack
on the native language of the Irish people, which is most
fortunately also the native language of half the world,
including England. Every election is fought on nationalist
grounds; every appointment is made on nationalist grounds;
every judge is a partisan in the nationalist conflict; every speech
is a dreary recapitulation of nationalist twaddle; every lecture
is a corruption of history to flatter nationalism or defame it;
every school is a recruiting station; every church is a barrack;
and every Irishman is unspeakably tired of the whole miserable
business, which nevertheless is and perforce must remain his
first business until Home Rule makes an end of it, and sweeps
the nationalist and the garrison back together into the dustbin.

There is indeed no greater curse to a nation than a nationalist movement, which is only the agonizing symptom of a
suppressed natural function. Conquered nations lose their
place in the world's march because they can do nothing but
strive to get rid of their nationalist movements by recovering
their national liberty. All demonstrations of the virtues of a

foreign government, though often conclusive, are as useless as demonstrations of the superiority of artificial teeth, glass eyes, silver windpipes, and patent wooden legs to the natural products. Like Democracy, national self-government is not for the good of the people: it is for the satisfaction of the people. One Antonine emperor, one St Louis, one Richelieu, may be worth ten democracies in point of what is called good government; but there is no satisfaction for the people in them. To deprive a dyspeptic of his dinner and hand it over to a man who can digest it better is a highly logical proceeding; but it is not a sensible one. To take the government of Ireland away from the Irish and hand it over to the English on the ground that they can govern better would be a precisely parallel case if the English had managed their own affairs so well as to place their superior faculty for governing beyond question. But as the English are avowed muddlers—rather proud of it, in fact—even the logic of that case against Home Rule is not complete. Read Mr Charles Booth's account of London, Mr Rowntree's account of York, and the latest official report on Dundee; and then pretend, if you can, that Englishmen and Scotchmen have not more cause to hand over their affairs to an Irish parliament than to clamor for another nation's cities to devastate and another people's business to mismanage.

A NATURAL RIGHT

The question is not one of logic at all, but of natural right. English universities have for some time past encouraged an extremely foolish academic exercise which consists in disproving the existence of natural rights on the ground that they cannot be deduced from the principles of any known political system. If they could, they would not be natural rights but acquired ones. Acquired rights are deduced from political constitutions; but political constitutions are deduced from natural rights. When a man insists on certain liberties without the slightest regard to demonstrations that they are not for his own good, nor for the public good, nor moral, nor reasonable, nor decent, nor compatible with the existing constitution of society, then he is said to claim a natural right to that liberty. When, for instance, he insists on living, in spite of the irrefutable demonstrations of many able pessimists, from the author of the book of Ecclesiastes to Schopenhauer, that life is an evil, he is asserting a natural right to live. When he insists on a vote in order that his country may be governed according to his ignorance instead of the wisdom of the Privy Council, he is asserting a natural right to self-government. When he insists on guiding himself at 21 by his own inexperience and folly and immaturity instead of by the experience and sagacity of his father, or the well-stored mind of his grandmother, he is asserting a natural right to independence. Even if Home Rule were as unhealthy as an Englishman's eating, as intemperate as his drinking, as filthy as his smoking, as licentious as his domesticity, as corrupt as his elections, as murderously greedy as his commerce, as cruel as his prisons, and as merciless as his streets, Ireland's claim to self-government would still be as good as England's. King James the First proved so cleverly and conclusively that the satisfaction of natural rights was incompatible with good government that his courtiers called him Solomon. We, more enlightened, call him Fool, solely because we have learnt that nations insist on being governed by their own consent—or, as they put it, by themselves and for themselves—and that they will finally upset a good government which denies them this even if the alternative be a bad government which at least creates and maintains an illusion of democracy. America, as far as one can ascertain, is much worse governed, and has a much more disgraceful political history than England under Charles I; but the American Republic is the stabler government because it starts from a formal concession of natural rights, and keeps up an illusion of safeguarding them by an elaborate machinery of democratic election. And the final reason why Ireland must have Home Rule is that she has a natural right to it.

A WARNING

Finally, some words of warning to both nations. Ireland has been deliberately ruined again and again by England. Unable to compete with us industrially, she has destroyed our industries by the brute force of prohibitive taxation. She was perfectly right. That brute force was a more honorable weapon than the poverty which we used to undersell her. We lived with and as our pigs, and let loose our wares in the Englishman's market at prices which he could compete with only by living like a pig himself. Having the alternative of stopping our industry altogether, he very naturally and properly availed himself of it. We should have done the same in his place. To bear malice against him on that score is to poison our blood and weaken our constitutions with unintelligent rancor. In wrecking all the industries that were based on the poverty of our people England did us an enormous service. In omitting to do the same on her own soil, she did herself a wrong that has rotted her almost to the marrow. I hope that when Home Rule is at last achieved, one of our first legislative acts will be to fortify the subsistence of our people behind the bulwark of a standard wage, and to impose crushing import duties on every English trade that flourishes in the slum and fattens on the starvation of our unfortunate English neighbors.

W. B. Yeats (1865-1939)

Cuchulain's Fight With the Sea[1]

A Man came slowly, from the setting sun,
To Emer, raddling[2] raiment in her dun,
And said, "I am that swineherd whom you bid
Go watch the road between the wood and tide,
But now I have no need to watch it more."

Then Emer cast the web upon the floor,
And raising arms all raddled with the dye,
Parted her lips with a loud sudden cry.
That swineherd stared upon her face and said,
"No man alive, no man among the dead,
Has won the gold his cars of battle bring."

"But if your master comes home triumphing
Why must you blench and shake from foot to crown?"

Thereon he shook the more and cast him down
Upon the web-heaped floor, and cried his word:
"With him is one sweet-throated like a bird."

---

[1] How Cuchulain unknowingly killed his own son is told in a ninth century story entitled "The Tragic Death of Connla" (see p. 61). Yeats' poem, however, is not based directly on the Old Irish tale but on later ballad versions in which the roles of Emer and Aife have been reversed and in which Cuchulain is deluded by a druid's spell into fighting the waves. Yeats dealt with the same story in his play On Baile's Strand (1904).

[2] Coloring coarsely with red or rouge. NED

"You dare me to my face," and thereupon
She smote with raddled fist, and where her son
Herded the cattle came with stumbling feet,
And cried with angry voice, "It is not meet
To idle life away, a common herd."

"I have long waited, mother, for that word:
But wherefore now?"
                    "There is a man to die;
You have the heaviest arm under the sky."

"Whether under its daylight or its stars
My father stands amid his battle-cars."

"But you have grown to be the taller man."

"Yet somewhere under starlight or the sun
My father stands."
                    "Aged, worn out with wars
On foot, on horseback or in battle-cars."

"I only ask what way my journey lies,
For He who made you bitter made you wise."

"The Red Branch camp in a great company
Between wood's rim and the horses of the sea.
Go there, and light a camp-fire at wood's rim;
But tell your name and lineage to him
Whose blade compels, and wait till they have found
Some feasting man that the same oath has bound."

Among those feasting men Cuchulain dwelt
And his young sweetheart close beside him knelt,
Stared on the mournful wonder of his eyes,
Even as Spring upon the ancient skies,
And pondered on the glory of his days;
And all around the harp-string told his praise,
And Conchubar, the Red Branch king of kings,
With his own fingers touched the brazen strings.

At last Cuchulain spake, "Some man has made
His evening fire amid the leafy shade.
I have often heard him singing to and fro,
I have often heard the sweet sound of his bow.
Seek out what man he is."
                                    One went and came.
"He bade me let all know he gives his name
At the sword-point, and waits till we have found
Some feasting man that the same oath has bound."

Cuchulain cried, "I am the only man
Of all this host so bound from childhood on."

After short fighting in the leafy shade,
He spake to the young man, "Is there no maid
Who loves you, no white arms to wrap you round,
Or do you long for the dim sleepy ground,
That you have come and dared me to my face?"

"The dooms of men are in God's hidden place."

"Your head a while seemed like a woman's head
That I loved once."
                                  Again the fighting sped,
But now the war-rage in Cuchulain woke,
And through that new blade's guard the old blade broke,
And pierced him.
                            "Speak before your breath is done."

"Cuchulain I, mighty Cuchulain's son."

"I put you from your pain. I can no more."

While day its burden on to evening bore,
With head bowed on his knees Cuchulain stayed;
Then Conchubar sent that sweet-throated maid,
And she, to win him, his grey hair caressed;
In vain her arms, in vain her soft white breast.
Then Conchubar, the subtlest of all men,
Ranking his Druids round him ten by ten,
Spake thus: "Cuchulain will dwell there and brood
For three days more in dreadful quietude,
And then arise, and raving slay us all.
Chaunt in his ear delusions magical,
That he may fight the horses of the sea."

The Druids took them to their mystery,
And chaunted for three days.
                                  Cuchulain stirred,
Stared on the horses of the sea, and heard
The cars of battle and his own name cried;
And fought with the invulnerable tide.

The Folly of Being Comforted

One that is ever kind said yesterday:
"Your well-belovèd's hair has threads of grey,
And little shadows come about her eyes;
Time can but make it easier to be wise
Though now it seems impossible, and so
All that you need is patience."

                             Heart cries, "No,
I have not a crumb of comfort, not a grain.
Time can but make her beauty over again:
Because of that great nobleness of hers
The fire that stirs about her, when she stirs,
Burns but more clearly. O she had not these ways
When all the wild summer was in her gaze."

O heart! O heart! if she'd but turn her head,
You'd know the folly of being comforted.

To A Shade

If you have revisited the town, thin Shade,
Whether to look upon your monument
(I wonder if the builder has been paid)
Or happier-thoughted when the day is spent
To drink of that salt breath out of the sea
When grey gulls flit about instead of men,
And the gaunt houses put on majesty:
Let these content you and be gone again;
For they are at their old tricks yet.

A man
Of your own passionate serving kind who had brought
In his full hands what, had they only known,
Had given their children's children loftier thought,
Sweeter emotion, working in their veins
Like gentle blood, has been driven from the place,
And insult heaped upon him for his pains,
And for his open-handedness, disgrace;
Your enemy, an old foul mouth, had set
The pack upon him.
                              Go, unquiet wanderer,
And gather the Glasnevin coverlet
About your head till the dust stops your ear,
The time for you to taste of that salt breath
And listen at the corners has not come;
You had enough of sorrow before death—
Away, away! You are safer in the tomb.
    September 29, 1913

In Memory of Major Robert Gregory

I

Now that we're almost settled in our house
I'll name the friends that cannot sup with us
Beside a fire of turf in th' ancient tower,
And having talked to some late hour
Climb up the narrow winding stairs to bed:
Discoverers of forgotten truth
Or mere companions of my youth,
All, all are in my thoughts to-night being dead.

II

Always we'd have the new friend meet the old
And we are hurt if either friend seem cold,
And there is salt to lengthen out the smart
In the affections of our heart,
And quarrels are blown up upon that head;
But not a friend that I would bring
This night would set us quarrelling,
For all that come into my mind are dead.

III

Lionel Johnson comes the first to mind,
That loved his learning better than mankind,
Though courteous to the worst; much falling he
Brooded upon sanctity
Till all his Greek and Latin learning seemed
A long blast upon the horn that brought
A little nearer to his thought
A measureless consummation that he dreamed.

IV

And that enquiring man John Synge comes next,
That dying chose the living world for text
And never could have rested in the tomb
But that, long travelling, he had come
Towards nightfall upon certain set apart
In a most desolate stony place,
Towards nightfall upon a race
Passionate and simple like his heart.

V

And then I think of old George Pollexfen,
In muscular youth well known to Mayo men
For horsemanship at meets or at racecourses,
That could have shown how pure-bred horses
And solid men, for all their passion, live
But as the outrageous stars incline
By opposition, square and trine;
Having grown sluggish and contemplative.

VI

They were my close companions many a year,
A portion of my mind and life, as it were,
And now their breathless faces seem to look
Out of some old picture-book;
I am accustomed to their lack of breath,
But not that my dear friend's dear son,
Our Sidney and our perfect man,
Could share in that discourtesy of death.

VII

For all things the delighted eye now sees
Were loved by him: the old storm-broken trees
That cast their shadows upon road and bridge;
The tower set on the stream's edge;
The ford where drinking cattle make a stir
Nightly, and startled by that sound
The water-hen must change her ground;
He might have been your heartiest welcomer.

VIII

When with the Galway foxhounds he would ride
From Castle Taylor to the Roxborough side
Or Esserkelly plain, few kept his pace;
At Mooneen he had leaped a place
So perilous that half the astonished meet
Had shut their eyes; and where was it
He rode a race without a bit?
And yet his mind outran the horses' feet.

IX

We dreamed that a great painter had been born
To cold Clare rock and Galway rock and thorn,
To that stern colour and that delicate line
That are our secret discipline
Wherein the gazing heart doubles her might.
Soldier, scholar, horseman, he,
And yet he had the intensity
To have published all to be a world's delight.

X

What other could so well have counselled us
In all lovely intricacies of a house
As he that practised or that understood
All work in metal or in wood,
In moulded plaster or in carven stone?
Soldier, scholar, horseman, he,
And all he did done perfectly
As though he had but that one trade alone.

XI

Some burn damp faggots, others may consume
The entire combustible world in one small room
As though dried straw, and if we turn about
The bare chimney is gone black out
Because the work had finished in that flare.
Soldier, scholar, horseman, he,
As 'twere all life's epitome.
What made us dream that he could comb grey hair?

XII

I had thought, seeing how bitter is that wind
That shakes the shutter, to have brought to mind
All those that manhood tried, or childhood loved
Or boyish intellect approved,
With some appropriate commentary on each;
Until imagination brought
A fitter welcome; but a thought
Of that late death took all my heart for speech.

Sailing to Byzantium

I

That is no country for old men. The young
In one another's arms, birds in the trees
—Those dying generations—at their song,
The salmon-falls, the mackerel-crowded seas,
Fish, flesh, or fowl, commend all summer long
Whatever is begotten, born, and dies.
Caught in that sensual music all neglect
Monuments of unageing intellect.

II

An aged man is but a paltry thing,
A tattered coat upon a stick, unless
Soul clap its hands and sing, and louder sing
For every tatter in its mortal dress,
Nor is there singing school but studying
Monuments of its own magnificence;
And therefore I have sailed the seas and come
To the holy city of Byzantium.

III

O sages standing in God's holy fire
As in the gold mosaic of a wall,
Come from the holy fire, perne in a gyre,
And be the singing-masters of my soul.
Consume my heart away; sick with desire
And fastened to a dying animal
It knows not what it is; and gather me
Into the artifice of eternity.

IV

Once out of nature I shall never take
My bodily form from any natural thing,
But such a form as Grecian goldsmiths make
Of hammered gold and gold enamelling
To keep a drowsy Emperor awake;
Or set upon a golden bough to sing
To lords and ladies of Byzantium
Of what is past, or passing, or to come.
            1927

Leda and the Swan

A sudden blow: the great wings beating still
Above the staggering girl, her thighs caressed
By the dark webs, her nape caught in his bill,
He holds her helpless breast upon his breast.

How can those terrified vague fingers push
The feathered glory from her loosening thighs?
And how can body, laid in that white rush,
But feel the strange heart beating where it lies?

A shudder in the loins engenders there
The broken wall, the burning roof and tower
And Agamemnon dead.
                    Being so caught up,
So mastered by the brute blood of the air,
Did she put on his knowledge with his power
Before the indifferent beak could let her drop?
    1923

Among School Children

I

I walk through the long school room questioning;
A kind old nun in a white hood replies;
The children learn to cipher and to sing,
To study reading-books and histories,
To cut and sew, be neat in everything
In the best modern way—the children's eyes
In momentary wonder stare upon
A sixty-year-old smiling public man.

II

I dream of a Ledaean body, bent
Above a sinking fire, a tale that she
Told of a harsh reproof, or trivial event
That changed some childish day to tragedy—
Told, and it seemed that our two natures blent
Into a sphere from youthful sympathy,
Or else, to alter Plato's parable,
Into the yolk and white of the one shell.

III

And thinking of that fit of grief or rage
I look upon one child or t'other there
And wonder if she stood so at that age—
For even daughters of the swan can share
Something of that paddler's heritage—
And had that colour upon cheek or hair,
And thereupon my heart is driven wild:
She stands before me as a living child.

IV

Her present image floats into the mind—
Did Quattrocento finger fashion it
Hollow of cheek as though it drank the wind
And took a mess of shadows for its meat?
And I though never of Ledaean kind
Had pretty plumage once—enough of that,
Better to smile on all that smile, and show
There is a comfortable kind of old scarecrow.

V

What youthful mother, a shape upon her lap
Honey of generation had betrayed,
And that must sleep, shriek, struggle to escape
As recollection or the drug decide,
Would think her son, did she but see that shape
With sixty or more winters on its head,
A compensation for the pang of his birth,
Or the uncertainty of his setting forth?

VI

Plato thought nature but a spume that plays
Upon a ghostly paradigm of things;
Soldier Aristotle played the taws
Upon the bottom of a king of kings;
World-famous golden-thighed Pythagoras
Fingered upon a fiddle-stick or strings
What a star sang and careless Muses heard:
Old clothes upon old sticks to scare a bird.

VII

Both nuns and mothers worship images,
But those the candles light are not as those
That animate a mother's reveries,
But keep a marble or a bronze repose.
And yet they too break hearts—O Presences
That passion, piety or affection knows,
And that all heavenly glory symbolise—
O self-born mockers of man's enterprise;

VIII

Labour is blossoming or dancing where
The body is not bruised to pleasure soul,
Nor beauty born out of its own despair,
Nor blear-eyed wisdom out of midnight oil.
O chestnut-tree, great-rooted blossomer,
Are you the leaf, the blossom or the bole?
O body swayed to music, O brightening glance,
How can we know the dancer from the dance?

The Wild Old Wicked Man

"Because I am mad about women
I am mad about the hills,"
Said that wild old wicked man
Who travels where God wills.
"Not to die on the straw at home,
Those hands to close these eyes,
That is all I ask, my dear,
From the old man in the skies.
      Daybreak and a candle-end.

"Kind are all your words, my dear,
Do not the rest withhold.
Who can know the year, my dear,
When an old man's blood grows cold?
I have what no young man can have
Because he loves too much.
Words I have that can pierce the heart,
But what can he do but touch?"
      Daybreak and a candle-end.

Then said she to that wild old man,
His stout stick under his hand,
"Love to give or to withhold
Is not at my command.
I gave it all to an older man:
That old man in the skies.
Hands that are busy with His beads
Can never close those eyes."
Daybreak and a candle-end.

"Go your ways, O go your ways,
I choose another mark,
Girls down on the seashore
Who understand the dark;
Bawdy talk for the fishermen;
A dance for the fisher-lads;
When dark hangs upon the water
They turn down their beds.
Daybreak and a candle-end.

"A young man in the dark am I,
But a wild old man in the light,
That can make a cat laugh, or
Can touch by mother wit
Things hid in their marrow-bones
From time long passed away,
Hid from all those warty lads
That by their bodies lay.
Daybreak and a candle-end.

"All men live in suffering,
I know as few can know,
Whether they take the upper road
Or stay content on the low,
Rower bent in his row-boat
Or weaver bent at his loom,
Horseman erect upon horseback
Or child hid in the womb.
    Daybreak and a candle-end.

"That some stream of lightning
From the old man in the skies
Can burn out that suffering
No right-taught man denies.
But a coarse old man am I,
I choose the second-best,
I forget it all awhile
Upon a woman's breast."
    Daybreak and a candle-end.

The Statues

Pythagoras planned it. Why did the people stare?
His numbers, though they moved or seemed to move
In marble or in bronze, lacked character.
But boys and girls, pale from the imagined love
Of solitary beds, knew what they were,
That passion could bring character enough,
And pressed at midnight in some public place
Live lips upon a plummet-measured face.

No! Greater than Pythagoras, for the men
That with a mallet or a chisel modelled these
Calculations that look but casual flesh, put down
All Asiatic vague immensities,
And not the banks of oars that swam upon
The many-headed foam at Salamis.
Europe put off that foam when Phidias
Gave women dreams and dreams their looking-glass.

One image crossed the many-headed, sat
Under the tropic shade, grew round and slow,
No Hamlet thin from eating flies, a fat
Dreamer of the Middle Ages. Empty eyeballs knew
That knowledge increases unreality, that
Mirror on mirror mirrored is all the show.
When gong and conch declare the hour to bless
Grimalkin crawls to Buddha's emptiness.

When Pearse[1] summoned Cuchulain to his side,
What stalked through the Post Office? What intellect,
What calculation, number, measurement, replied?
We Irish, born into that ancient sect
But thrown upon this filthy modern tide
And by its formless spawning fury wrecked,
Climb to our proper dark, that we may trace
The lineaments of a plummet-measured face.
        April 9, 1938

---

[1] Padraic Pearse (1879-1916) was one of the leaders in the Rising of 1916, when the General Post Office in Dublin was occupied by the insurrectionists and besieged by English forces.

AE (George Russell) (1867-1935)

Truth

THE hero first thought it
To him 'twas a deed:
To those who retaught it,
A chain on their speed.

The fire that we kindled,
A beacon by night,
When darkness has dwindled
Grows pale in the light.

For life has no glory
Stays long in one dwelling,
And time has no story
That's true twice in telling.

And only the teaching
That never was spoken
Is worthy thy reaching,
The fountain unbroken.

The Twilight of Earth

THE wonder of the world is o'er:
  The magic from the sea is gone:
There is no unimagined shore,
  No islet yet to venture on.
The Sacred Hazels' blooms are shed,
The Nuts of Knowledge harvested.

Oh, what is worth this lore of age
 If time shall never bring us back
Our battle with the gods to wage
 Reeling along the starry track.
The battle rapture here goes by
In warring upon things that die.

Let be the tale of him whose love
 Was sighed between white Deirdre's breasts,
It will not lift the heart above
 The sodden clay on which it rests.
Love once had power the gods to bring
All rapt on its wild wandering.

We shiver in the falling dew,
 And seek a shelter from the storm:
When man these elder brothers knew
 He found the mother nature warm,
A hearth fire blazing through it all,
A home without a circling wall.

We dwindle down beneath the skies,
 And from ourselves we pass away:
The paradise of memories
 Grows ever fainter day by day.
The shepherd stars have shrunk within,
The world's great night will soon begin.

Will no one, ere it is too late,
 Ere fades the last memorial gleam,
Recall for us our earlier state?
 For nothing but so vast a dream
That it would scale the steeps of air
Could rouse us from so vast despair.

The power is ours to make or mar
    Our fate as on the earliest morn,
The Darkness and the Radiance are
    Creatures within the spirit born.
Yet, bathed in gloom too long, we might
Forget how we imagined light.

Not yet are fixed the prison bars;
    The hidden light the spirit owns
If blown to flame would dim the stars
    And they who rule them from their thrones:
And the proud sceptred spirits thence
Would bow to pay us reverence.

Oh, while the glory sinks within
    Let us not wait on earth behind,
But follow where it flies, and win
    The glow again, and we may find
Beyond the Gateways of the Day
Dominion and ancestral sway.

On Behalf of Some Irishmen
Not Followers of Tradition

THEY call us aliens, we are told,
Because our wayward visions stray
From that dim banner they unfold,
The dreams of worn-out yesterday.
The sum of all the past is theirs,
The creeds, the deeds, the fame, the name,
Whose death-created glory flares
And dims the spark of living flame.
They weave the necromancer's spell,
And burst the graves where martyrs slept,
Their ancient story to retell,

Renewing tears the dead have wept.
And they would have us join their dirge,
This worship of an extinct fire
In which they drift beyond the verge
Where races all outworn expire.
The worship of the dead is not
A worship that our hearts allow,
Though every famous shade were wrought
With woven thorns above the brow.
We fling our answer back in scorn:
"We are less children of this clime
Than of some nation yet unborn
Or empire in the womb of time.
We hold the Ireland in the heart
More than the land our eyes have seen,
And love the goal for which we start
More than the tale of what has been."
The generations as they rise
May live the life men lived before,
Still hold the thought once held as wise,
Go in and out by the same door.
We leave the easy peace it brings:
The few we are shall still unite
In fealty to unseen kings
Or unimaginable light.
We would no Irish sign efface,
But yet our lips would gladlier hail
The firstborn of the Coming Race
Than the last splendour of the Gael.
No blazoned banner we unfold—
One charge alone we give to youth,
Against the sceptred myth to hold
The golden heresy of truth.

A Prisoner

Brixton, September 1920

SEE, though the oil be low, more purely still and higher
The flame burns in the body's lamp. The watchers still
Gaze with unseeing eyes while the Promethean will,
The Uncreated Light, the Everlasting Fire,
Sustain themselves against the torturer's desire,
Even as the fabled Titan chained upon the hill.
Burn on, shine here, thou immortality, until
We too can light our lamps at the funereal pyre;
Till we too can be noble, unshakeable, undismayed
Till we too can burn with the holy flame, and know
There is that within us can conquer the dragon pain,
And go to death alone, slowly and unafraid.
The candles of God already are burning row on row:
Farewell, light-bringer; fly to thy fountain again.

The King of Ireland's Son

BY Nora Hopper (1871-1906)

All the way to Tir na n'Og are many roads that run,
But the darkest road is trodden by the King of Ireland's Son.
The world wears on to sundown, and love is lost and won,
But he recks not of loss or gain, the King of Ireland's Son.
He follows on for ever, when all your chase is done,
He follows after shadows—the King of Ireland's Son.

From Deirdre of the Sorrows[1]

BY J. M. Synge (1871-1909)

ACT III

SCENE. *Tent below Emain, with shabby skins and benches. There is an opening at each side and at back, the latter closed. Old Woman comes in with food and fruits and arranges them on table. Conchubor comes in on right.*

CONCHUBOR (*sharply*). Has no one come with news for me?

OLD WOMAN. I've seen no one at all, Conchubor.

CONCHUBOR (*watches her working for a moment, then makes sure opening at back is closed*). Go up then to Emain, you're not wanting here. (*A noise heard left.*) Who is that?

OLD WOMAN (*going left*). It's Lavarcham coming again. She's a great wonder for jogging back and forward through the world, and I made certain she'd be off to meet them; but she's coming alone, Conchubor, my dear child Deirdre isn't with her at all.

CONCHUBOR. Go up so and leave us.

OLD WOMAN (*pleadingly*). I'd be well pleased to set my eyes on Deirdre if she's coming this night, as we're told.

---

[1] See p. 76 for the story from Old Irish literature upon which Synge's play is based. The third act begins at the point where Deirdre, her nurse Lavarcham and the sons of Usna have just returned to Emain Macha after their exile in Scotland. King Conchubor, from whom the lovers fled seven years before, has promised no harm to them if they will return and has sent Fergus to accompany them as surety. From the beginning Deirdre has looked with suspicion on the king's offer of a safe return. The first inkling Naisi has that they are to be betrayed comes when Fergus is separated from the lovers as soon as they arrive in Ireland by an offer of a feast, which he is under taboo not to refuse.

CONCHUBOR (*impatiently*).   It's not long till you'll see her. But I've matters with Lavarcham, and let you go now, I'm saying.

[*He shows her out right, as Lavarcham comes in on the left.*]

LAVARCHAM (*looking round her with suspicion*).   This is a queer place to find you, and it's a queer place to be lodging Naisi and his brothers, and Deirdre with them, and the lot of us tired out with the long way we have been walking.

CONCHUBOR.   You've come along with them the whole journey?

LAVARCHAM.   I have, then, though I've no call now to be wandering that length to a wedding or a burial, or the two together. (*She sits down wearily.*) It's a poor thing the way me and you is getting old, Conchubor, and I'm thinking you yourself have no call to be loitering this place getting your death, maybe, in the cold of night.

CONCHUBOR.   I'm waiting only to know is Fergus stopped in the north.

LAVARCHAM (*more sharply*).   He's stopped, surely, and that's a trick has me thinking you have it in mind to bring trouble this night on Emain and Ireland and the big world's east beyond them. (*She goes to him.*) And yet you'd do well to be going to your dun, and not putting shame on her meeting the High King, and she seamed and sweaty and in great disorder from the dust of many roads. (*Laughing derisively*). Ah, Conchubor, my lad, beauty goes quickly in the woods, and you'd let a great gasp, I tell you, if you set your eyes this night on Deirdre.

CONCHUBOR (*fiercely*).   It's little I care if she's white and worn, for it's I did rear her from a child. I should have a good right to meet and see her always.

LAVARCHAM.   A good right, is it?   Haven't the blind a good right to be seeing, and the lame to be dancing, and the dummies[1] singing tunes? It's that right you have to be looking for gaiety on Deirdre's lips. (*Coaxingly.*) Come on to your dun, I'm saying, and leave her quiet for one night itself.

---

[1] The dumb.

CONCHUBOR (*with sudden anger*). I'll not go, when it's long enough I am above in my dun stretching east and west without a comrade, and I more needy, maybe, than the thieves of Meath. . . . You think I'm old and wise, but I tell you the wise know the old must die, and they'll leave no chance for a thing slipping from them they've set their blood to win.

LAVARCHAM (*nodding her head*). If you're old and wise, it's I'm the same, Conchubor, and I'm telling you you'll not have her though you're ready to destroy mankind and skin the gods to win her. There's things a king can't have, Conchubor, and if you go rampaging this night you'll be apt to win nothing but death for many, and a sloppy face of trouble on your own self before the day will come.

CONCHUBOR. It's too much talk you have. (*Goes right.*) Where is Owen? Did you see him no place and you coming the road?

LAVARCHAM. I seen him surely. He went spying on Naisi, and now the worms is spying on his own inside.

CONCHUBOR (*exultingly*). Naisi killed him?

LAVARCHAM. He did not, then. It was Owen destroyed himself running mad because of Deirdre. Fools and kings and scholars are all one in a story with her like, and Owen thought he'd be a great man, being the first corpse in the game you'll play this night in Emain.

CONCHUBOR. It's yourself should be the first corpse, but my other messengers are coming, men from the clans that hated Usna.

LAVARCHAM (*drawing back hopelessly*). Then the gods have pity on us all!

[*Men with weapons come in.*]

CONCHUBOR (*to Soldiers*). Are Ainnle and Ardan separate from Naisi?

MEN. They are, Conchubor. We've got them off, saying they were needed to make ready Deirdre's house.

CONCHUBOR. And Naisi and Deirdre are coming?

SOLDIER. Naisi's coming, surely, and a woman with him is putting out the glory of the moon is rising and the sun is going down.

CONCHUBOR (*looking at Lavarcham*). That's your story that
she's seamed and ugly?

SOLDIER. I have more news. (*Pointing to Lavarcham.*) When
that woman heard you were bringing Naisi this place, she
sent a horse-boy to call Fergus from the north.

CONCHUBOR (*to Lavarcham*). It's for that you've been playing your tricks, but what you've won is a nearer death for
Naisi. (*To Soldiers.*) Go up and call my fighters, and take
that woman up to Emain.

LAVARCHAM. I'd liefer stay this place. I've done my best, but
if a bad end is coming, surely it would be a good thing maybe
I was here to tend her.

CONCHUBOR (*fiercely*). Take her to Emain; it's too many
tricks she's tried this day already. (*A Soldier goes to her.*)

LAVARCHAM. Don't touch me. (*She puts her cloak round her
and catches Conchubor's arm.*) I thought to stay your hand
with my stories till Fergus would come to be beside them,
the way I'd save yourself, Conchubor, and Naisi and Emain
Macha; but I'll walk up now into your halls, and I'll say
(*with a gesture*) it's here nettles will be growing, and beyond
thistles and docks. I'll go into your high chambers, where
you've been figuring yourself stretching out your neck for
the kisses of a queen of women; and I'll say it's here there'll
be deer stirring and goats scratching, and sheep waking and
coughing when there is a great wind from the north. (*Shaking herself loose. Conchubor makes a sign to Soldiers.*) I'm
going, surely. In a short space I'll be sitting up with many
listening to the flames crackling, and the beams breaking,
and I looking on the great blaze will be the end of Emain.
[*She goes out.*]

CONCHUBOR (*looking out*). I see two people in the trees; it
should be Naisi and Deirdre. (*To Soldier.*) Let you tell them
they'll lodge here to-night.
[*Conchubor goes out right. Naisi and Deirdre come in on
left, very weary.*]

NAISI (*to Soldiers*). Is it this place he's made ready for myself
and Deirdre?

SOLDIER. The Red Branch House is being aired and swept and you'll be called there when a space is by; till then you'd find fruits and drink on this table, and so the gods be with you.

[*Goes out right.*]

NAISI (*looking round*). It's a strange place he's put us camping and we come back as his friends.

DEIRDRE. He's likely making up a welcome for us, having curtains shaken out and rich rooms put in order; and it's right he'd have great state to meet us, and you his sister's son.

NAISI (*gloomily*). It's little we want with state or rich rooms or curtains, when we're used to the ferns only and cold streams and they making a stir.

DEIRDRE (*roaming round room*). We want what is our right in Emain (*looking at hangings*), and though he's riches in store for us it's a shabby, ragged place he's put us waiting, with frayed rugs and skins are eaten by the moths.

NAISI (*a little impatiently*). There are few would worry over skins and moths on this first night that we've come back to Emain.

DEIRDRE (*brightly*). You should be well pleased it's for that I'd worry all times, when it's I have kept your tent these seven years as tidy as a bee-hive or a linnet's nest. If Conchubor'd a queen like me in Emain he'd not have stretched these rags to meet us. (*She pulls hanging, and it opens.*) There's new earth on the ground and a trench dug. . . . It's a grave, Naisi, that is wide and deep.

NAISI (*goes over and pulls back curtain showing grave*). And that'll be our home in Emain. . . . He's dug it wisely at the butt of a hill, with fallen trees to hide it. He'll want to have us killed and buried before Fergus comes.

DEIRDRE. Take me away. . . . Take me to hide in the rocks, for the night is coming quickly.

NAISI (*pulling himself together*). I will not leave my brothers.

DEIRDRE (*vehemently*). It's of us two he's jealous. Come away to the places where we're used to have our company. . . .

Wouldn't it be a good thing to lie hid in the high ferns to-gether? (*She pulls him left.*) I hear strange words in the trees.

NAISI.   It should be the strange fighters of Conchubor. I saw them passing as we came.

DEIRDRE (*pulling him towards the right*).   Come to this side. Listen, Naisi!

NAISI.   There are more of them. . . . We are shut in, and I have not Ainnle and Ardan to stand near me. Isn't it a hard thing that we three who have conquered many may not die together?

DEIRDRE (*sinking down*).   And isn't it a hard thing that you and I are in this place by our opened grave; though none have lived had happiness like ours those days in Alban that went by so quick?

NAISI.   It's a hard thing, surely, we've lost those days for ever; and yet it's a good thing, maybe, that all goes quick, for when I'm in that grave it's soon a day'll come you'll be too wearied to be crying out, and that day'll bring you ease.

DEIRDRE.   I'll not be here to know if that is true.

NAISI.   It's our three selves he'll kill to-night, and then in two months or three you'll see him walking down for court-ship with yourself.

DEIRDRE.   I'll not be here.

NAISI (*hard*).   You'd best keep him off, maybe, and then, when the time comes, make your way to some place west in Donegal, and it's there you'll get used to stretching out lonesome at the fall of night, and waking lonesome for the day.

DEIRDRE.   Let you not be saying things are worse than death.

NAISI (*a little recklessly*).   I've one word left. If a day comes in the west that the larks are cocking their crests on the edge of the clouds, and the cuckoos making a stir, and there's a man you'd fancy, let you not be thinking that day I'd be well pleased you'd go on keening always.

DEIRDRE (*turning to look at him*).   And if it was I that died, Naisi, would you take another woman to fill up my place?

NAISI (*very mournfully*). It's little I know, saving only that it's a hard and bitter thing leaving the earth, and a worse and harder thing leaving yourself alone and desolate to be making lamentation on its face always.

DEIRDRE. I'll die when you do, Naisi. I'd not have come here from Alban but I knew I'd be along with you in Emain, and you living or dead. . . . Yet this night it's strange and distant talk you're making only.

NAISI. There's nothing, surely, the like of a new grave of open earth for putting a great space between two friends that love.

DEIRDRE. If there isn't, it's that grave when it's closed will make us one for ever, and we two lovers have had great space without weariness or growing old or any sadness of the mind.

CONCHUBOR (*coming in on right*). I'd bid you welcome, Naisi.

NAISI (*standing up*). You're welcome, Conchubor. I'm well pleased you've come.

CONCHUBOR (*blandly*). Let you not think bad of this place where I've put you till other rooms are readied.

NAISI (*breaking out*). We know the room you've readied. We know what stirred you to send your seals and Fergus into Alban and stop him in the north, (*opening curtain and pointing to the grave*) and dig that grave before us. Now I ask what brought you here?

CONCHUBOR. I've come to look on Deirdre.

NAISI. Look on her. You're a knacky fancier, and it's well you chose the one you'd lure from Alban. Look on her, I tell you, and when you've looked I've got ten fingers will squeeze your mottled goose neck, though you're king itself.

DEIRDRE (*coming between them*). Hush, Naisi! Maybe Conchubor'll make peace. . . . Do not mind him, Conchubor; he has cause to rage.

CONCHUBOR. It's little I heed his raging, when a call would bring my fighters from the trees. . . . But what do you say, Deirdre?

DEIRDRE. I'll say so near that grave we seem three lonesome

people, and by a new made grave there's no man will keep brooding on a woman's lips, or on the man he hates. It's not long till your own grave will be dug in Emain, and you'd go down to it more easy if you'd let call Ainnle and Ardan, the way we'd have a supper all together, and fill that grave, and you'll be well pleased from this out, having four new friends the like of us in Emain.

CONCHUBOR (*looking at her for a moment*). That's the first friendly word I've heard you speaking, Deirdre. A game the like of yours should be the proper thing for softening the heart and putting sweetness in the tongue; and yet this night when I hear you I've small blame left for Naisi that he stole you off from Ulster.

DEIRDRE (*to Naisi*). Now, Naisi, answer gently, and we'll be friends to-night.

NAISI (*doggedly*). I have no call but to be friendly. I'll answer what you will.

DEIRDRE (*taking Naisi's hand*). Then you'll call Conchubor your friend and king, the man who reared me up upon Slieve Fuadh.

[*As Conchubor is going to clasp Naisi's hand cries are heard behind.*]

CONCHUBOR. What noise is that?

AINNLE (*behind*). Naisi. . . . Naisi! Come to us; we are betrayed and broken.

NAISI. It's Ainnle crying out in a battle.

CONCHUBOR. I was near won this night, but death's between us now.

[*He goes out.*]

DEIRDRE (*clinging to Naisi*). There is no battle. . . . Do not leave me, Naisi.

NAISI. I must go to them.

DEIRDRE (*beseechingly*). Do not leave me, Naisi. Let us creep up in the darkness behind the grave. If there's a battle, maybe the strange fighters will be destroyed, when Ainnle and Ardan are against them.

[*Cries heard.*]

NAISI (*wildly*).   I hear Ardan crying out. Do not hold me from my brothers.

DEIRDRE.   Do not leave me, Naisi. Do not leave me broken and alone.

NAISI.   I cannot leave my brothers when it is I who have defied the king.

DEIRDRE.   I will go with you.

NAISI.   You cannot come. Do not hold me from the fight. [*He throws her aside almost roughly.*]

DEIRDRE (*with restraint*).   Go to your brothers. For seven years you have been kindly, but the hardness of death has come between us.

NAISI (*looking at her aghast*).   And you'll have me meet death with a hard word from your lips in my ear?

DEIRDRE.   We've had a dream, but this night has waked us surely. In a little while we've lived too long, Naisi, and isn't it a poor thing we should miss the safety of the grave, and we trampling its edge?

AINNLE (*behind*).   Naisi, Naisi, we are attacked and ruined!

DEIRDRE.   Let you go where they are calling. (*She looks at him for an instant coldly.*) Have you no shame loitering and talking, and a cruel death facing Ainnle and Ardan in the woods?

NAISI (*frantic*).   They'll not get a death that's cruel, and they with men alone. It's women that have loved are cruel only; and if I went on living from this day I'd be putting a curse on the lot of them I'd meet walking in the east or west, putting a curse on the sun that gave them beauty, and on the madder and the stonecrop[1] put red upon their cloaks.

DEIRDRE (*bitterly*).   I'm well pleased there's no one in this place to make a story that Naisi was a laughing-stock the night he died.

NAISI.   There'd not be many'd make a story, for that mockery is in your eyes this night will spot the face of Emain with a plague of pitted graves.

[*He goes out.*]

---

[1] Plants from which reddish die is extracted.

CONCHUBOR (*outside*). This is Naisi. Strike him! (*Tumult.
Deirdre crouches down on Naisi's cloak. Conchubor comes
in hurriedly.*) They've met their death—the three that stole
you, Deirdre, and from this out you'll be my queen in
Emain.

[*A keen of men's voices is heard behind.*]

DEIRDRE (*bewildered and terrified*).   It is not I will be a queen.

CONCHUBOR.   Make your lamentation a short while if you will,
but it isn't long till a day'll come when you begin pitying a
man is old and desolate, and High King also. . . . Let you not
fear me, for it's I'm well pleased you have a store of pity
for the three that were your friends in Alban.

DEIRDRE.   I have pity, surely. . . . It's the way pity has me this
night, when I think of Naisi, that I could set my teeth into
the heart of a king.

CONCHUBOR.   I know well pity's cruel, when it was my pity for
my own self destroyed Naisi.

DEIRDRE (*more wildly*).   It was my words without pity gave
Naisi a death will have no match until the ends of life and
time. (*Breaking out into a keen.*) But who'll pity Deirdre
has lost the lips of Naisi from her neck and from her cheek
for ever? Who'll pity Deirdre has lost the twilight in the
woods with Naisi, when beech-trees were silver and copper,
and ash-trees were fine gold?

CONCHUBOR (*bewildered*).   It's I'll know the way to pity and
care you, and I with a share of troubles has me thinking this
night it would be a good bargain if it was I was in the grave,
and Deirdre crying over me, and it was Naisi who was old
and desolate.

[*Keen heard.*]

DEIRDRE (*wild with sorrow*).   It is I who am desolate; I,
Deirdre, that will not live till I am old.

CONCHUBOR.   It's not long you'll be desolate, and I seven
years saying, "It's a bright day for Deirdre in the woods of
Alban"; or saying again, "What way will Deirdre be sleeping this night, and wet leaves and branches driving from the

north?" Let you not break the thing I've set my life on, and
you giving yourself up to your sorrow when it's joy and sor
row do burn out like straw blazing in an east wind.

DEIRDRE (*turning on him*). Was it that way with your sorrow, when I and Naisi went northward from Slieve Fuadh
and let raise our sails for Alban?

CONCHUBOR. There's one sorrow has no end surely—that's
being old and lonesome. (*With extraordinary pleading.*) But
you and I will have a little peace in Emain, with harps playing, and old men telling stories at the fall of night. I've let
build rooms for our two selves, Deirdre, with red gold upon
the walls and ceilings that are set with bronze. There was
never a queen in the east had a house the like of your house,
that's waiting for yourself in Emain.

SOLDIER (*running in*). Emain is in flames. Fergus has come
back and is setting fire to the world. Come up, Conchubor,
or your state will be destroyed!

CONCHUBOR (*angry and regal again*). Are the Sons of Usna
buried?

SOLDIER. They are in their grave, but no earth is thrown.

CONCHUBOR. Let me see them. Open the tent! (*Soldier opens
back of tent and shows grave.*) Where are my fighters?

SOLDIER. They are gone to Emain.

CONCHUBOR (*to Deirdre*). There are none to harm you. Stay
here until I come again.

[*Goes out with Soldier. Deirdre looks round for a moment,
then goes up slowly and looks into grave. She crouches down
and begins swaying herself backwards and forwards, keening
softly. At first her words are not heard, then they become
clear.*]

DEIRDRE. It's you three will not see age or death coming—
you that were my company when the fires on the hill-tops
were put out and the stars were our friends only. I'll turn my
thoughts back from this night, that's pitiful for want of pity,
to the time it was your rods and cloaks made a little tent for
me where there'd be a birch tree making shelter and a dry

stone; though from this day my own fingers will be making a
tent for me, spreading out my hairs and they knotted with
the rain.

[*Lavarcham and Old Woman come in stealthily on right.*]

DEIRDRE (*not seeing them*). It is I, Deirdre, will be crouching in a dark place; I, Deirdre, that was young with Naisi, and
brought sorrow to his grave in Emain.

OLD WOMAN. Is that Deirdre broken down that was so light
and airy?

LAVARCHAM. It is, surely, crying out over their grave.
[*She goes to Deirdre.*]

DEIRDRE. It will be my share from this out to be making
lamentation on this stone always, and I crying for a love
will be the like of a star shining on a little harbour by the
sea.

LAVARCHAM (*coming forward*). Let you rise up, Deirdre, and
come off while there are none to heed us, the way I'll find
you shelter and some friend to guard you.

DEIRDRE. To what place would I go away from Naisi? What
are the woods without Naisi or the sea shore?

LAVARCHAM (*very coaxingly*). If it is that way you'd be, come
till I find you a sunny place where you'll be a great wonder
they'll call the queen of sorrows; and you'll begin taking a
pride to be sitting up pausing and dreaming when the summer comes.

DEIRDRE. It was the voice of Naisi that was strong in summer
—the voice of Naisi that was sweeter than pipes playing, but
from this day will be dumb always.

LAVARCHAM (*to Old Woman*). She doesn't heed us at all.
We'll be hard set to rouse her.

OLD WOMAN. If we don't the High King will rouse her, coming down beside her with the rage of battle in his blood, for
how could Fergus stand against him?

LAVARCHAM (*touching Deirdre with her hand*). There's a
score of woman's years in store for you, and you'd best choose
will you start living them beside the man you hate, or being
your own mistress in the west or south?

DEIRDRE.   It is not I will go on living after Ainnle and after Ardan. After Naisi I will not have a lifetime in the world.

OLD WOMAN (with excitement).   Look, Lavarcham! There's a light leaving the Red Branch. Conchubor and his lot will be coming quickly with a torch of bog-deal for her marriage, throwing a light on her three comrades.

DEIRDRE (startled).   Let us throw down clay on my three comrades. Let us cover up Naisi along with Ainnle and Ardan, they that were the pride of Emain. (Throwing in clay.) There is Naisi was the best of three, the choicest of the choice of many. It was a clean death was your share, Naisi; and it is not I will quit your head, when it's many a dark night among the snipe and plover that you and I were whispering together. It is not I will quit your head, Naisi, when it's many a night we saw the stars among the clear trees of Glen da Ruadh, or the moon pausing to rest her on the edges of the hills.

OLD WOMAN.   Conchubor is coming, surely. I see the glare of flames throwing a light upon his cloak.

LAVARCHAM (eagerly).   Rise up, Deirdre, and come to Fergus, or be the High King's slave for ever!

DEIRDRE (imperiously).   I will not leave Naisi, who has left the whole world scorched and desolate. I will not go away when there is no light in the heavens, and no flower in the earth under them, but is saying to me that it is Naisi who is gone for ever.

CONCHUBOR (behind).   She is here. Stay a little back. (Lavarcham and Old Woman go into the shadow on left as Conchubor comes in. With excitement, to Deirdre.) Come forward and leave Naisi the way I've left charred timber and a smell of burning in Emain Macha, and a heap of rubbish in the storehouse of many crowns.

DEIRDRE (more awake to what is round her).   What are crowns and Emain Macha, when the head that gave them glory is this place, Conchubor, and it stretched upon the gravel will be my bed to-night?

CONCHUBOR.   Make an end of talk of Naisi, for I've come to bring you to Dundealgan since Emain is destroyed.

[*Conchubor makes a movement towards her.*]

DEIRDRE (*with a tone that stops him*).   Draw a little back from
Naisi, who is young for ever. Draw a little back from the
white bodies I am putting under a mound of clay and grasses
that are withered—a mound will have a nook for my own
self when the end is come.

CONCHUBOR (*roughly.*)   Let you rise up and come along with
me in place of growing crazy with your wailings here.

DEIRDRE.   It's yourself has made a crazy story, and let you go
back to your arms, Conchubor, and to councils where your
name is great, for in this place you are an old man and a fool
only.

CONCHUBOR.   If I've folly, I've sense left not to lose the thing
I've bought with sorrow and the deaths of many.

[*He moves towards her.*]

DEIRDRE.   Do not raise a hand to touch me.

CONCHUBOR.   There are other hands to touch you. My fighters
are set round in among the trees.

DEIRDRE.   Who'll fight the grave, Conchubor, and it opened
on a dark night?

LAVARCHAM (*eagerly*).   There are steps in the wood. I hear the
call of Fergus and his men.

CONCHUBOR (*furiously*).   Fergus cannot stop me. I am more
powerful than he is, though I am defeated and old.

FERGUS (*comes in to Deirdre; a red glow is seen behind the
grove*).   I have destroyed Emain, and now I'll guard you all
times, Deirdre, though it was I, without knowledge, brought
Naisi to his grave.

CONCHUBOR.   It's not you will guard her, for my whole armies
are gathering. Rise up, Deirdre, for you are mine surely.

FERGUS (*coming between them*).   I am come between you.

CONCHUBOR (*wildly*).   When I've killed Naisi and his brothers,
is there any man that I will spare? And is it you will stand
against me, Fergus, when it's seven years you've seen me
getting my death with rage in Emain?

FERGUS.   It's I, surely, will stand against a thief and a traitor.

DEIRDRE (*stands up and sees the light from Emain*). Draw a little back with the squabbling of fools when I am broken up with misery. (*She turns round.*) I see the flames of Emain starting upward in the dark night; and because of me there will be weasels and wild cats crying on a lonely wall where there were queens and armies and red gold, the way there will be a story told of a ruined city and a raving king and a woman will be young for ever. (*She looks round.*) I see the trees naked and bare, and the moon shining. Little moon, little moon of Alban, it's lonesome you'll be this night, and to-morrow night, and long nights after, and you pacing the woods beyond Glen Laoi, looking every place for Deirdre and Naisi, the two lovers who slept so sweetly with each other.

FERGUS (*going to Conchubor's right and whispering*). Keep back, or you will have the shame of pushing a bolt on a queen who is out of her wits.

CONCHUBOR. It is I who am out of my wits, with Emain in flames, and Deirdre raving, and my own heart gone within me.

DEIRDRE (*in a high and quiet tone*). I have put away sorrow like a shoe that is worn out and muddy, for it is I have had a life that will be envied by great companies. It was not by a low birth I made kings uneasy, and they sitting in the halls of Emain. It was not a low thing to be chosen by Conchubor, who was wise, and Naisi had no match for bravery. It is not a small thing to be rid of grey hairs, and the loosening of the teeth. (*With a sort of triumph.*) It was the choice of lives we had in the clear woods, and in the grave, we're safe, surely. . . .

CONCHUBOR. She will do herself harm.

DEIRDRE (*showing Naisi's knife*). I have a little key to unlock the prison of Naisi you'd shut upon his youth for ever. Keep back, Conchubor; for the High King who is your master has put his hands between us. (*She half turns to the grave.*) It was sorrows were foretold, but great joys were my share always;

yet it is a cold place I must go to be with you, Naisi; and it's cold your arms will be this night that were warm about my neck so often. . . . It's a pitiful thing to be talking out when your ears are shut to me. It's a pitiful thing, Conchubor, you have done this night in Emain; yet a thing will be a joy and triumph to the ends of life and time.

[*She presses knife into her heart and sinks into the grave. Conchubor and Fergus go forward. The red glow fades, leaving stage very dark.*]

FERGUS.   Four white bodies are laid down together; four clear lights are quenched in Ireland. (*He throws his sword into the grave.*)   There is my sword that could not shield you— my four friends that were the dearest always. The names of Emain have gone out: Deirdre is dead and there is none to keen her. That is the fate of Deirdre and the children of Usna, and for this night, Conchubor, our war is ended.

[*He goes out.*]

LAVARCHAM.   I have a little hut where you can rest, Conchubor; there is a great dew falling.

CONCHUBOR (*with the voice of an old man*).   Take me with you. I'm hard set to see the way before me.

OLD WOMAN.   This way, Conchubor.

[*They go out.*]

LAVARCHAM (*beside the grave*).   Deirdre is dead, and Naisi is dead; and if the oaks and stars could die for sorrow, it's a dark sky and a hard and naked earth we'd have this night in Emain.

CURTAIN

Oliver St. John Gogarty (1878-   )

The Crab Tree

Here is the crab tree,
Firm and erect,
In spite of the thin soil,
In spite of neglect.
The twisted root grapples
For sap with the rock,
And draws the hard juice
To the succulent top:
Here are wild apples,
Here's a tart crop!

No outlandish grafting
That ever grew soft
In a sweet air of Persia,
Or safe Roman croft;
Unsheltered by steading,
Rock-rooted and grown,
A great tree of Erin,
It stands up alone,
A forest tree spreading
Where forests are gone.

Of all who pass by it
How few in it see
A westering remnant
Of days when Lough Neagh
Flowed up the long dingles
Its blossom had lit,
Old days of glory
Time cannot repeat;
And therefore it mingles
The bitter and sweet.

It takes from the West Wind
The thrust of the main;
It makes from the tension
Of sky and of plain,
Of what clay enacted,
Of living alarm,
A vitalised symbol
Of earth and of storm,
Of Chaos contracted
To intricate form.

Unbreakable wrestler!
What sapling or herb
Has core of such sweetness
And fruit so acerb?
So grim a transmitter
Of life through mishap,
That one wonders whether
If that in the sap,
Is sweet or is bitter
Which makes it stand up.

Ringsend

(After Reading Tolstoi)

I will live in Ringsend
With a red-headed whore,
And the fan-light gone in
Where it lights the hall-door;
And listen each night
For her querulous shout,
As at last she streels in
And the pubs empty out.

To soothe that wild breast
With my old-fangled songs,
Till she feels it redressed
From inordinate wrongs,
Imagined, outrageous,
Preposterous wrongs,
Till peace at last comes,
Shall be all I will do,
Where the little lamp blooms
Like a rose in the stew;
And up the back-garden
The sound comes to me
Of the lapsing, unsoilable,
Whispering sea.

Exorcism

To banish your shape from my mind
I thought of the dangerous wood
Where a man might wander and find,
By a stream in the solitude,
The Queen it is death if one sees,
Death by a merciless dart;
But how could that bring me release,
Shot as I am to the heart?

Beauty will cure me, I cried;
By Beauty is Beauty dislodged.
And I worked on a dream till I eyed
The Queens whom the young man judged.
But the vision faded and slipt;
And the cure was a cure of no worth;
For I said, when the Queens were stript,
I have given the prize to a fourth.

Ugliness, Chaos and War
I know, but I would not invoke;
They would feed you as darkness a star,
And strengthen the beam of my yoke.
If Love be reborn in a song
I with my fate will not quarrel,
But you, if you do him a wrong,
May be changed to a reed or a laurel.

To the Liffey With the Swans[1]

Keep you these calm and lovely things,
    And float them on your clearest water;
For one would not disgrace a King's
    Transformed beloved and buoyant daughter.

And with her goes this sprightly swan,
    A bird of more than royal feather,
With alban beauty clothed upon:
    O keep them fair and well together!

As fair as was that doubled Bird,
    By love of Leda so besotten,
That she was all with wonder stirred,
    And the Twin Sportsmen were begotten!

---

[1] The poet, imprisoned in a deserted house on the edge of the Liffey, escaped from his enemies by plunging into the water. As he swam the stream he promised it, in return for safe passage, two swans. Later, in the presence of W. B. Yeats, he fulfilled his vow.

Per Iter Tenebricosum

Enough! Why should a man bemoan
A Fate that leads the natural way?
Or think himself a worthier one
Than those who braved it in their day?
If only gladiators died,
Or Heroes, Death would be his pride;
But have not little maidens gone,
And Lesbia's sparrow—all alone?

Verse

What should we know,
For better or worse,
Of the Long Ago,
Were it not for Verse:
What ships went down;
What walls were razed;
Who won the crown;
What lads were praised?
A fallen stone,
Or a waste of sands;
And all is known
Of Art-less lands.
But you need not delve
By the sea-side hills
Where the Muse herself
All Time fulfils,
Who cuts with his scythe
All things but hers;
All but the blithe
Hexameters.

To the Maids Not to Walk
In the Wind

When the wind blows, walk not abroad,
For, Maids, you may not know
The mad, quaint thoughts which incommode
Me when the winds do blow.

What though the tresses of the treen
In doubled beauty move,
With silver added to their green,
They were not made for Love.

But when your clothes reveal your thighs
And surge around your knees,
Until from foam you seem to rise,
As Venus from the seas . . .

Though ye are fair, it is not fair!
Unless you will be kind,
Till I am dead, and changed to AIR,
O walk not in the wind!

To W. B. Yeats Who Says That
His Castle of Ballylee
Is His Monument

To stones trust not your monument
To make a living fame endure.
Who built Dun Angus battlement?
O'Flaherty is forgotten in Auchnanure.

And he who told how Troy was sacked
And what men clipt the lovely Burd,[1]
Had seven Mayors to swear, in fact,
Their towns first heard his babbling word.

Leda and the Swan

Though her Mother told her
  Not to go a-bathing,
Leda loved the river
  And she could not keep away:
Wading in its freshets
  When the noon was heavy;
Walking by the water
  At the close of day.

Where between its waterfalls,
  Underneath the beeches,
Gently flows a broader
  Hardly moving stream,
And the balanced trout lie
  In the quiet reaches;
Taking all her clothes off,
  Leda went to swim.

There was not a flag-lead
  By the river's margin
That might be a shelter
  From a passer-by;
And a sudden whiteness
  In the quiet darkness,
Let alone the splashing,
  Was enough to catch an eye.

---

[1] Lady, i.e., Helen.

But the place was lonely,
    And her clothes were hidden;
Even cattle walking
    In the ford had gone away;
Every single farm-hand
    Sleeping after dinner,—
What's the use of talking?
    There was no one in the way.

In, without a stitch on,
    Peaty water yielded,
Till her head was lifted
    With its ropes of hair;
It was more surprising
    Than a lily gilded
Just to see how golden
    Was her body there:

Lolling in the water,
    Lazily uplifting
Limbs that on the surface
    Whitened into snow;
Leaning on the water,
    Indolently drifting,
Hardly any faster
    Than the foamy bubbles go.

You would say to see her
    Swimming in the lonely
Pool, or after, dryer,
    Putting on her clothes:
"O but she is lovely,
    Not a soul to see her,
And how lovely only
    Leda's Mother knows!"

Under moving branches
   Leisurely she dresses,
And the leafy sunlight
   Made you wonder were
All its woven shadows
   But her golden tresses,
Or a smock of sunlight
   For her body bare.

When on earth great beauty
   Goes exempt from danger,
It will be endangered
   From a source on high;
When unearthly stillness
   Falls on leaves, the ranger,
In his wood-lore anxious,
   Gazes at the sky.

While her hair was drying,
   Came a gentle languor,
Whether from the bathing
   Or the breeze she didn't know.
Anyway she lay there,
   And her Mother's anger
(Worse if she had wet hair)
   Could not make her dress and go.

Whitest of all earthly
   Things, the white that's rarest,
Is the snow on mountains
   Standing in the sun;
Next the clouds above them,
   Then the down is fairest
On the breast and pinions
   Of a proudly sailing swan.

And she saw him sailing
  On the pool where lately
She had stretched unnoticed,
  As she thought, and swum;
And she never wondered
  Why, erect and stately,
Where no river weed was
  Such a bird had come.

What was it she called him:
  Goosey-goosey gander?
For she knew no better
  Way to call a swan;
And the bird responding
  Seemed to understand her,
For he left his sailing
  For the bank to waddle on.

Apple blossoms under
  Hills of Lacedæmon,
With the snow beyond them
  In the still blue air,
To the swan who hid them
  With his wings asunder,
Than the breasts of Leda,
  Were not lovelier!

Of the tales that daughters
  Tell their poor old mothers,
Which by all accounts are
  Often very odd;
Leda's was a story
  Stranger than all others.
What was there to say but:
  Glory be to God?

And she half-believed her,
   For she knew her daughter;
And she saw the swan-down
   Tangled in her hair.
Though she knew how deeply
   Runs the stillest water;
How could she protect her
   From the winged air?

Why is it effects are
   Greater than their causes?
Why should causes often
   Differ from effects?
Why should what is lovely
   Fill the world with harness?
And the most deceived be
   She who least suspects?

When the hyacinthine
   Eggs were in the basket,—
Blue as at the whiteness
   Where a cloud begins;
Who would dream there lay there
   All that Trojan brightness:
Agamemnon murdered:
   And the mighty Twins?

Joseph Campbell (1879-1944)

The Old Age Pensioner

He sits over the glimmering coal
With ancient face and folded hands:
His eye glasses his quiet soul,
He blinks and nods and understands.
In dew wetted, in tempest blown,
A Lear at last come to his own.

For fifty years he trenched his field
That he might eat a freeman's bread:
The seasons balked him of their yield,
His children's children wished him dead.
But ransom came to him at length
At the ebb-tide of life and strength.

And so he sits with folded hands
Over the flag of amber fire:
He blinks and nods and understands,
He has his very soul's desire.
In dew wetted, in tempest blown,
A Lear at last come to his own.

The Unfrocked Priest

He leant at the door
    In his priest's clothes—
Greasy black they were:
    And he bled at the nose.

He leant at the door,
    And the blood trickled down:
A man of the country,
    More than the town.

He was of God's anointed,
    A priest, no less:
But he had been unfrocked
    For drunkenness.

For that, or worse,
    And flesh is only human,
For some wrong-doing
    With a woman.

And in his father's house
    He lived at ease,
Reading his books,
    As quiet as the trees.

No one troubled him
    As he went in and out,
And he smoked his clay,
    And he grew stout.

And he tramped the parish
    In the summer days,
Thinking high thoughts
    And giving God praise.

None but blessed him
    As he walked the hills,
For he gave to the poor
    And he cured their ills.

There was no herb
    That grew in the grass,
But he saw its virtue
    As in a glass.

No rath, no Mass-bush
    No ogham stone,
But he knew its story
    As his own.

He had a scholar's knowledge
    Of Greek
And dabbled in Hebrew
    And Arabic.

And in his time
    (He died in 'eighty-seven)
He wrote two epics
    And a "Dream of Heaven."

I saw him once only
    In his priest's clothes
At his father's door:
    And he bled at the nose.

I Am the Mountainy Singer

I am the mountainy singer—
The voice of the peasant's dream,
The cry of the wind on the wooded hill,
The leap of the fish in the stream.

Quiet and love I sing—
The carn[1] on the mountain crest,
The cailin[2] in her lover's arms,
The child at its mother's breast.

Beauty and peace I sing—
The fire on the open hearth,
The cailleach[3] spinning at her wheel,
The plough in the broken earth.

Travail and pain I sing—
The bride on the childing bed,
The dark man laboring at his rhymes,
The ewe in the lambing shed.

---

[1] Cairn—a pyramid of rough stones raised as a memorial or a sepulchral monument. NED
[2] Colleen, girl.
[3] Old woman.

Sorrow and death I sing—
The canker come on the corn,
The fisher lost in the mountain loch,
The cry at the mouth of morn.

No other life I sing,
For I am sprung of the stock
That broke the hilly land for bread,
And built the nest in the rock!

I Am the Gilly of Christ

I AM the gilly[1] of Christ,
The mate of Mary's Son;
I run the roads at seeding time,
And when the harvest's done.

I sleep among the hills,
The heather is my bed;
I dip the termon[2]-well for drink,
And pull the sloe for bread.

No eye has ever seen me,
But shepherds hear me pass,
Singing at fall of even
Along the shadowed grass.

The beetle is my bellman,
The meadow-fire my guide,
The bee and bat my ambling nags
When I have need to ride.

---

[1] Servant.
[2] Land belonging to a religious house. NED

All know me only the Stranger,
Who sits on the Saxons' height:
He burned the bacach's[1] little house
On last St. Brigid's Night.

He sups off silver dishes,
And drinks in a golden horn,
But he will wake a wiser man
Upon the Judgment Morn!

I am the gilly of Christ,
The mate of Mary's Son;
I run the roads at seeding time,
And when the harvest's done.

The seed I sow is lucky,
The corn I reap is red,
And whoso sings the Gilly's Rann[2]
Will never cry for bread.

As I Came Over the Grey, Grey Hills

As I came over the grey, grey hills
And over the grey, grey water,
I saw the gilly leading on,
And the white Christ following after.

Where and where does the gilly lead?
And where is the white Christ faring?
They've travelled the four grey sounds of Orc,
And the four grey seas of Eirinn.

---

[1] Lame man's.
[2] A verse, quatrain or stanza.

The moon it set and the wind's away,
And the song in the grass is dying,
And a silver cloud on the silent sea
Like a shrouding sheet is lying.

But Christ and the gilly will follow on
Till the ring in the east is showing,
And the awny[1] corn is red on the hills,
And the golden light is glowing!

I Will Go With My Father

A-Ploughing

I will go with my father a-ploughing
To the green field by the sea,
And the rooks and the crows and the seagulls
Will come flocking after me.
I will sing to the patient horses
With the lark in the white of the air,
And my father will sing the plough-song
That blesses the cleaving share.

I will go with my father a-sowing
To the red field by the sea,
And the rooks and the gulls and the starlings
Will come flocking after me.
I will sing to the striding sowers
With the finch on the flowering sloe,
And my father will sing the seed-song
That only the wise men know.

---

[1] Bearded, bristly.

I will go with my father a-reaping
To the brown field by the sea,
And the geese and the crows and the children
Will come flocking after me.
I will sing to the weary reapers
With the wren in the heat of the sun,
And my father will sing the scythe-song
That joys for the harvest done.

The Herb-Leech

I HAVE gathered luss[1]
At the wane of the moon,
And supped its sap
With a yewen[2] spoon.
I have set a spell
By the carn of Medb,
And smelt the mould
Of the red queen's grave.
I have dreamed a dearth
In the darkened sun,
And felt the hand
Of the Evil One.
I have fathomed war
In the comet's tail,
And heard the crying
Of Gall[3] and Gael.
I have seen the spume
On the dead priest's lips,
And the "holy fire"
On the spars of ships;
And the shooting stars

---

[1] Foxglove.
[2] Made of yew.
[3] Englishman.

On Barthelmy's Night,
Blanching the dark
With ghostly light;
And the corpse-candle
Of the seer's dream,
Bigger in girth
Than a weaver's beam;
And the shy hearth-fairies
About the grate,
Blowing the turves
To a whiter heat.
All things on earth
To me are known,
For I have the gift
Of the Murrain Stone!

The Raid[1]

BY Sean O'Casey (1880-   )

THE cold beauty of frost glittered everywhere outside, unseen, unfelt, for the slum was asleep. An uneasy silence echoed over the house, for awake or asleep, everyone knew that death with his comrade, the inflictor of wounds, roamed the darkened streets. Stretched out in a truckle bed in a tenement room, its murky window facing on to the street, Sean thought of the tapestry of the day. He could see the street stretching along outside, its roughly cobbled roadway beset with empty match-boxes, tattered straws, tattered papers, scattered mounds of horse-dung, and sprinkled deep with slumbering dust waiting for an idle wind to come and raise it to irritating life again. Lean-looking gas-lamps stood at regular intervals on the foot-

[1] The action takes place during the Anglo-Irish war (1918-1921). The Black and Tans, so called because they wore makeshift uniforms of half English khaki and half Royal Irish Constabulary black, were temporary policemen. The Auxiliaries were recruited from ex-officers of the Royal Navy, Army and Air Force and were a military force.

paths, many of them deformed from the play of swinging children, bending over like old men standing to gasp, and wait for
a pain in the back to go. The melancholy pathway meandered
along by the side of the tall houses, leading everywhere to tar-
nishing labour, to consumption's cough, to the writhings of
fever, to bitter mutterings against life, and frantic calls on St.
Anthony, The Little Flower, and Bernadette of Missabielle to
be absent helps in time of trouble. Upon these stones, I will
build my church.

There were the houses, too—a long, lurching row of dis-
contented incurables, smirched with the age-long marks of
ague, fevers, cancer, and consumption, the soured tears of little
children, and the sighs of disappointed newly-married girls.
The doors were scarred with time's spit and anger's hasty
knocking; the pillars by their sides were shaky, their stuccoed
bloom long since peeled away, and they looked like crutches
keeping the trembling doors standing on their palsied feet.
The gummy-eyed windows blinked dimly out, lacquered by a
year's tired dust from the troubled street below. Dirt and
disease were the big sacraments here—outward and visible
signs of an inward and spiritual disgrace. The people bought
the cheapest things in food they could find in order to live,
to work, to worship: the cheapest spuds, the cheapest tea, the
cheapest meat, the cheapest fat; and waited for unsold bread
to grow stale that they might buy that cheaper, too. Here they
gathered up the fragments so that nothing would be lost. The
streets were long haggard corridors of rottenness and ruin.
What wonderful mind of memory could link this shrinking
wretchedness with the flaunting gorgeousness of silk and satin;
with bloom of rose and scent of lavender? A thousand years
must have passed since the last lavender lady was carried out
feet first from the last surviving one of them. Even the sun
shudders now when she touches a roof, for she feels some evil
has chilled the glow of her garment. The flower that here once
bloomed is dead forever. No wallflower here has crept into a
favoured cranny; sight and sign of the primrose were far away;
no room here for a dance of daffodils; no swallow twittering

under a shady eave; and it was sad to see an odd sparrow seeking a yellow grain from the mocking dust; not even a spiky-headed thistle, purple mitred, could find a corner here for a sturdy life. No Wordsworth here wandered about as lonely as a cloud.

> The decent dead provoke no blood-congealing fear,
> Like the dread death that lives to fester here.
> Here children, lost to every sense but life,
> Indulge in play that mimics social strife;
> And learn from strenuous practice that they may
> Act well their part at home some future day:
> The girl trains her lungs to scream and shout,
> The boy his arms to knock a wife about.

And yet his riddled horridness had given root to the passion flower. What had been lost was found; what had been dead came to life again. The spirit beneath the coat brocaded, with slender sword quivering, had come into being again, not in brocade, but in rags; not with sword or dainty phrases, elegant in comedy and satire; but with bitter curses, blows as hard as an arm can give, and a rank, savage spit into a master's face. Fought these frantic fools did, led by Larkin and by Connolly; fought till the day-star arose in their shivering hearts, the new and glorious light, the red evangel, the light of the knowledge of the glory of God, manifested in the active mind and vital bodies of men and women and little children. And now something stronger than bare hands were in the battle. Many a spearpoint flame from a gun frightened a dark corner or a shadowy street, making armed men in khaki or black crouch low in their rushing lorries, firing rapidly back at the street grown shadowy again, or the corner now darker than ever before.

Now the old house was still. Comely Bessie Ballynoy, on her way up, had knocked; but finding Sean in bed, had bid goodnight, and gone. Lazy sleep had crawled in by the dark hallway to soothe restlessness and to hush the clamour from the attic above to the basement below. A lousy sleep, dreary-eyed, in loosely slippered feet, torn and muddy, calling in a shoddy whisper for quietness; creeping in yawning, leaving no-one on watch, though every night now was a perilous night for Dublin. In all the rooms, all the cheap crockery stood quiet on the shelves; the chairs leaned against the shaky walls; rosy-faced fires had all gone pale; the patter of children's feet had long since ceased; only dreams crept slyly in to fill the ugly rooms with sparkling peace for a few dark moments, clothing the sleepers with a cautious splendour; setting them, maybe, to sip rare wines from bulging bottles, or led them to yellow sands bordering a playful sea. A younger lass, perhaps, dreamed of scanty night attire between snowy sheets, with a colour-robed prince by the bedroom door in haste to come in, and bid her a choice goodnight; while the younger men saw themselves, sword in hand, driving the khaki cut-throats out of Eire's five beautiful fields.

Every guardian angel relaxed now, and nodded sleepily by tattered counterpane and ragged sheet, for sin usually curled up like a dog to sleep at their feet, waiting for the tenement life to go on again in the morning. So after Curfew the silent tenement slept, unconscious even that every whining wail of every passing motor sang a song of death to someone; for in sleep the slimy roof above them had slid aside, and left the stars but a hand's breadth out of reach.

When will the day break in Eirinn; when will her day-star arise? How often had he heard these words sung in a languishing voice after an eight-hand reel or a high-cauled cap at ceilidh or sgoruidheacht! Well, no day would ever break here, nor would the shadows ever flee away. Sean's eyes were closing, and dimming thoughts swooned faintly from his mind into the humming whine of motor-engines coming quick along the road outside. Up on his elbow he shot as he heard the sound of braking, telling him that the lorries were outside of his house, or of those on either side. Then he shot down again to hide as a blinding beam from a searchlight poured through

the window, skimming the cream of the darkness out of the
room. It silvered the old walls for a few moments, then withdrew like a receding tide to send its beam on another part
of the house. Then there was a volley of battering blows on
the obstinate wooden door, mingled with the crash of falling
glass that told Sean the panels on each side of it had been
shattered by hammer or rifle-butt.

A raid! All the winsome dreams of the house had vanished;
sleep had gone; and children dug arms and legs into the tens-
ing bodies of their mothers.

Which were they—the Tommies or the Tans? Tans,
thought Sean, for the Tommies would not shout so soullessly,
nor smash the glass panels so suddenly; they would hammer
on the door with a rifle-butt, and wait for it to be opened.
No; these were the Tans.

He heard the quick pit-put, pit-put of stockinged feet, faint
as it was, coming down the stairs, turning left at the bottom
of them, and hurrying along the hall towards the back-yard.
His ears were so cocked that he heard the soft, silkly pad of
the hurrying feet plainly through the storm of blows falling
on the street door; then he thought he heard the back door
open softly and gently close again.

—·Who could that be? he thought. Might be anyone of
the men. Those who didn't take part in ambushes often carried
ammunition to those who did; and the dockers and seamen
gave a ready hand to the smuggling in of arms. If it wasn't for
his own poor sight, he'd probably be doing it himself. All were
friendly, save the thin and delicate husband of Mrs. Ballynoy,
who cared for no manner of politics. Someone, anyway, slipping into the back to dodge over the wall into the dark lanes,
with fear but without fuss. The Dublin slums at war with the
British Empire; all the power of an army, flanked by gangs of
ruthless ruffians; all the ordered honour of a regal cabinet and
the mighty-moneyed banks fighting the ragged tits of the tenements. An unequal fight, by God, but the slums would win!
There goes the door!

A great crash shook the old house and shook the heart of
Sean, for well he knew the ordeal that might be in front of
him once the light from a Tan's torch smote the darkness of
the room. A mad rush of heavy feet went past his door, to
spread over the stilly house; for no-one had come from a room
to risk sudden death in the dark and draughty hallway. He
remembered the two boys brought bound from Dublin Castle
to a dump-field on the edge of the city by two Auxie-Tan
officers, who set them sitting against an old stone wall, extin-
guishing each young head under an old bucket picked from
a rubbish heap. Then going away forty paces or so, they fired
away at the buckets till they were full of holes, leaving what
they had done behind them to put the fear of the Tans into
the hearts of the surviving I.R.A. men. He thought, too, of
Clancy, Clune, and McKee, caught and brought to the Castle,
where the Tans interviewed them with the stimulant of bayonets, prodding them gamely till none of the three could sigh
any longer, for each at last was dead. Now he could hear
neither sound nor murmur—all had gone quiet after the crashing fall of the door. No sound even of a child's protest, though
that wasn't surprising, for all of them would be too frightened
to squeal till a gun exploded somewhere: all was quiet—the
sad silence of a sleeping slum. Yet Sean knew that the house
must be alive with crawling men, slinking up and down the
stairs, hovering outside this door or that one, each with a gun
tensed to the last hair, with a ready finger touching the trigger.
He guessed that a part of them were the Auxies, the classic
members of sibilant and sinister raiders. The Tans alone would
make more noise, slamming themselves into a room, shouting
to shake off the fear that slashed many of their faces. The
Auxies were too proud to show a sign of it. The Tommies
would be warm, always hesitant at knocking a woman's room
about; they would even be jocular in their funny English way,
encouraging the women and even the children to grumble
at being taken away from their proper sleep.

All Sean could do was to try to lie dead still, digging down deeper without a sound into the hard mattress of his truckle bed; stifling any desire to steal to the door to listen; to try to modify his breathing till it became unnoticed by himself; for a profound silence might make the Tans disinclined to probe a way in to find out the cause of it; though the Auxies cared nothing for silence, but would lift a corpse from a coffin to search for a gun. He always left his door unlocked now, for past experience had shown him that the slightest obstacle to a swift entrance to a room always irritated them.

From the corner of an eye he could see through the window the searchlight gliding, now up, now down the street, and once for a few moments it blinded him by flooding the room. Then he heard sullen, but loud, thuds of heavy iron falling on heavy wood, coming from the back, and he guessed they were breaking in the entrance to the large shed that was said to be used as a carpenter's shop, and in which Mrs. Ballynoy's husband sometimes worked. Now he heard soft, sly steps going down the hallway to the back. After whomsoever had crept away while the door was being broken down. He had climbed the wall, thought Sean, and somewhere—maybe just behind it— crouched silently in the darkest corner of the narrow lane, a revolver tight in his hand, his shoes slung round his neck, so that, if he had to run, no sound of running feet would give an enemy a cue of a direction through which to send a hail of bullets: a bitter night for a pair of bare feet.

Sean could sense the women, and, maybe, the men, praying while the hammering lasted, to cease at once when silence came again, for it wouldn't serve them to let the Auxies hear them trying to talk to God. These silences were the worst: during the hammering one knew where they were; throughout the silences one didn't. Then they might be anywhere; might be opening his very own door snakily, softly, now; some of them might be even in the room, for their black uniforms fitted the darkness they loved, and black juices, smeared over their cheeks and brows, mixed them cosily with the darker shadows of the night. Any moment a brilliant torch might blind his slatted eyes, and a string of shouted questions blast his ear; a pressed-in, cold pistol barrel make a tiny livid rim on his naked chest. He tried to forget thought, making his mind one with the darkness, losing his fear in the vastness of space; but it was no use, for thought never got farther than that the Tans were there, and his mind came back to think of how it would feel to have a bullet burning a swift channel through the middle of his belly.

Azrael, Azrael, gentle, dignified being of spirit, graceful spirit of death, come, and minister unto us, and save us merry gentlemen!

> Come lovely and soothing death,
> Undulate round the world, serenely arriving,
> Arriving
> In the day, in the night, to all, to each,
> Sooner or later, delicate death.

Ah! Whitman, Walt Whitman, you never knew the Tans! Death doesn't arrive serenely here, his hands are desperate, and neither is delicately formed. Here the angel of death is a biting bitch!

The silence was startled by the sound of a motor-engine warming up, getting ready to go. He heard steps now in the hall, and the sound of bravura jests from a few voices. They were going. They mightn't be, though: they pretended that at times, driving the lorries away a bit, but leaving the men behind, to come with a rush into the house again among foolish people hurrying in their nightclothes out of their rooms to ask questions of each other. Stay still; don't move; not a stir: some of them still might be just beyond the door.

He lay there for what seemed a long time, the sweat of fear damping his body, and making him shiver. Stay still; don't move—someone was beside the door. He heard the handle

giving a faint, brassy murmur. Soon, a black-clothed arm
would thrust itself within, and a shot might go off that he
would never hear. He silently squirmed deeper into the bed,
and left the rest to God.

—Eh! he heard the voice of Mrs. Ballynoy whisper from
the darkness, Are you there, or did they take you? Are you
gone, or are you asleep, or wha'?

—That woman again! he thought resentfully—what a fright
she gave me! Awake, Mrs. Ballynoy, he whispered back.

—Well, she said softly, you can take your ayse now, an'
sleep tranquil, or get up, an' talk about th' queer things done
in a Christian age.

—Wait till I light a candle, he said, making a great creak
as he heaved himself out of the bed's hollow.

—You'll light no candle while I'm here, young man, said
her voice, dressed in a titter, for a slip of overall's th' only
shelter between me and a piercin' look from a young man's
eyes; an' it wouldn't be good to go from one exthreme to
another on an identical night.

—Did they discover anything? asked Sean.

—Not a thing, though they took two o' th' men away with
them. A sudden end to them all, an' a short fall to th' hottest
hob that hell can heat! Don't light that candle yet, she added,
for minds that have safely passed a danger near them are often
reckless in their dealin' with an innocent female; though you're
not that kind of a man, I know.

He heard the door softly closing and her hand fumbling
with the lock. He hoped she wasn't going to stay. Ah! here's
the key, for it's safer to put a locked door between eyes that
pry into other people's affairs day an' night, tintin' everything
with the colour of their own minds.

—Hadn't you better go back to your room, Mrs. Ballynoy,
he warned. You need all the sleep you can get these days. We
all do; and someone might be prowlin' round an' see an' think
th' worst.

—Ay, she said; bad minds, th' lot o' them—that's why I've
locked th' door. An' call me Nellie, for you know me well
enough be now. Light th' candle now you can, but leave it on
th' far side of where I'll be, for it's only a flimsy apron-overall
I have between me an' all harm; and she tittered gaily as Sean
very slowly lighted a candle on a box beside his bed.

She was a fine-looking heifer, right enough: long reddish
hair coiled up into a bunch that rested neatly on the nape of
a white neck; a well-chiselled, pale face, with large grey innocent eyes that seemed to be shrouded in a mist from the valley
of the Missabielle; a fine figure set these charms off, and when
she slyly waved this sweet figure in front of a man, he no longer
saw, or wanted to see, the mist of Missabielle. A rose of Tralee,
without the flower's serenity, maybe; but certainly a lovely rose
of the tenements. But Sean was in no mood now to enjoy
the charm of her fine figure and face. Once let a soul see she
had been in his room and the whole house would be declaring
that he was carrying on with Mrs. Ballynoy. He should have
had the courage to get up and push her out. He almost wished
now that the Auxies had stayed a little longer.

In the sober light of the candle he saw that she had just
decorated her delightful body in a pair of brown slippers and
a flowered overall reaching only half-way down her thighs, and
showing a wide part of her white swelling bosom; a show
that was very charming, but damned uncomfortable to one
who was determined to take no notice of it.

—Oh! There y'are, she said, when the candle-light got
steady, nice an' snug an' all alone. She came over and sat down
on the edge of the bed beside him. I'm askin' meself why a
land, overflowin' with prayer an' devotion, should be so often
plunged into dhread in the dead o' night for nothin'? An'
they tellin' me it's for Ireland's sake. Them politics'll be the
death of us some day. I feel terrible shy in this get-up, she said
suddenly. Afther washin' the one good nightgown I have, I
was sleepin' in me skin, an' this overall was th' first thing I
laid hands on when the Tans came thundherin' at the door.

Pansies on it, she said, giggling, pulling it a little from her thigh, pansies for thought! and she poked Sean in the breast, playfully, with a hand reddened by the soda she used in the washing of clothes.

—Isn't Mr. Ballynoy at home, said Sean, trying to get her mind away from the overall, while he thought of a way to get rid of her.

—Didn't I tell you this mornin', on the stairs, that he was on a counthry job! He would be when the Tans come; though it's little good he'd be in any emergency, bein' born timid, with a daisy in his mouth. So I'm a poor lone lassie now, and she gave him another poke—this time in the thigh.

Don't you think you ought to get back, he warned; the Tans might come again.

—Ay, indeed, they might; a body can never know what them fellas'll do. An' it only a little way from Christmas, too. Ah! she said suddenly, looking away into a dream distance; it's good to be near one of your own: th' only two protestants in th' house, not countin' me husband. Of the crowd, not countin' him, only two who have th' proper way o' worshippin' an' are able to foresee th' genuine meanin' of th' holy text.

—There's me for you, said Sean, thinking neither you nor your husband bothered about religion, one way or another.

—Then you're sadly mistaken. I can't remember a year we missed feelin' the curious chantin' glow in th' air of a Christmas mornin', an' us on our way to church. In a proper mood, an' that was often, I could see what you'd think's th' star, ashine on the tip of the spire's top; an' me ears can hear th' dull plod of the three camels' feet in th' deep sand, bearin' th' three kings with th' three rich gifts from Persia, or some other place in th' wilds of a faraway world; an' all th' time an anxious man seekin' shelter for his good woman, with the valleys levelled an' th' hills hidden be th' fallin' snow, dyein' her rich hair grey with its fallin' flakes, a sly soft carpet for her sandalled feet, an' sore they were from th' sting in its frosty tendherness; while th' tired Joseph thrudged demented behind, wondherin'

if they'd find their lodgins only on the cowld, cowld ground.
But God was good, an' found the shelther of a stable for the
bewildhered, half-perished man, with his thin gown sodden,
his toil-marked hands a hot ache, an' his poor feet blue with
the bitther penetration of th' clingin' snow; an' afther Joseph
had shooed th' puzzled animals to a safe an' ordherly distance,
th' little fella was soon snug in a manger on top o' warm heaps
of sainfoin, thyme, rosemary, an' lavender.

—You're wrong there, said Sean; for how in such a bitther
season could anyone come on spring and summer plants like
those?

—I dunno, she murmured, unless God turned th' hay an'
th' sthraw into th' sweet-savourin' herbs. But it's far betther
not to thry to go into them things. Are you afraid to look at
me, or what? she ejaculated, turning away from her dream;
for Sean had turned his head away to escape the charm of the
white bosom and soft thighs. As long as you don't make too
free, I don't mind, though I feel a little shy in this scarce
get-up.

A shoulder-band of the overall had slipped down, and she
had saucily drawn an arm out of it altogether so that near half
of her body to the waist was bare, and he saw a breast, rather
lovely in the light of the candle, looking like a golden cup with
a misty ruby in its centre. If he only had her in a shady corner
of the Phoenix Park, or in a room of his own in a house where
she wasn't known, the world would be well lost for a period
of ecstasy. But not here.

—Your husband's a good fellow, he said trying to keep his
mind off her, and would rejoice to see you as you are now. He
thinks a lot of you.

—He oughtn't, she said sarcastically; where'd he get another
like me? He means well, poor man, but honest, it's pathetic
when we're alone, an' he thries to get goin'. Askin' me to tell
him when he's hurtin' me! She went into a soft, gay, gurgling
laugh, putting a hand over her mouth to quench the merry
sound of it. It's funny to talk of it here, but maddenin' when

I'm with him. I'm often near worn out thryin', thryin' to coax
a little flash of endeavour outa him. He does his best, but the
little sting he once had's gone with the wind—joy go with it!
She now laughed venomously and loud, making Sean fearful
of someone hearing her. Wait till I tell you, she went on—
you'll die laughin'! You should see Charlie when he's at the
he-man business—are you sure you won't get faint, Nellie?
Don't forget to say if I'm hurtin' you, dearie! One night, when
he was—you know—I jerked him clean outa th' bed on to
th' floor—th' bump shook th' house! D'ye know, honest t'God,
he just lay stunned there. Put th' heart across me. Ever afther,
d'ye know, I've had to handle him like a delicate piece of
china! No; poor Charlie's style's too shy for me. Not like Jim
Achree's. J'ever hear o' his?

She slid down till she was half lying over him, and sang
sedulously beside his ear:

> Jim Achree's style has a wondherful way with it,
> All th' girls' minds are in sad disarray with it;
> Whenever they venture to have a short play with it,
> Good girls want to stay with it, ever an' aye.
> Oh! Jimmy Achree, shure your style is your own,
> Amazin' th' way it has flourished an' grown,
> With lovely threats shakin,' tense with mischief makin',
> Knockin' poor women flat like a gorgeous cyclone!

—Looka, she said breathlessly, th' least bit o' fondlin' now,
an' I'd swoon away, helpless an' benighted.

—In the midst of death we are in life, thought Sean. He
tried to turn his head away so that he wouldn't be prompted
by the white breast that was like a golden cup with a misty
ruby in its centre; but his head refused to stir. Instead, he
found his hand sliding over her fair bosom. He felt her arm
pushing a way under his head till it was firmly round his neck,
while the other pushed the clothes from covering him. He was
lost, unless he yelled for help, and that he couldn't do.

—You're a good young man, he heard her whispering, an' would never take advantage of a woman alone in your room in th' dead o' night, with but a loose slip between you an' a swift lie-down on a bed o' meadow-sweet. Don't sthruggle, man, or you'll upset things! Why'r you thryin' to keep me from gettin' the clothes down? You've far too many on you; a little cool air'll do you good. Take th' good things while they're goin'. She whipped the clothes down with a fierce jerk, and lying beside him, pressed her mouth to his. Her big innocent eyes looked frantic now.

—G'won, she muttered, panting, be as rough as you like with me—it's what I'm longin' for for weeks! And half mad himself now, he gripped her like a vice, and sank his fingers into her flesh.

Then they suddenly went still as death, listening; listening to the whine of a motor-engine cruising down the road outside. Then another whine followed that, and another, the last, till they mingled into one shrill, threatening whine that went echoing round the walls of the old house.

—Out in strength tonight, thought Sean; more'n three of them; each of them crooning a song of death to someone. Ireland's modern, senseless Tanshee!

Suddenly the shrill whine lifted into a shrill, quavering scream, the scream fading into the throb, throb of active engines as the lorries stopped outside, or very near, the house.

—They've stopped at this house, or th' next one! said Nellie, loosening her arm from around his neck, and sliding swift from the bed to the door. Who' ha' thought th' bastards would bother to come twice th' same night? Christ! It's this house they're makin' for! And swiftly came a great hammering on the door again. Nellie frantically twisted and turned at the key, but she couldn't get the door of the room open.

—In they'll come, she squealed softly, an' I'll be exposed to th' world as a fast woman. She tugged and writhed till the slip fell from her shoulders, leaving her naked, fuming, at the door. You it was, she half shouted, turning a red and bitter face towards Sean, that lured me into this predicament, never able to let any decent woman pass without thryin' to meddle her!

Sean as eager as she was herself that she should go unseen, leaped out of bed, hurried over, and with a hard twist, turned the key. Snatching up her flowered overall, she whipped the door open, rushed out, and up the stairs, without another word. Shutting the door again, he fled back to bed, digging himself down deep into it once again, listening to hear if it was Tan or Tommy who had entered the house.

The door spun open, and a torchlight shot terror into his eyes. Silently he waited for a blow or a shot, but neither came. He opened his eyes, and saw a young khaki-clad officer just inside the door, a torch in one hand, a revolver in the other. Behind him were two soldiers with rifles at ready. The officer stared at Sean, then slowly returned the gun to a holster, and the soldiers, at this sign, stood at ease, and rested the butts of the rifles on the dirty floor.

—Get up; dress; go out to the street, said the officer tersely; this house has to be searched room by room. Don't try to go farther than the wire cordon ringing the district: orders are to fire on any who do. He watched Sean dressing, and when he saw him clap a cap on his head, asked, Haven't you an overcoat?

—A sort of a one, said Sean.

—Better than nothing; you'd better put it on—it's damned cold outside.

—Decent man, thought Sean, putting on his old coat; has an occasional thought for others. Thank God, the Tans are absent!

He went out into the dark hall, and near bumped into a Tan standing there, fingering a heavy revolver. A cold shiver trickled down his spine

—Where are you going? he asked.

—Outside to street—officer's orders, said Sean.

—What officer? asked the Tan.

—Military officer, sir.

—Oh! Military officer, eh? Well, we give the orders here—
understand?

—Yessir, said Sean promptly.

—Are you a Sinn Feiner? he questioned, twisting the gun
in his hand.

—A Sinn Feiner? Me? No fear.

—You were one, then.

—No; never, said Sean emphatically. Thank God, thought
Sean, he didn't ask if I had ever been a Republican. The ignorant English bastard doesn't know the difference.

—Well, you're an Irishman, anyway—you can't deny that!

—No, sir, I can't deny that: I'm an Irishman, right enough.

—Well, shout To Hell with Ireland, and you can go—no
mutter, but a shout the house can hear. Now!

But Sean fell silent. God damn him if he'd do that! He
knew his face was white; he felt his legs tremble; but he fell
silent, with a stubborn look on his face.

—Go on, you Sinn Fein rat, shout it!

A streak of light fell on them, and Sean saw the young
officer coming to them. He stopped, looked at Sean, then
looked at the Tan.

—What's wrong here? he asked. Let that man go into the
street.

—You mind your own damned business, snarled the Tan.

—I am minding it, said the young officer. I happen to be an
Irishman, too. Have you any objection to it?

—I don't take orders from you! said the Tan roughly.

—I'm not sorry for that, the officer said; but this man does
—didn't I give you an order to go into the street? he asked,
turning to Sean.

—Yessir.

—Carry it out, then, he said sharply; and Sean, turning
swiftly, made a quick march through the hall, out by the door,
into the street.

It was very cold, and from the timid gleams from a waning moon, Sean saw that path and road were white with a covering of rich rime frost. Groups of people were standing, huddled up against the railings of the houses, while more were oozing sleepily out of the remaining ones, shepherded into bunches by armed soldiers. The women were trying to coax warmth into their tearful and shivering children by wrapping flimsy rags round their shoulders, and tucking the little ones under them into their arms.

Several searchlights wandered through the street, flashing over the groups of people, or tinselling along the walls of the houses. At one end stood an armoured car, the lids raised, showing the heads of several Tommies who were quietly chanting an advice to the shivering people to pack up their troubles in their old kit-bags. Along the road, over the calm, quiet chastity of the white frost, slid a diamond-shaped tank, looking like a dirty, dangerous crawling slug, machine-guns sticking out from slits, like ugly protruding eyes staring at the cowering people.

He saw a commotion round the door of the house he lived in. He mooched over till he was beside the steps to look over the shoulders of a rank of soldiers. A prisoner! Who could it be? He whisperingly asked the soldier in front of him what had happened.

—An awrsenal! whispered the soldier hoarsely. Rear of th' ouse, an awrsenal discovered! 'Nough gelignite to blow up 'ole neighbourhood. A blighter there drew a gun, but was shot through hand afore 'ee could pull trigger. 'Ere's the bawstard coming!

Amid a group of soldiers with rifles at the ready marched a thin forlorn figure, but the lips in the pale face were tight together, and the small head was held high. Peering closer, Sean saw that handcuffs kept the two small hands locked together, and that from one of them red blobs were dripping on to the white frost on the path, leaving little spots behind like crimson berries that had fallen on to snow. In the hall he heard the voice of Nellie shouting.

—That's me husband! he heard her shout; a good man an' a brave one! Yous'll never shoot the life outa Ireland, yous gang o' armed ruffians! Here, take me, too, if yous aren't afraid. Keep your pecker up, Charlie—Ireland's with you!

Sean peered closer. Good God—the prisoner was the timid, insignificant Charlie Ballynoy who took no interest in politics! A lorry, full of soldiers, swirled into the kerb. The handcuffed prisoner was pushed and lifted into it. Standing there in the middle of the soldiers, with the searchlight covering him with glory, he held up his iron-locked hands from which clouts of blood still dripped.

—Up th' Republic! he shouted with the full force of his voice.

The lorry drove off, and the red specks in the rime turned brown and lonely. Heads that had lifted bent again, and all was quiet once more. A bleak dawn at last began to peel the deeper darkness from the sky, and the scene crept into a ghostly glamour, brightened by the pale faces of the waiting people; the pale moon sinking deeper into a surly sky, and the rimy frost on pathway, road, and roof grew whiter. Dirty-yellow-clad figures moved into the whiteness from one dark doorway, to move out of it again into another blacker still; while the brown, slug-like tank crept up and down the road, charring the dainty rime with its grinding treads—the new leviathan that God could ne'er control.

Padraic Colum (1881-)

A Drover

To Meath of the pastures,
From wet hills by the sea,
Through Leitrim and Longford,
Go my cattle and me.

I hear in the darkness
Their slipping and breathing—
I name them the by-ways
They're to pass without heeding;

Then the wet, winding roads,
Brown bogs with black water,
And my thoughts on white ships
And the King o' Spain's daughter.

O farmer, strong farmer!
You can spend at the fair,
But your face you must turn
To your crops and your care;

And soldiers, red soldiers!
You've seen many lands,
But you walk two by two,
And by captain's commands!

O the smell of the beasts,
The wet wind in the morn,
And the proud and hard earth
Never broken for corn!

And the crowds at the fair,
The herds loosened and blind,
Loud words and dark faces,
And the wild blood behind!

(O strong men with your best
I would strive breast to breast,
I could quiet your herds
With my words, with my words!)

I will bring you, my kine,
Where there's grass to the knee,
But you'll think of scant croppings
Harsh with salt of the sea.

A Poor Scholar of the 'Forties

My eyelids red and heavy are
With bending o'er the smold'ring peat.
I know the Æneid now by heart,
My Virgil read in cold and heat,
In loneliness and hunger smart.
 And I know Homer, too, I ween,
 As Munster poets know Ossian.

And I must walk this road that winds
'Twixt bog and bog, while east there lies
A city with its men and books;
With treasures open to the wise,
Heart-words from equals, comrade-looks;
 Down here they have but tale and song,
 They talk Repeal[1] the whole night long.

---

[1] Repeal of the Act of Union (1800) which disestablished the
Irish Parliament and provided Ireland instead with representation at
Westminster.

"You teach Greek verbs and Latin nouns,"
The dreamer of Young Ireland said,
"You do not hear the muffled call,
The sword being forged, the far-off tread
Of hosts to meet as Gael and Gall—
    What good to us your wisdom-store,
    Your Latin verse, your Grecian lore?"

And what to me is Gael or Gall?
Less than the Latin or the Greek—
I teach these by the dim rush-light
In smoky cabins night and week.
But what avail my teaching slight?
    Years hence, in rustic speech, a phrase,
    As in wild earth a Grecian vase!

James Stephens (1882-1950)

The Wind

The wind stood up, and gave a shout;
He whistled on his fingers, and

Kicked the withered leaves about,
And thumped the branches with his hand,

And said he'll kill, and kill, and kill;
And so he will! And so he will!

The College of Surgeons

As I stood at the door
Sheltered out of the wind,
Something flew in
Which I hardly could find.

In the dim gloomy doorway
I searched till I found
A dry withered leaf
Lying down on the ground.

With thin pointed claws
And a dry dusty skin,
—Sure, a hall is no place
For a leaf to be in!

Oh where is your tree,
And your summer and all,
Poor dusty leaf,
Whistled into a hall!

Check

The Night was creeping on the ground!
She crept and did not make a sound,

Until she reached the tree: And then
She covered it, and stole again

Along the grass beside the wall!
—I heard the rustling of her shawl

As she threw blackness everywhere
Along the sky, the ground, the air,

And in the room where I was hid!
But, no matter what she did

To everything that was without,
She could not put my candle out!

So I stared at the Night! And she
Stared back solemnly at me!

The Crest Jewel

(1)

The leaf will wrinkle to decay,
And crumble into dust away!

The rose, the lily, grow to eld,
And are, and are no more, beheld!

Nothing will stay! For, as the eye
Rests upon an object nigh,

It is not there to look upon!
It is mysteriously gone!

And, in its place, another thing
Apes its shape and fashioning!

(2)

All that the sun will breath to-day
The moon will lip and wear away

To-night! And all will re-begin
To-morrow as the dawn comes in!

Is no beginning, middle-trend,
Or argument to that, or end!

No cause and no effect, and no
Reason why it should be so!

Or why it might be otherwise
To other minds, or other eyes!

(3)

The soul can dream itself to be
Adrift upon an endless sea

Of day and night! The soul can seem
To be all things that it can dream!

Yet needs but look within to find
That which is steady in the wind!

That which the fire does not appal!
Which good and ill move not at all!

Which does not seek, or lack, or try!
And was not born, and cannot die!

(4)

It has been writ in wisdom old—
This is the last word to be told:

—There is no dissolution! No
Creation! There are none in woe!

There is no teacher, teaching, taught!
Are none who long for, lack for aught!

Are none who pine for freedom! None
Are liberated under sun!

—And this is absolutely true
In Him who dreams in me and you.

Ivy Day in the Committee Room

BY James Joyce (1882-1941)

OLD JACK raked the cinders together with a piece of cardboard and spread them judiciously over the whitening dome
of coals. When the dome was thinly covered his face lapsed
into darkness but, as he set himself to fan the fire again, his
crouching shadow ascended the opposite wall and his face
slowly re-emerged into light. It was an old man's face, very
bony and hairy. The moist blue eyes blinked at the fire and
the moist mouth fell open at times, munching once or twice
mechanically when it closed. When the cinders had caught
he laid the piece of cardboard against the wall, sighed and said:

"That's better now, Mr. O'Connor."

Mr. O'Connor, a grey-haired young man, whose face was
disfigured by many blotches and pimples, had just brought
the tobacco for a cigarette into a shapely cylinder but when
spoken to he undid his handiwork meditatively. Then he began

to roll the tobacco again meditatively and after a moment's thought decided to lick the paper.

"Did Mr. Tierney say when he'd be back?" he asked in a husky falsetto.

"He didn't say."

Mr. O'Connor put his cigarette into his mouth and began to search his pockets. He took out a pack of thin pasteboard cards.

"I'll get you a match," said the old man.

"Never mind, this'll do," said Mr. O'Connor.

He selected one of the cards and read what was printed on it:

MUNICIPAL ELECTIONS

Royal Exchange Ward

Mr. Richard J. Tierney, P.L.G., respectfully solicits the favour of your vote and influence at the coming election in the Royal Exchange Ward.

Mr. O'Connor had been engaged by Tierney's agent to canvass one part of the ward but, as the weather was inclement and his boots let in the wet, he spent a great part of the day sitting by the fire in the Committee Room in Wicklow Street with Jack, the old caretaker. They had been sitting thus since the short day had grown dark. It was the sixth of October, dismal and cold out of doors.

Mr. O'Connor tore a strip off the card and, lighting it, lit his cigarette. As he did so the flame lit up a leaf of dark glossy ivy in the lapel of his coat. The old man watched him attentively and then, taking up the piece of cardboard again, began to fan the fire slowly while his companion smoked.

"Ah, yes," he said, continuing, "it's hard to know what way to bring up children. Now who'd think he'd turn out like that! I sent him to the Christian Brothers and I done what I could for him, and there he goes boosing about. I tried to make him someway decent."

He replaced the cardboard wearily.

"Only I'm an old man now I'd change his tune for him. I'd take the stick to his back and beat him while I could stand over him—as I done many a time before. The mother, you know, she cocks him up with this and that. . . ."

"That's what ruins children," said Mr. O'Connor.

"To be sure it is," said the old man. "And little thanks you get for it, only impudence. He takes th'upper hand of me whenever he sees I've a sup taken. What's the world coming to when sons speaks that way to their fathers?"

"What age is he?" said Mr. O'Connor.

"Nineteen," said the old man.

"Why don't you put him to something?"

"Sure, amn't I never done at the drunken bowsy ever since he left school? 'I won't keep you,' I says. 'You must get a job for yourself.' But, sure, it's worse whenever he gets a job; he drinks it all."

Mr. O'Connor shook his head in sympathy, and the old man fell silent, gazing into the fire. Someone opened the door of the room and called out:

"Hello! Is this a Freemason's meeting?"

"Who's that?" said the old man.

"What are you doing in the dark?" asked a voice.

"Is that you, Hynes?" asked Mr. O'Connor.

"Yes. What are you doing in the dark?" said Mr. Hynes, advancing into the light of the fire.

He was a tall, slender young man with a light brown moustache. Imminent little drops of rain hung at the brim of his hat and the collar of his jacket-coat was turned up.

"Well, Mat," he said to Mr. O'Connor, "how goes it?"

Mr. O'Connor shook his head. The old man left the hearth, and after stumbling about the room returned with two candle-sticks which he thrust one after the other into the fire and carried to the table. A denuded room came into view and the fire lost all its cheerful colour. The walls of the room were bare except for a copy of an election address. In the middle of the room was a small table on which papers were heaped.

Mr. Hynes leaned against the mantelpiece and asked:

"Has he paid you yet?"

"Not yet," said Mr. O'Connor. "I hope to God he'll not leave us in the lurch to-night."

Mr. Hynes laughed.

"O, he'll pay you. Never fear," he said.

"I hope he'll look smart about it if he means business," said Mr. O'Connor.

"What do you think, Jack?" said Mr. Hynes satirically to the old man.

The old man returned to his seat by the fire, saying:

"It isn't but he has it, anyway. Not like the other tinker."

"What other tinker?" said Mr Hynes.

"Colgan," said the old man scornfully.

"It is because Colgan's a working-man you say that? What's the difference between a good honest bricklayer and a publican —eh? Hasn't the working-man as good as right to be in the Corporation as anyone else—ay, and a better right than those shoneens that are always hat in hand before any fellow with a handle to his name? Isn't that so, Mat?" said Mr. Hynes, ad-dressing Mr. O'Connor.

"I think you're right," said Mr. O'Connor.

"One man is a plain honest man with no hunker-sliding about him. He goes in to represent the labour classes. This fellow you're working for only wants to get some job or other."

"Of course, the working-classes should be represented," said the old man.

"The working-man," said Mr. Hynes, "gets all kicks and no halfpence. But it's labour produces everything. The working-man is not looking for fat jobs for his sons and nephews and cousins. The working-man is not going to drag the honour of Dublin in the mud to please a German monarch."

"How's that?" said the old man.

"Don't you know they want to present an address of welcome to Edward Rex if he comes here next year? What do we want kowtowing to a foreign king?"

"Our man won't vote for the address," said Mr. O'Connor. "He goes in on the Nationalist ticket."

"Won't he?" said Mr. Hynes. "Wait till you see whether he will or not. I know him. Is it Tricky Dicky Tierney?"

"By God! perhaps you're right, Joe," said Mr. O'Connor. "Anyway, I wish he'd turn up with the spondulics."

The three men fell silent. The old man began to rake more cinders together. Mr. Hynes took off his hat, shook it and then turned down the collar of his coat, displaying, as he did so, an ivy leaf in the lapel.

"If this man was alive," he said, pointing to the leaf, "we'd have no talk of an address of welcome."

"That's true," said Mr. O'Connor.

"Musha, God be with them times!" said the old man. "There was some life in it then."

The room was silent again. Then a bustling little man with a snuffling nose and very cold ears pushed in the door. He walked over quickly to the fire, rubbing his hands as if he intended to produce a spark from them.

"No money, boys," he said.

"Sit down here, Mr. Henchy," said the old man, offering him his chair.

"O, don't stir, Jack, don't stir," said Mr. Henchy.

He nodded curtly to Mr. Hynes and sat down on the chair which the old man vacated.

"Did you serve Aungier Street?" he asked Mr. O'Connor.

"Yes," said Mr. O'Connor, beginning to search his pockets for memoranda.

"Did you call on Grimes?"

"I did."

"Well? How does he stand?"

"He wouldn't promise. He said: 'I won't tell anyone what way I'm going to vote.' But I think he'll be all right."

"Why so?"

"He asked me who the nominators were; and I told him. I mentioned Father Burke's name. I think it'll be all right."

Mr. Henchy began to snuffle and to rub his hands over the fire at a terrific speed. Then he said:

"For the love of God, Jack, bring us a bit of coal. There must be some left."

The old man went out of the room.

"It's no go," said Mr. Henchy, shaking his head. "I asked the little shoeboy, but he said: 'O, now, Mr. Henchy, when I see the work going on properly I won't forget you, you may be sure.' Mean little tinker! 'Usha, how could he be anything else?"

"What did I tell you, Mat?" said Mr. Hynes. "Tricky Dicky Tierney."

"O, he's as tricky as they make 'em," said Mr. Henchy. "He hasn't got those little pigs' eyes for nothing. Blast his soul! Couldn't he pay up like a man instead of: 'O, now, Mr. Henchy, I must speak to Mr. Fanning. . . . I've spent a lot of money'? Mean little schoolboy of hell! I suppose he forgets the time his little old father kept the hand-me-down shop in Mary's Lane."

"But is that a fact?" asked Mr. O'Connor.

"God, yes," said Mr. Henchy. "Did you never hear that? And the men used to go in on Sunday morning before the houses were open to buy a waistcoat or a trousers—moya! But Tricky Dicky's little old father always had a tricky little black bottle up in a corner. Do you mind now? That's that. That's where he first saw the light."

The old man returned with a few lumps of coal which he placed here and there on the fire.

"That's a nice how-do-you-do," said Mr. O'Connor. "How does he expect us to work for him if he won't stump up?"

"I can't help it," said Mr. Henchy. "I expect to find the bailiffs in the hall when I go home."

Mr. Hynes laughed and, shoving himself away from the mantelpiece with the aid of his shoulders, made ready to leave.

"It'll be all right when King Eddie comes," he said. "Well, boys, I'm off for the present. See you later. 'Bye, 'bye."

He went out of the room slowly. Neither Mr. Henchy nor the old man said anything, but, just as the door was closing, Mr. O'Connor, who had been staring moodily into the fire, called out suddenly:

" 'Bye, Joe."

Mr. Henchy waited a few moments and then nodded in the direction of the door.

"Tell me," he said across the fire, "what brings our friend in here? What does he want?"

" 'Usha, poor Joe!" said Mr. O'Connor, throwing the end of his cigarette into the fire, "he's hard up, like the rest of us."

Mr. Henchy snuffled vigorously and spat so copiously that he nearly put out the fire, which uttered a hissing protest.

"To tell you my private and candid opinion," he said, "I think he's a man from the other camp. He's a spy of Colgan's, if you ask me. Just go round and try and find out how they're getting on. They won't suspect you. Do you twig?"

"Ah, poor Joe is a decent skin," said Mr. O'Connor.

"His father was a decent, respectable man," Mr. Henchy admitted. "Poor old Larry Hynes! Many a good turn he did in his day! But I'm greatly afraid our friend is not nineteen carat. Damn it, I can understand a fellow being hard up, but what I can't understand is a fellow sponging. Couldn't he have some spark of manhood about him?"

"He doesn't get a warm welcome from me when he comes," said the old man. "Let him work for his own side and not come spying around here."

"I don't know," said Mr. O'Connor dubiously, as he took out cigarette-papers and tobacco. "I think Joe Hynes is a straight man. He's a clever chap, too, with the pen. Do you remember that thing he wrote . . . ?"

"Some of these hillsiders and fenians are a bit too clever if you ask me," said Mr. Henchy. "Do you know what my private

and candid opinion is about some of those little jokers? I believe half of them are in the pay of the Castle."

"There's no knowing," said the old man.

"O, but I know it for a fact," said Mr. Henchy. "They're
Castle hacks. . . . I don't say Hynes. . . . No, damn it, I think
he's a stroke above that. . . . But there's a certain little noble-
man with a cock-eye—you know the patriot I'm alluding to?"

Mr. O'Connor nodded.

"There's a lineal descendant of Major Sirr[1] for you if you
like! O, the heart's blood of a patriot! That's a fellow now
that'd sell his country for fourpence—ay—and go down on
his bended knees and thank the Almighty Christ he had a
country to sell."

There was a knock at the door.

"Come in!" said Mr. Henchy.

A person resembling a poor clergyman or a poor actor appeared in the doorway. His black clothes were tightly buttoned
on his short body and it was impossible to say whether he
wore a clergyman's collar or a layman's, because the collar of
his shabby frock-coat, the uncovered buttons of which reflected
the candlelight, was turned up about his neck. He wore a
round hat of hard black felt. His face, shining with raindrops,
had the appearance of damp yellow cheese save where two rosy
spots indicated the cheekbones. He opened his very long
mouth suddenly to express disappointment and at the same
time opened wide his very bright blue eyes to express pleasure
and surprise.

"O Father Keon!" said Mr. Henchy, jumping up from his
chair. "Is that you? Come in!"

"O, no, no, no!" said Father Keon quickly, pursing his lips
as if he were addressing a child.

"Won't you come in and sit down?"

"No, no, no!" said Father Keon, speaking in a discreet, in-
dulgent, velvety voice. "Don't let me disturb you now! I'm
just looking for Mr. Fanning. . . ."

---

[1] The capturer of Robert Emmet.

"He's round at the *Black Eagle*," said Mr. Henchy. "But won't you come in and sit down a minute?"

"No, no, thank you. It was just a little business matter," said Father Keon. "Thank you, indeed."

He retreated from the doorway and Mr. Henchy, seizing one of the candlesticks, went to the door to light him downstairs.

"O, don't trouble, I beg!"

"No, but the stairs is so dark."

"No, no, I can see. . . . Thank you, indeed."

"Are you right now?"

"All right, thanks. . . . Thanks."

Mr. Henchy returned with the candlestick and put it on the table. He sat down again at the fire. There was silence for a few moments.

"Tell me, John," said Mr. O'Connor, lighting his cigarette with another pasteboard card.

"Hm?"

"What he is exactly?"

"Ask me an easier one," said Mr. Henchy.

"Fanning and himself seem to me very thick. They're often in Kavanagh's together. Is he a priest at all?"

" 'Mmmyes, I believe so. . . . I think he's what you call a black sheep. We haven't many of them, thank God! but we have a few. . . . He's an unfortunate man of some kind. . . ."

"And how does he knock it out?" asked Mr. O'Connor.

"That's another mystery."

"Is he attached to any chapel or church or institution or—"

"No," said Mr. Henchy, "I think he's travelling on his own account. . . . God forgive me," he added, "I thought he was the dozen of stout."

"Is there any chance of a drink itself?" asked Mr. O'Connor.

"I'm dry too," said the old man.

"I asked that little shoeboy three times," said Mr. Henchy, "would he send up a dozen of stout. I asked him again now, but he was leaning on the counter in his shirt-sleeves having a deep goster with Alderman Cowley."

"Why didn't you remind him?" said Mr. O'Connor.

"Well, I couldn't go over while he was talking to Alderman Cowley. I just waited till I caught his eye, and said: 'About that little matter I was speaking to you about. . . .' 'That'll be all right, Mr. H.,' he said. Yerra, sure the little hop-o'-my-thumb has forgotten all about it."

"There's some deal on in that quarter," said Mr. O'Connor thoughtfully. "I saw the three of them hard at it yesterday at Suffolk Street corner."

"I think I know the little game they're at," said Mr. Henchy. "You must owe the City Fathers money nowadays if you want to be made Lord Mayor. Then they'll make you Lord Mayor. By God! I'm thinking seriously of becoming a City Father myself. What do you think? Would I do for the job?"

Mr. O'Connor laughed.

"So far as owing money goes. . . ."

"Driving out of the Mansion House," said Mr. Henchy, "in all my vermin, with Jack here standing up behind me in a powdered wig—eh?"

"And make me your private secretary, John."

"Yes. And I'll make Father Keon my private chaplain. We'll have a family party."

"Faith, Mr. Henchy," said the old man, "you'd keep up better style then some of them. I was talking one day to old Keegan, the porter. 'And how do you like your new master, Pat?' says I to him. 'You haven't much entertaining now,' says I. 'Entertaining!' says he. 'He'd live on the smell of an oil-rag.' And do you know what he told me? Now, I declare to God, I didn't believe him."

"What?" said Mr. Henchy and Mr. O'Connor.

"He told me: 'What do you think of a Lord Mayor of Dublin sending out for a pound of chops for his dinner? How's that for high living?' says he. 'Wisha! wisha,' says I. 'A pound of chops,' says he, 'coming into the Mansion House.' 'Wisha!' says I, 'what kind of people is going at all now?' "

At this point there was a knock at the door, and a boy put in his head.

"What is it?" said the old man.

"From the *Black Eagle*," said the boy, walking in sideways and depositing a basket on the floor with a noise of shaken bottles.

The old man helped the boy to transfer the bottles from the basket to the table and counted the full tally. After the transfer the boy put his basket on his arm and asked:

"Any bottles?"

"What bottles?" said the old man.

"Won't you let us drink them first?" said Mr. Henchy.

"I was told to ask for bottles."

"Come back to-morrow," said the old man.

"Here, boy!" said Mr. Henchy, "will you run over to O'Farrell's and ask him to lend us a corkscrew—for Mr. Henchy, say. Tell him we won't keep it a minute. Leave the basket there."

The boy went out and Mr. Henchy began to rub his hands cheerfully, saying:

"Ah, well, he's not so bad after all. He's as good as his word, anyhow."

"There's no tumblers," said the old man.

"O, don't let that trouble you, Jack," said Mr. Henchy. "Many's the good man before now drank out of the bottle."

"Anyway, it's better than nothing," said Mr. O'Connor.

"He's not a bad sort," said Mr. Henchy, "only Fanning has such a loan of him. He means well, you know, in his own tin-pot way."

The boy came back with the corkscrew. The old man opened three bottles and was handing back the corkscrew when Mr. Henchy said to the boy,

"Would you like a drink, boy?"

"If you please, sir," said the boy.

The old man opened another bottle grudgingly, and handed it to the boy.

"What age are you?" he asked.

"Seventeen," said the boy.

As the old man said nothing further, the boy took the bottle, said: "Here's my best respects, sir, to Mr. Henchy," drank the contents, put the bottle back on the table and wiped his mouth with his sleeve. Then he took up the corkscrew and went out of the door sideways, muttering some form of salutation.

"That's the way it begins," said the old man.

"The thin edge of the wedge," said Mr. Henchy.

The old man distributed the three bottles which he had opened and the men drank from them simultaneously. After having drank each placed his bottle on the mantelpiece within hand's reach and drew in a long breath of satisfaction.

"Well, I did a good day's work to-day," said Mr. Henchy, after a pause.

"That so, John?"

"Yes. I got him one or two sure things in Dawson Street, Crofton and myself. Between ourselves, you know, Crofton (he's a decent chap, of course), but he's not worth a damn as a canvasser. He hasn't a word to throw to a dog. He stands and looks at the people while I do the talking."

Here two men entered the room. One of them was a very fat man, whose blue serge clothes seemed to be in danger of falling from his sloping figure. He had a big face which resembled a young ox's face in expression, staring blue eyes and a grizzled moustache. The other man, who was much younger and frailer, had a thin, clean-shaven face. He wore a very high double collar and a wide-brimmed bowler hat.

"Hello, Crofton!" said Mr. Henchy to the fat man. "Talk of the devil . . ."

"Where did the boose come from?" asked the young man. "Did the cow calve?"

"O, of course, Lyons spots the drink first thing!" said Mr. O'Connor, laughing.

"Is that the way you chaps canvass," said Mr. Lyons, "and Crofton and I out in the cold and rain looking for votes?"

"Why, blast your soul," said Mr. Henchy, "I'd get more votes in five minutes than you two'd get in a week."

"Open two bottles of stout, Jack," said Mr. O'Connor.

"How can I?" said the old man, "when there's no cork screw?"

"Wait now, wait now!" said Mr. Henchy, getting up quickly. "Did you ever see this little trick?"

He took two bottles from the table and, carrying them to the fire, put them on the hob. Then he sat down again by the fire and took another drink from his bottle. Mr. Lyons sat on the edge of the table, pushed his hat towards the nape of his neck and began to swing his legs.

"Which is my bottle?" he asked.

"This, lad," said Mr. Henchy.

Mr. Crofton sat down on a box and looked fixedly at the other bottle on the hob. He was silent for two reasons. The first reason, sufficient in itself, was that he had nothing to say; the second reason was that he considered his companions beneath him. He had been a canvasser for Wilkins, the Conservative, but when the Conservatives had withdrawn their man and, choosing the lesser of two evils, given their support to the Nationalist candidate, he had been engaged to work for Mr. Tierney.

In a few minutes an apologetic "Pok!" was heard as the cork flew out of Mr. Lyons' bottle. Mr. Lyons jumped off the table, went to the fire, took his bottle and carried it back to the table.

"I was just telling them, Crofton," said Mr. Henchy, "that we got a good few votes to-day."

"Who did you get?" asked Mr. Lyons.

"Well, I got Parkes for one, and I got Atkinson for two, and I got Ward of Dawson Street. Fine old chap he is, too—regular old toff, old Conservative! 'But isn't your candidate a Nationalist?' said he. 'He's a respectable man,' said I. 'He's in favour of whatever will benefit this country. He's a big ratepayer,' I said. 'He has extensive house property in the city and three places of business and isn't it to his own advantage to keep down the rates? He's a prominent and respected citizen,' said I, 'and a Poor Law Guardian, and he doesn't belong to any party, good, bad, or indifferent.' That's the way to talk to 'em."

"And what about the address to the King?" said Mr. Lyons, after drinking and smacking his lips.

"Listen to me," said Mr. Henchy. "What we want in this country, as I said to old Ward, is capital. The King's coming here will mean an influx of money into this country. The citizens of Dublin will benefit by it. Look at all the factories down by the quays there, idle! Look at all the money there is in the country if we only worked the old industries, the mills, the ship-building yards and factories. It's capital we want."

"But look here, John," said Mr. O'Connor. "Why should we welcome the King of England? Didn't Parnell himself . . ."

"Parnell," said Mr. Henchy, "is dead. Now, here's the way I look at it. Here's this chap come to the throne after his old mother keeping him out of it till the man was grey. He's a man of the world, and he means well by us. He's a jolly fine decent fellow, if you ask me, and no damn nonsense about him. He just says to himself: 'The old one never went to see these wild Irish. By Christ, I'll go myself and see what they're like.' And are we going to insult the man when he comes over here on a friendly visit? Eh? Isn't that right, Crofton?"

Mr. Crofton nodded his head.

"But after all now," said Mr. Lyons argumentatively, "King Edward's life, you know, is not the very . . ."

"Let bygones be bygones," said Mr. Henchy. "I admire the man personally. He's just an ordinary knockabout like you and me. He's fond of his glass of grog and he's a bit of a rake, perhaps, and he's a good sportsman. Damn it, can't we Irish play fair?"

"That's all very fine," said Mr. Lyons. "But look at the case of Parnell now."

"In the name of God," said Mr. Henchy, "where's the analogy between the two cases?"

"What I mean," said Mr. Lyons, "is we have our ideals. Why, now, would we welcome a man like that? Do you think now after what he did Parnell was a fit man to lead us? And why, then, would we do it for Edward the Seventh?"

"This is Parnell's anniversary," said Mr. O'Connor, "and don't let us stir up any bad blood. We all respect him now that he's dead and gone—even the Conservatives," he added, turning to Mr. Crofton.

Pok! The tardy cork flew out of Mr. Crofton's bottle. Mr. Crofton got up from his box and went to the fire. As he returned with his capture he said in a deep voice:

"Our side of the house respects him, because he was a gentleman."

"Right you are, Crofton!" said Mr. Henchy fiercely. "He was the only man that could keep that bag of cats in order. 'Down, ye dogs! Lie down, ye curs!' That's the way he treated them. Come in Joe! Come in!" he called out, catching sight of Mr. Hynes in the doorway.

Mr. Hynes came in slowly.

"Open another bottle of stout, Jack," said Mr. Henchy. "O, I forgot there's no corkscrew. Here, show me one here and I'll put it at the fire."

The old man handed him another bottle and he placed it on the hob.

"Sit down, Joe," said Mr. O'Connor, "we're just talking about the Chief."

"Ay, ay!" said Mr. Henchy.

Mr. Hynes sat on the side of the table near Mr. Lyons but said nothing.

"There's one of them, anyhow," said Mr. Henchy, "that didn't renege him. By God, I'll say for you, Joe! No, by God, you stuck to him like a man!"

"O, Joe," said Mr. O'Connor suddenly. "Give us that thing you wrote—do you remember? Have you got it on you?"

"O, ay!" said Mr. Henchy. "Give us that. Did you ever hear that, Crofton? Listen to this now: splendid thing."

"Go on," said Mr. O'Connor. "Fire away, Joe."

Mr. Hynes did not seem to remember at once the piece to which they were alluding, but, after reflecting a while, he said:

"O, that thing is it. . . . Sure, that's old now."

"Out with it, man!" said Mr. O'Connor.

" 'Sh, 'sh," said Mr. Henchy. "Now, Joe!"

Mr. Hynes hesitated a little longer. Then amid the silence he took off his hat, laid it on the table and stood up. He seemed to be rehearsing the piece in his mind. After a rather long pause he announced:

THE DEATH OF PARNELL

6th October, 1891

He cleared his throat once or twice and then began to recite:

> He is dead. Our Uncrowned King is dead.
>   O, Erin, mourn with grief and woe
> For he lies dead whom the fell gang
>   Of modern hypocrites laid low.
>
> He lies slain by the coward hounds
>   He raised to glory from the mire;
> And Erin's hopes and Erin's dreams
>   Perish upon her monarch's pyre.
>
> In palace, cabin or in cot
>   The Irish heart where'er it be
> Is bowed with woe—for he is gone
>   Who would have wrought her destiny.
>
> He would have had his Erin famed,
>   The green flag gloriously unfurled,
> Her statesmen, bards and warriors raised
>   Before the nations of the World.
>
> He dreamed (alas, 'twas but a dream!)
>   Of Liberty: but as he strove
> To clutch that idol, treachery
>   Sundered him from the thing he loved.

Shame on the coward, caitiff hands
   That smote their Lord or with a kiss
Betrayed him to the rabble-rout
   Of fawning priests—no friends of his.

May everlasting shame consume
   The memory of those who tried
To befoul and smear the exalted name
   Of one who spurned them in his pride.

He fell as fall the mighty ones,
   Nobly undaunted to the last,
And death has now united him
   With Erin's heroes of the past.

No sound of strife disturb his sleep!
   Calmly he rests: no human pain
Or high ambition spurs him now
   The peaks of glory to attain.

They had their way: they laid him low.
   But Erin, list, his spirit may
Rise, like the Phœnix from the flames,
   When breaks the dawning of the day,

The day that brings us Freedom's reign.
   And on that day may Erin well
Pledge in the cup she lifts to Joy
   One grief—the memory of Parnell.

Mr. Hynes sat down again on the table. When he had
finished his recitation there was a silence and then a burst of
clapping: even Mr. Lyons clapped. The applause continued for
a little time. When it had ceased all the auditors drank from
their bottles in silence.

Pok! The cork flew out of Mr. Hynes' bottle, but Mr. Hynes
remained sitting flushed and bareheaded on the table. He did
not seem to have heard the invitation.

"Good man, Joe!" said Mr. O'Connor, taking out his cigarette papers and pouch the better to hide his emotion.

"What do you think of that, Crofton?" cried Mr. Henchy. "Isn't that fine? What?"

Mr. Crofton said that it was a very fine piece of writing.

Austin Clarke (1896-   )

Night And Morning

I know the injured pride of sleep,
The strippers at the mocking-post,
The insult in the house of Caesar
And every moment that can hold
In brief the miserable act
Of centuries. Thought can but share
Belief—and the tormented soul,
Changing confession to despair,
Must wear a borrowed robe.

Morning has moved the dreadful candle,
Appointed shadows cross the nave;
Unlocked by the secular hand,
The very elements remain
Appearances upon the altar.
Adoring priest has turned his back
Of gold upon the congregation.
All saints have had their day at last,
But thought still lives in pain.

How many councils and decrees
Have perished in the simple prayer
That gave obedience to the knee;
Trampling of rostrum, feathering
Of pens at cock-rise, sum of reason
To elevate a common soul:
Forgotten as the minds that bled
For us, the miracle that raised
A language from the dead.

O when all Europe was astir
With echo of learned controversy,
The voice of logic led the choir.
Such quality was in all being,
The forks of heaven and this earth
Had met, town-walled, in mortal view
And in the pride that we ignore,
The holy rage of argument,
God was made man once more.

Tenebrae

This is the hour that we must mourn
With tallows on the black triangle,
Night has a napkin deep in fold
To keep the cup; yet who dare pray
If all in reason should be lost,
The agony of man betrayed
At every station of the cross?

O when the forehead is too young,
Those centuries of mortal anguish,
Dabbed by a consecrated thumb
That crumbles into dust, will bring
Despair with all that we can know;
And there is nothing left to sing,
Remembering our innocence.

I hammer on that common door,
Too frantic in my superstition,
Transfix with nails that I have broken,
The angry notice of the mind.
Close as the thought that suffers him,
The habit every man in time
Must wear beneath his ironed shirt.

An open mind disturbs the soul,
And in disdain I turn my back
Upon the sun that makes a show
Of half the world, yet still deny
The pain that lives within the past,
The flame sinking upon the spike,
Darkness that man must dread at last.

The Straying Student

On a holy day when sails were blowing southward,
A bishop sang the Mass at Inishmore,
Men took one side, their wives were on the other
But I heard the woman coming from the shore:
And wild in despair my parents cried aloud
For they saw the vision draw me to the doorway.

Long had she lived in Rome when Popes were bad,
The wealth of every age she makes her own,
Yet smiled on me in eager admiration,
And for a summer taught me all I know,
Banishing shame with her great laugh that rang
As if a pillar caught it back alone.

I learned the prouder counsel of her throat,
My mind was growing bold as light in Greece;
And when in sleep her stirring limbs were shown,
I blessed the noonday rock that knew no tree:
And for an hour the mountain was her throne,
Although her eyes were bright with mockery.

They say I was sent back from Salamanca
And failed in logic, but I wrote her praise
Nine times upon a college wall in France.
She laid her hand at darkfall on my page
That I might read the heavens in a glance
And I knew every star the Moors have named.

Awake or in my sleep, I have no peace now,
Before the ball is struck, my breath has gone,
And yet I tremble lest she may deceive me
And leave me in this land, where every woman's son
Must carry his own coffin and believe
In dread, all that the clergy teach the young.

F. R. Higgins (1896-1941)

An Old Air

As I was walking I met a woman
   And she side-saddled on a horse,
Most proudly riding the road to Moyrus
   On a stallion worthy of a fine race-course.

The horse it sidled; I asked her kindly,
   With a timid hand on the jolting rein,
"Now are you Niamh[1] or Grace O'Maille,[2]
   Or a female grandee from the fields of Spain?"

She merely fondled those bridled fingers
   And little fearing sweetly replied,
"Among my people you'd grow so noble
   That none would know you did here abide:

"Then live with me, man, and I will give you
   The run of twelve hills with a still in each."
Her eyes were craving that rainy evening
   While a gentle air was in her speech.

"But O, my darling, who is your father?
   Ah, would your mother take kindly to me?"
And then she told me, "My folk ride over
   The silver flowering of a green-lit sea."

---

1 See "Oisin in the Land of Youth," p. 105.
2 Grania O'Malley was a chieftainess of the 16th century who made
war on English armies and fleets along the Connaught seaboard. Cele-
brated in song and story, her name became a synonym of Ireland.

At those strange words then I did remember
　　Her folk they were of no good sort,
So I bid good evening to that young woman
　　And she took herself to the woods of Gort!

Song for the Clatter-Bones

God rest that Jewy woman,
Queen Jezebel, the bitch
Who peeled the clothes from her shoulder-bones
Down to her spent teats
As she stretched out of the window
Among the geraniums, where
She chaffed and laughed like one half daft
Titivating her painted hair—

King Jehu he drove to her,
She tipped him a fancy beck;
But he from his knacky side-car spoke,
"Who'll break that dewlapped neck?"
And so she was thrown from the window;
Like Lucifer she fell
Beneath the feet of the horses and they beat
The light out of Jezebel.

That corpse wasn't planted in clover;
Ah, nothing of her was found
Save those grey bones that Hare-foot Mike
Gave me for their lovely sound;
And as once her dancing body
Made star-lit princes sweat,
So I'll just clack: though her ghost lacks a back
There's music in the old bones yet.

The Wild Sow

BY Liam O'Flaherty (1896-   )

OLD Neddy the fisherman, of Kilmillick, bought a sow pig one day in Kilmurrage. He put the pig in a bag, dropped it into one of his donkey's creels and brought it home to his cabin. It was just six weeks old, a little black pig, with a long back, and big ears that dropped over its eyes and a little tail curled up in a knot.

The neighbours were surprised when they heard that Neddy had bought the pig, for he was an old man and lived alone in his two-roomed cabin and he had no land except a little patch in front of his door that grew enough potatoes to last him the year round. He was, too, very fond of drink, and whenever he had any money he stayed in Kilmurrage until he had spent it. So that the neighbours wondered what possessed him to buy the pig. In fact Martin Conroy came into Neddy's cabin and said, "Brother, it's plain that they fooled you into buying that young pig, so if ye'll throw ten rockfish into the bargain with it, I'll give you a pound for it."

Neddy hitched up his belt, glanced at Conroy with his little grey eyes and told him to get out of his cabin. Then he shook his fist after Conroy and said, "I'll have money while I have that pig and that's why I bought it. So may the devil choke the lot of you."

He made a straw bed for the little pig in the corner of his kitchen and sawed off the lower part of a barrel in which he salted his fish to make a trough for it. For a while he looked after it carefully and gave it plenty of potatoes, dry fish and whatever sour milk he could get from the neighbours. So that the sow got big and fat until it was six months old and fit for sale. But when a jobber came to look at it and asked Neddy what price did he want, Neddy told him to get out of his cabin. "I have money," he said, "while I have that pig, so I'll keep it."

That was in the month of April and Neddy's stock of potatoes had been all eaten by the sow and most of his dried fish along with the potatoes, so he turned the sow loose on the roadside to eat grass, saying, "Now feed yerself and may the devil choke you." And he took his basket and his fishing lines and went away to fish.

The sow wandered about on the road all the forenoon, smelling at everything, snorting furiously and making little short runs that make her foot joints snap under her fat body like hard biscuits being cracked, when a horse or a peasant driving a cow went past. She rooted among the grass until her head was caked with earth up to her eyes. Then towards her feeding time at midday she trotted back to the cabin, but the door was locked. For a time she waited at the door grunting and with her ears cocked listening to every sound, sniffing the air with her twitching hairy snout and tossing her head now and again in vexation. Then, when nobody opened the door, she began to whine with the hunger. She stood there motionless and whining until Neddy came back at dusk and let her into the cabin. He only gave her fish guts and potato peelings for her supper. "From now on," he said, "you'll have to fend for yourself, and may the devil choke you."

That went on for a fortnight with Neddy away fishing every day, and then the sow got thinner and wild with hunger. She began to eat grass by the roadside and roamed over the crags picking nettles and everything she could get hold of. She no longer snorted when horses or cows passed her. Her bristles grew rough and strong and her ears lost their tender transparency. Her eyes were hardly visible through the caked dirt that gathered around them. She used to run out of the cabin in the morning and never come near it again until dusk.

At first she roamed about the village of Kilmillick, eating grass and nettles, tearing up the ground for roots, chewing everything she found in rubbish heaps, old fish bones, rags, boots and potato skins. Then, as the summer grew, the heat and the long days tempted her farther, down the beach and along the lanes and the road leading to Kilmurrage. Often she never came back to the cabin for two or three days at a stretch, but would spend the night among the sandhills about the beach where the wild grass was very sweet and there was always a dog-fish or a piece of mackerel cast up by the sea among the weeds. Her bristles were now as stiff and thick as needles, and her black skin beneath them was cracked by the sun and scarred in places where dogs bit her or boys struck her with stones and dried sea rods when they cornered her in narrow lanes. All her flesh had hardened into muscle. She was lean like a hound and nearly as tall as a year-old donkey.

Towards the end of summer a jobber came again to Neddy and asked him would he sell the sow. "She's not much good now," said the jobber, "so I'll give ye a pound for her. I might be able to soften her a bit and get a litter from her." "Get out of my cabin," said Neddy, "and may the devil choke you. I have money while I have that pig, so I'll keep the pig." But the fishing was bad that year and he had to sell his donkey in order to buy flour for the winter. Still he wouldn't sell the pig. "It's like having money in a bank," he would say, "a pig is always money. I often heard my father say so."

But when winter came on and the ocean winds swept the crags viciously and sea foam was falling like snow over the cabins, the sow could go out no more, but sat on her haunches on her straw litter in Neddy's kitchen grunting and whining with the hunger.

Then one stormy day Neddy went into Kilmurrage to sell his dried pollock. He turned the pig out of the cabin and locked the door. Then he went away. The sow roamed about for awhile shivering with the cold and weak with hunger. Her stomach was drawn up into her back so that she looked like a cat that is stretching itself. She could discover nothing to eat around the village so she came back to the cabin.

She got on her knees at the door and began to gnaw at the bottom until she made a hole for her snout; then she seemed to go mad and tore at the door with her teeth and battered it with her head until she burst it off its hinges and she pushed right under it into the cabin. The door hung on one hinge and the sow's right ear was gashed down the middle by a nail in the jamb.

She stood in the middle of the kitchen grunting, with her snout to the ground and with blood dripping from her ear in a steady stream. Then she tossed her head and rushed at Neddy's bedroom door. Sticking her snout at the bottom near the jamb, she pushed and burst the string with which the door was fastened and got into the bedroom. Neddy's potatoes were lying in the far corner with a little wall of stones around them. His sack of flour stood against the wall near the potatoes. His dried rockfish were stacked on pieces of paper under the wooden bedstead. The sow began to eat. Snorting and tossing her head she ran from the flour to the potatoes and then to the rockfish, swallowing huge mouthfuls without chewing, and making a noise like a horse pulling her hoof out of a bog, until her stomach swelled out to a point at each side.

Then a big potato stuck in her throat.

When Neddy came in that evening he found her lying on her side, stone dead.

A Difficult Question

BY Kate O'Brien (1898-   )

ON Wednesdays the chaplain addressed the school for forty
minutes on Christian doctrine. This lecture took place at half-
past five in the *salle d'études*, his hearers sitting as for marks
in a "hairpin," very orderly and with gloves on. It was an ordeal
for a young man, when every mannerism was pounced upon
and giggled at, week after week, by the school wags. Indeed,
Reverend Mother thought it a questionable tradition that in
this Irish house the chaplain was always so young. Elsewhere
in the order's convents he was usually an old and experienced
priest, hardened to folly and indifferent to giggles. But here
in this rural parish the duties of chaplaincy fell ex officio on
the second curate of the village, which meant a succession of
nervous young men for budding feminine wits to lacerate.

The Wednesday lecture was made additionally painful for
the chaplain by the ceremony which preceded it, of drinking
tea in St Anthony's parlour, waited on by Reverend Mother.
This custom held throughout the order and was based on the
supposed need of chaplain and Mother Superior to discuss
such problems of spirit or character as might have struck either
in dealing with the school. But as week after week, year after
year, Reverend Mother poured tea for and offered buttered
toast to a succession of shy or truculent young Irishmen she
smiled wryly to herself at the characteristically Latin idea which
justified the stiff reflection. No Irish boy just out of college
was going to be drawn into other than the most perfunctory
generalisations on the character or spiritual difficulties of a pack
of schoolgirls. Nor, indeed, did she blame the successive young
chaplains for their negative resolution. Still, she had to obey
custom and torture them with her half-hour of politeness. But
as she really believed in discipline, for herself and all human
creatures, she thought it no harm that the curates should have

to sit for one half-hour each week and make conversation with her, when she knew they really feared and disliked it.

Father Conroy was the third chaplain she had known in her four years in Ireland and the one with whom she felt least sympathy.

The two were nervous and at sea with each other.

"Well, Reverend Mother—that's a nice hare your friend Joe Chamberlain is making of himself these days!"

"*My* friend, Father Conroy?"

"Oh well—he's English; that's all I meant."

"I come of a Liberal family, Father. I have never known any statesmen, but if you were to speak of Mr Chamberlain's opponent, Mr Asquith, as 'my friend,' I mightn't be so startled."

"Aha! So you think there is some good in Asquith, Reverend Mother? I am surprised to hear that. Six of one and half a dozen of the other, if you ask me."

"Nothing of the kind, if you ask me," said Reverend Mother amiably.

"Well, well—we must agree to differ there. But tariff reform, God help us!"

"You ought to be delighted with Mr Chamberlain's tariff reform, Father."

"I—delighted?"

"Because it is a pernicious, greedy conception which will very likely cost the present government its office. And then Home Rule will become a near possibility again, surely?"

"Yah, Home Rule. What good would that be to us, Reverend Mother?"

"It is difficult to say." She spoke with faint malice, but he did not see the mild joke. "In any case, what should a nun know of these matters?" she amended gently.

"Ah, that's the trouble," he said, and as he went on she conceded that there was real trouble and some diffidence in his voice and face. "Nuns shouldn't trouble themselves with these secular things, I suppose. And yet you know, Reverend Mother, a convent like this wields great influence—through its girls afterward—in the world."

"We are very conscious of that, Father Conroy."

She realised wearily that he was circling, as usual, round the Irish hierarchy's distrust of an independent religious order. It was a patent exasperation to the authoritarian bishop that, short of grave scandal, he had no power to counsel or direct the Compagnie de la Sainte Famille. And this exceptional privilege of the order increased the offence of its forgiveness; in fact, Reverend Mother knew very well that, as far as his lordship was to be reckoned with, the independence of this house was the sole safeguard of its peculiar tradition, which the bishop called "exotic" and démodé and which he would have overthrown without hesitation had he the power.

The bishop had some of the weapons of an intellectual to his hand, but Father Conroy had only an untutored, unbridled nationalism. He disliked the spirit of Sainte Famille, Reverend Mother suspected, solely because it was governed by an English-woman. And as such an emotional and bad ellipsis of argument was distasteful to her in anyone but incomprehensible in a consecrated priest, spiritual communication between the two was impossible.

"To be sure you are, Reverend Mother. And the young ladies of Sainte Famille are beautifully educated—we all know that. But times are changing here, and somehow——"

"Somehow what, Father Conroy?"

The cold English tone annoyed him.

"Somehow it's a bit of a pity, it seems to me, Reverend Mother, to be training Irish girls as suitable wives for English majors and colonial governors!"

He spoke angrily because he was afraid of his own audacity.

"We educate our children in the Christian virtues and graces. If these appeal to English majors, why, so much the better for those gentlemen!"

"Our young girls must be educated nationally now, Reverend Mother—to be the wives of Irishmen and to meet the changing times!"

"We do what we can about that, Father. But if the 'changing

times' you are so sure of are to have no place for Christian
discipline and common politeness, I can only say I'm glad I
shall not see very much of them."

She spoke very coldly and offered the young man some cakes.

"No, thank you, Reverend Mother," he said. "It's a terror
the way you won't see what I mean at all."

"I do see what you mean, Father—and I find you are rude
and officious. But you are, after all, very young."

He looked so startled and indignant that at once she was
ashamed of herself and distressed in her turn at the cruel enmity
she felt toward him. As she sought a way of apology there was
a knock on the parlour door.

Anna Murphy came in.

"Yes, Anna, that's right—come along. I told her to come
to the parlour to you this evening, Father, as she appears now
to understand her catechism well, and you may wish—after
you've talked with her—to arrange her instructions for first
confession. She will be seven next month."

"On April fifth," said Anna.

"Will you now?" said Father Conroy. "You're a small girl
for that—aren't you, Anna?"

Anna drew near.

"Still, I'd like to make my first confession, please," she said.

"Well, I expect we'll let you. On April fifth you will have
reached the age of reason, Anna—and even now you sound
reasonable enough, God bless you!"

Reverend Mother smiled.

"Reasonableness is her forte at present, Father."

"Would you like a biscuit, Anna? May I give her one, Reverend Mother? Which kind will you have?"

"The one that's like a piece of orange, please."

Father Conroy handed her the yellow-sugared biscuit shaped
like a piece of orange.

"Thank you, Father Conroy."

"Now, Anna, we must prepare you for first confession, so
that you can make it about April fifth. You know I come to hear

the other girls' confessions every Saturday at half-past five. This
Saturday I'll come at five—if I may, Reverend Mother?—and
have a talk with you about Christian doctrine and what confession is. Then on this day week we could have another talk,
I suppose, Reverend Mother? And when we have talked together about six times I think you will be able to receive the
sacrament of penance. You know it *is* a sacrament, don't you?"

Anna nodded.

"I'm doing that chapter now in catechism. I had two questions about contrition to learn today."

"Oh, good girl. You're quite far on in your catechism. You've
learned the Ten Commandments then and the explanations of
them?"

"Well—yes."

The frowning uncertainty which entered her face made both
nun and priest smile faintly.

"You mustn't worry if you don't completely understand
them all," Father Conroy said. "You couldn't expect it yet.
They cover a wide field."

"I can see that," said Anna. "Still——"

"Still—what?"

"Well, since they really are *commandments*, I think I should
have a rough idea—and Mother Felicita too, I think she
should. After all, she's *old*."

"And what's bothering yourself and Mother Felicita, may I
ask?"

"We don't know what adultery is. Either of us. What is it?"

Reverend Mother sat very still, anxiety in her heart. The
awkward, not to say loutish, young priest was in charge of this
conversation. He was the spiritual director, and Anna had
rightly put her query to him. He must answer as his wit directed, but the child who questioned him was not easy to
hoodwink, and the questing ease of her mind was, in Reverend
Mother's eyes, a very delicate and cherishable thing. As she
waited alert for the sequence of dialogue one region of her
heart was rapidly flooded with uneasy prayer. If this little child

were told a lie or made to suspect already, by any clumsiness, the sordid hush-hush of sexual troubles—— The nun winced with anxiety as she searched, without any clue, the broad, unsubtle face of the young priest.

"Are you sure Mother Felicita doesn't know the meaning of adultery?" Father Conroy asked Anna.

"Oh yes. She didn't exactly say so, but anyone could tell it muddles her."

The priest nodded.

"Well, of course, being a nun, she wouldn't have to know, as it doesn't have anything to do with her, in her life. And until you are grown up it won't be any concern of yours."

"Still—it's in my catechism, after all——"

"Yes—and I'm going to tell you what it is. I was only explaining to you why Mother Felicita might happen not to understand about it. You see, it isn't everyone's business. But when you are grown up, left school, you will perhaps decide to be a nun and live entirely for the glory of God; or you may decide to live alone in the world, devoting yourself to work or study of some kind; or, very likely, you will feel that you do not want to live always alone, that you would like a husband and children. In that case you will choose some man who will also choose you; you'll choose each other by what is called 'falling ing love'—which means you will find that you love each other more than you love other people. And so you'll receive to- gether the sacrament of marriage—you've learned about that? —and, having promised in that sacrament to love each other always, you live together and have children. Well—if after- ward either of you should stop loving the other and begin to let yourself love another person more than the one you had promised to love best always—that is adultery."

"I think it might be very easy to commit," Anna said.

"Why do you think that?"

"Well—how could you be sure of loving anyone best always?"

"You couldn't be sure, I suppose—on our own steam we

can't be sure of anything. But marriage is a sacrament—which is, you know, a special way of receiving special grace from God. God helps us a very great deal in difficulties, as you'll discover when you grow up, young lady. Well, are you clear in your mind now about the sixth commandment?"

"Oh yes. Thank you very much. Do you mind if I explain it to Mother Felicita?"

"Not at all. But after all, it has nothing to do with her."

"But she's *teaching* catechism. I think it'd be better if she understood—for another time."

"Perhaps. Well, off with you now and eat your sugar biscuit. And remember, on Saturday at five I'll examine you on the first two chapters of the catechism."

"I'll remember. Good-bye, Father Conroy. Good-bye, Reverend Mother."

Anna shook hands with the priest and bowed to Reverend Mother, who smiled at her as she withdrew.

The bell for religious instruction rang, and Father Conroy rose from his chair.

As the nun ascended the broad staircase with him on the way to the *salle d'études* she pondered in bitter humility. This priest whom she judged crude and unwise had just shown himself gentle and wise and a good, honest teacher. He had shown perfect understanding of innocence and intelligence and had spoken to them out of peace and humour and without a shadow of evasiveness in word or implication. She was ashamed of her earlier extreme severity with him; she felt very grateful to him for the guarded sensibility with which he had impressed her as he replied to the good sense of childhood. She racked her brain for a way of expressing friendliness and repentance. She decided that the only just course was to apologise for having sought to humiliate him.

"I hope you will forgive me for having spoken unjustly a few moments ago, Father. But I fear I lose my sense of proportion and of justice when I think people want to make a political weapon of the education of children."

But he thought he saw a further thrust at himself in this piece of self-explanation—and he was still rankling with dislike of her.

"To be sure, Reverend Mother. But isn't that exactly what you English have done all the same, all over the globe?"

"I was only speaking for myself," she answered wearily.

Genevieve Ahern opened the swing door of the *salle d'études*, and as the chaplain and Reverend Mother entered the school stood up and bowed.

My Grander

BY Sean O'Faolain (1900-   )

"HE was a vain man," somebody who knew him once said to me, "and ambitious; but very weak in the carnalities."

I must say all the "carnalities" I ever saw in him at that time was when he would be with his friend Arty Tinsley, and I after him with young Christy Tinsley, in and out of every pub in the city of Cork, and rain, hail, or snow, every third Sunday of the month galloping out the country in wagonettes, decorating the graves of the Fenian dead. Then we would be, the four of us with his friends, over a pub fire in Kilcrea or Ovens or Kilcroney, the talk floating up the chimney with the steam of our legs, while the rain hissed into the misty grass and the pokers hissed in the mulled stout, surrounded by a procession of names, hour by hour, corner to corner, Rossa and O'Neill-Crowley, Land and Labour, Davitt and the Tory "hoors"; a drink to Lomasney, who was found in his own clots of gore on the mud of the Isle of Dogs after floating down from London Bridge that he had tried to blow up—nothing less would appease his wild imagination, I suppose; and a drink to the men who swung for the agent they sunk in a bog near Tipperary; and a drink to His Lordship of Cashel who talked up to the Pope when he went to Rome *ad audiendum verbum* . . . all ending with the road thick with night and a singing born of liquor, and Christy Tinsley and myself wrapped into one another with cold and sleep.

Then came the day when old Arty Tinsley died. It was a wretched rain-down of a southern evening when my grander and myself set off to the cemetery on the Douglas Road, that was for some crazy reason called the Botanic Gardens, to fix about the burial. I was not sad but frightened, for this was the first real death I knew. But my grander took my dread for sorrow and as a reward he packed me with Shandon Mixtures and Peggy's Leg until I was sick in the stomach and sticky around the mouth as I stood under the yews of the graveyard. In the Gothic porch of the gate lodge—smelling of laurels and wood-smoke—my grander was discussing the details of the funeral with a long dreep of a caretaker who kept on remembering all the Tinsleys who ever came in the gate on the flat of their backs. Then we went into the lodge itself, very small with its red and black tiles and even more odorous of the fallen leaves and the damp wood-smoke; and I was looking at a photograph of a bishop, and at the framed photos of the sons in their red coats holding their arms very stiff to show the sergeant's stripes, when I suddenly felt a strange silence and saw my grander over the book, making slow circles with the pen in his hand.

"That's the way, sir," the foxy caretaker was saying, "that's grand, now, Mister Crone, religion now, sir, enter the religion of the deceased."

"He was born a Catholic," said my grander.

"Down with it, sir," said Foxer.

"But . . . I don't know what he might be, now."

The man looked at him in surprise, as if he was asking himself: "Does the ould lad think there's no religion in heaven?"

"Fill it in, sir," he said politely.

"Yes, grander," said I. "C—A—T—H——"

"Go out, boy, and wait outside," says he very shortly.

But I was soon sick of the misty hills and the swaying wet

yews around the marbles—ever since I have hated that white
Carrara marble for outdoor monuments—and I returned to
the porch. There, inside, was a terrible argument going on
between the two of them, and my old grandfather shouting:

"What I say is, if an unfortunate Fenian isn't left in peace
by the clergy when he's alive, then they should leave him in
peace anyway when he's dead."

And the man crying out:

"For God's sake, now, Mister Crone, fill in the two words—
R.C.—and be done with it—the Church is wise, Mister Crone
—the Church has to look after us all, dead and alive—and for
God's sake and God is the best judge of all those things and
God will judge you and me . . ."

"What I say is, the Church wouldn't admit he was a Catholic
when he was alive, so why should the Church want to say he's
a Catholic because he's dead?" (I knew what he was at—the
Church had banned Fenianism in Ireland.)

"My dear good sir," said the man, beyond all patience,
"I'm not the Church and you're not the Church, and if the
Church says he was a Catholic, then it's dogma, and a Catholic
he is, and no wan can get behind that. Write it down—R.C."

"The Church never admitted he was a Catholic. It denied
him the sacraments. It now wants to deny him Christian
burial."

The foxy man held out his index finger as if he were balanc-
ing a pin on the ball of it. Solemnly he looked at it; solemnly
he looked at my grander; then he tapped that finger with the
tip of another, saying quietly but finally:

"Did the Church say he was a Protestant?"

"No."

He tapped his second finger. "Did the Church say he was
excommunicated?"

"No!"

The man drew out a sail of a handkerchief and blew his nose.

"Write down R.C.," he ordered, like a Pope.

"NO!" said my grander, and he flung down the pen in a

fury. "The Church never said yiss or no to Arthur Tinsley.
But you know and I know and everybody knows that no Fenian
could get absolution in confession or the sacrament from the
altar unless he retracted his oath to live and die for his country.
And . . ."

"Mister Crone . . ."

"And . . ."

"Excuse me, one moment, mister. . . ."

"AND if Arthur Tinsley was asked here and now whether
he would retract that oath . . ."

"There's nobody asking him. . . ."

". . . whether, to obtain burial in this bloody cemetery, he
would bow the knee to the Church, and the first question
they'd put to him would be, Do you admit that oath was a
sin?—what would he say? What would he say?"

The man walked away to the door.

"What would he say?" roared my grander. "He'd say: 'I
wo'NOT!' And what would they say?" he bellowed, with a
great sweep of his hand through the air. "They'd say: 'Then
we'll have nothing to do with yeh, and yeh can go to hell!' "

"This cemetery," said the caretaker loftily, "is a Catholic
cemetery."

"Then," sobbed my grander, "where will I bury him?"

"Look here," said the man in a kindly voice, and he picked
up the pen. "I'll sign it, R.C."

"NO!" cried ould Ten-to-Wan. "NO!"

"Very well," said the man. "You can put it to the Cemetery
Committee. I won't have anything to do with it." And he
walked out about his business.

"Come on, boy," said the old lad, and away we went, I with
big eyes and beating heart, he muttering his rage:

"Damn the Committee! Damn the Committee!"

In the Train

BY Frank O'Connor (1903-   )

I

"There!" said the sergeant's wife. "You would hurry me."

"I always like to be in time for a train," replied the sergeant with the equability of one who has many times before explained the guiding principle of his existence.

"I'd have had heaps of time to buy the hat," added his wife.

The sergeant sighed and opened his evening paper. His wife looked out on the dark platform, pitted with pale lights under which faces and faces passed, lit up and dimmed again. A uniformed lad strode up and down with a tray of periodicals and chocolates. Farther up the platform a drunken man was being seen off by his friends.

"I'm very fond of Michael O'Leary," he shouted. "He is the most sincere man I know."

"I have no life," sighed the sergeant's wife. "No life at all! There isn't a soul to speak to, nothing to look at all day but bogs and mountains and rain—always rain! And the people! Well, we've had a fine sample of them, haven't we?"

The sergeant continued to read.

"Just for the few days it's been like heaven. Such interesting people! Oh, I thought Mr Boyle had a glorious face! And his voice—it went through me."

The sergeant lowered his paper, took off his peaked cap, laid it on the seat beside him, and lit his pipe. He lit it in the old-fashioned way, ceremoniously, his eyes blinking pleasurably like a sleepy cat's in the match-flame. His wife scrutinised each face that passed, and it was plain that for her life meant faces and people and things and nothing more.

"Oh dear!" she said again. "I simply have no existence. I was educated in a convent and play the piano; my father was a literary man, and yet I am compelled to associate with the lowest types of humanity. If it was even a decent town, but a village!"

"Ah," said the sergeant, gapping his reply with anxious puffs, "maybe with God's help we'll get a shift one of these days." But he said it without conviction, and it was also plain that he was well pleased with himself, with the prospect of returning home, with his pipe and with his paper.

"Here are Magner and the others," said his wife as four other policemen passed the barrier. "I hope they'll have sense enough to let us alone. . . . How do you do? How do you do? Had a nice time, boys?" she called with sudden animation, and her pale, sullen face became warm and vivacious. The policemen smiled and touched their caps but did not halt.

"They might have stopped to say good evening," she added sharply, and her face sank into it old expression of boredom and dissatisfaction. "I don't think I'll ask Delancey to tea again. The others make an attempt, but really, Delancey is hopeless. When I smile and say 'Guard Delancey, wouldn't you like to use the butter-knife?' he just scowls at me from under his shaggy brows and says without a moment's hesitation 'I would not.'"

"Ah, Delancey is a poor slob," said the sergeant affectionately.

"Oh yes, but that's not enough, Jonathon. Slob or no slob, he should make an attempt. He's a young man; he should have a dinner-jacket at least. What sort of wife will he get if he won't even wear a dinner-jacket?"

"He's easy, I'd say. He's after a farm in Waterford!"

"Oh, a farm! A farm! The wife is only an incidental, I suppose?"

"Well, now from all I hear she's a damn nice little incidental."

"Yes, I suppose many a nice little incidental came from a farm," answered his wife, raising her pale brows. But the irony was lost on him.

"Indeed, yes; indeed, yes," he said fervently.

"And here," she added in biting tones, "come our charming neighbours."

Into the pale lamplight stepped a group of peasants. Not such as one sees in the environs of a capital but in the mountains and along the coasts. Gnarled, wild, with turbulent faces, their ill-cut clothes full of character, the women in pale brown shawls, the men wearing black sombreros and carrying big sticks, they swept in, ill at ease, laughing and shouting defiantly. And, so much part of their natural environment were they, that for a moment they seemed to create about themselves rocks and bushes, tarns, turf-ricks and sea.

With a prim smile the sergeant's wife bowed to them through the open window.

"How do you do? How do you do?" she called. "Had a nice time?"

At the same moment the train gave a jolt and there was a rush in which the excited peasants were carried away. Some minutes passed; the influx of passengers almost ceased, and a porter began to slam the doors. The drunken man's voice rose in a cry of exultation.

"You can't possibly beat O'Leary!" he declared. "I'd lay down my life for Michael O'Leary."

Then, just as the train was about to start, a young woman in a brown shawl rushed through the barrier. The shawl, which came low enough to hide her eyes, she held firmly across her mouth, leaving visible only a long thin nose with a hint of pale flesh at either side. Beneath the shawl she was carrying a large parcel.

She looked hastily around, a porter shouted to her and pushed her towards the nearest compartment which happened to be that occupied by the sergeant and his wife. He had actually seized the handle of the door when the sergeant's wife sat up and screamed.

"Quick! Quick!" she cried. "Look who it is! She's coming in! Jonathon! Jonathon!"

The sergeant rose with a look of alarm on his broad red face. The porter threw open the door, with his free hand grasping the woman's elbow. But when she laid eyes on the sergeant's startled countenance, she stepped back, tore herself free, and ran crazily up the platform. The engine shrieked, the porter slammed the door with a curse, somewhere another door opened and shut, and the row of watchers, frozen into effigies of farewell, now dark now bright, began to glide gently past the window, and the stale, smoky air was charged with the breath of open fields.

II

The four policemen spread themselves out in a separate compartment and lit cigarettes.

"Ah, poor old Delancey!" said Magner with his reckless laugh. "He's cracked on her all right."

"Cracked on her," agreed Fox. "Did ye see the eye he gave her?"

Delancey smiled sheepishly. He was a tall, handsome, black-haired young man with the thick eyebrows described by the sergeant's wife. He was new to the force and suffered from a mixture of natural gentleness and country awkwardness.

"I am," he said in his husky voice, "cracked on her. The devil admire me, I never hated anyone yet, but I think I hate the living sight of her."

"Oh, now! Oh, now!" protested Magner.

"I do. I think the Almighty God must have put that one in the world with the one main object of persecuting me."

"Well, indeed," said Foley, "I don't know how the sergeant puts up with the same damsel. If any woman up and called me by an outlandish name like Jonathon when all knew my name was plain John, I'd do fourteen days for her—by God, I would, and a calendar month!"

The four men were now launched on a favourite topic that held them for more than an hour. None of them liked the sergeant's wife, and all had stories to tell against her. From these there emerged the fact that she was an incurable scandal-monger and mischief-maker, who couldn't keep quiet about her own business, much less that of her neighbours. And while they talked the train dragged across a dark plain, the heart of Ireland, and in the moonless night tiny cottage windows blew past like sparks from a fire, and a pale simulacrum of the lighted carriages leaped and frolicked over hedges and fields. Magner shut the window, and the compartment began to fill with smoke.

"She'll never rest till she's out of Farranchreesht," he said.

"That she mightn't!" groaned Delancey.

"How would you like the city yourself, Dan?" asked Magner.

"Man, dear," exclaimed Delancey with sudden brightness, "I'd like it fine. There's great life in a city."

"You can have it and welcome," said Foley, folding his hands across his paunch.

"Why so?"

"I'm well content where I am."

"But the life!"

"Ah, life be damned! What sort of life is it when you're always under someone's eye? Look at the poor devils in court!"

"True enough, true enough," said Fox.

"Ah, yes, yes," said Delancey, "but the adventures they have!"

"What adventures!"

"Look now, there was a sergeant in court only yesterday telling me about a miser, an old maid without a soul in the world that died in an ould loft on the quays. Well, this sergeant I'm talking about put a new man on duty outside the door while he went back to report, and all this fellow had to do was to kick the door and frighten off the rats."

"That's enough, that's enough!" cried Foley.

"Yes, yes, but listen now, listen, can't you? He was there about ten minutes with a bit of candle in his hand and all at once the door at the foot of the stairs began to open. 'Who's there?' says he, giving a start. 'Who's there I say?' There

was no answer and still the door kept opening quietly. Then
he gave a laugh. What was it but a cat? 'Puss, puss,' says he,
'come on up, puss!' Thinking, you know, the ould cat would
be company. Up comes the cat, pitter-patter on the stairs, and
then whatever look he gave the door the hair stood up on his
head. What was coming in but another cat? 'Coosh!' says
he, stamping his foot and kicking the door to frighten them.
'Coosh away to hell out of that!' And then another cat came
in and then another, and in his fright he dropped the candle
and kicked out right and left. The cats began to hiss and bawl,
and that robbed him of the last stitch of sense. He bolted
down the stairs, and as he did he trod on one of the brutes,
and before he knew where he was he slipped and fell head
over heels, and when he put out his hand to grip something
'twas a cat he gripped, and he felt the claws tearing his hands
and face. He had strength enough to pull himself up and run,
but when he reached the barrack gate down he dropped in a
fit. He was a raving lunatic for three weeks after."

"And that," said Foley with bitter restraint, "is what you
call adventure!"

"Dear knows," added Magner, drawing himself up with a
shiver, " 'tis a great consolation to be able to put on your cap
and go out for a drink any hour of the night you like."

" 'Tis of course," drawled Foley scornfully. "And to know
the worst case you'll have in ten years is a bit of a scrap about
politics."

"I dunno," sighed Delancey dreamily. "I'm telling you
there's great charm about the Criminal Courts."

"Damn the much charm they had for you when you were
in the box," growled Foley.

"I know, sure, I know," admitted Delancey, crestfallen.

"Shutting his eyes," said Magner with a laugh, "like a kid
afraid he was going to get a box across the ears."

"And still," said Delancey, "this sergeant fellow I'm talking
about, he said, after a while you wouldn't mind it no more
than if 'twas a card party, but talk up to the judge himself."

"I suppose you would," agreed Magner pensively.

There was silence in the smoky compartment that jolted and rocked on its way across Ireland, and the four occupants, each touched with that morning wit which afflicts no one so much as state witnesses, thought of how they would speak to the judge if only they had him before them now. They looked up to see a fat red face behind the door, and a moment later it was dragged back.

"Is thish my carriage, gentlemen?" asked a meek and boozy voice.

"No, 'tisn't. Go on with you!" snapped Magner.

"I had as nice a carriage as ever was put on a railway thrain," said the drunk, leaning in, "a handsome carriage, and 'tis losht."

"Try farther on," suggested Delancey.

"Excuse me interrupting yeer conversation, gentlemen."

"That's all right, that's all right."

"I'm very melancholic. Me besht friend, I parted him thish very night, and 'tish known to no wan, only the Almighty and Merciful God (here the drunk reverently raised his bowler hat and let it slide down the back of his neck to the floor), if I'll ever lay eyes on him agin in thish world. Good night, gentlemen, and thanks, thanks for all yeer kindness."

As the drunk slithered away up the corridor Delancey laughed. Fox resumed the conversation where it had left off.

"I'll admit," he said, "Delancey wasn't the only one."

"He was not," agreed Foley. "Even the sergeant was shook. When he caught up the mug he was trembling all over, and before he could let it down it danced a jig on the table."

"Ah, dear God! Dear God!" sighed Delancey, "what killed me most entirely was the bloody ould model of the house. I didn't mind anything else but the house. There it was, a living likeness, with the bit of grass in front and the shutter hanging loose, and every time I looked down I was in the back lane in Farranchreesht, hooshing the hens and smelling the turf, and then I'd look up and see the lean fellow in the wig pointing his finger at me."

"Well, thank God," said Foley with simple devotion, "this time to-morrow I'll be sitting in Ned Ivers' back with a pint in my fist."

Delancey shook his head, a dreamy smile playing upon his dark face.

"I dunno," he said. " 'Tis a small place, Farranchreesht, a small, mangy ould fothrach[1] of a place with no interest or advancement in it."

"There's something to be said on both sides," added Magner judicially. "I wouldn't say you're wrong, Foley, but I wouldn't say Delancey was wrong either."

"Here's the sergeant now," said Delancey, drawing himself up with a smile of welcome. "Ask him."

"He wasn't long getting tired of Julietta," whispered Magner maliciously.

The door was pushed back and the sergeant entered, loosening the collar of his tunic. He fell into a corner seat, crossed his legs and accepted the cigarette which Delancey proffered.

"Well, lads," he exclaimed. "What about a jorum!"

"By Gor," said Foley, "isn't it remarkable? I was only talking about it!"

"I have noted before now, Peter," said the sergeant, "that you and me have what might be called a simultaneous thirst."

III

The country folk were silent and exhausted. Kendillon drowsed now and again, but he suffered from blood-pressure, and after a while his breathing grew thicker and stronger until at last it exploded in a snort, and then he started up, broad awake and angry. In the silence rain spluttered and tapped along the roof, and the dark window-panes streamed with shining runnels of water that trickled on to the floor. Moll Mor scowled, her lower lip thrust out. She was a great flop of a woman with a big coarse powerful face. The other two women, who kept their eyes closed, had their brown shawls drawn tight about their heads, but Moll's was round her

[1] Ruin.

shoulders and the gap above her breasts was filled by a blaze of scarlet.

"Where are we?" asked Kendillon crossly, starting awake after one of his drowsing fits.

Moll Mor glowered at him.

"Aren't we home yet?" he asked again.

"No," she answered. "Nor won't be. What scour is on you?"

"Me little house," moaned Kendillon.

"Me little house," mimicked Moll. " 'Twasn't enough for you to board the windows and put barbed wire on the ould bit of a gate!"

" 'Tis all dom well for you," he snarled, "that have someone to mind yours for you."

One of the women laughed softly and turned a haggard virginal face within the cowl of her shawl.

" 'Tis that same have me laughing," she explained apologetically. "Tim Dwyer this week past at the stirabout pot!"

"And making the beds!" chimed in the third woman.

"And washing the children's faces! Glory be to God, he'll blast creation!"

"Ay," snorted Moll, "and his chickens running off with Thade Kendillon's roof."

"My roof, is it?"

"Ay, your roof."

" 'Tis a good roof. 'Tis a better roof than ever was seen over your head since the day you married."

"Oh, Mary Mother!" sighed Moll, " 'tis a great pity of me this three hours and I looking at the likes of you instead of me own fine bouncing man."

" 'Tis a new thing to hear you praising your man, then," said a woman.

"I wronged him," said Moll contritely. "I did so. I wronged him before the world."

At this moment the drunken man pulled back the door of the compartment and looked from face to face with an expression of deepening melancholy.

"She'sh not here," he said in disappointment.

"Who's not here, mister?" asked Moll with a wink at the others.

"I'm looking for me own carriage, ma'am," said the drunk with melancholy dignity, "and, whatever the bloody hell they done with it, 'tish losht. The railways in thish counthry are gone to hell."

"Wisha, if 'tis nothing else is worrying you wouldn't you sit here with me?" asked Moll.

"I would with very great pleasure," replied the drunk, "but 'tishn't on'y the carriage, 'tish me thravelling companion. . . . I'm a lonely man, I parted me besht friend this very night, I found wan to console me, and then when I turned me back— God took her!"

And with a dramatic gesture the drunk closed the door and continued on his way. The country folk sat up, blinking. The smoke of the men's pipes filled the compartment, and the heavy air was laden with the smell of homespun and turf smoke, the sweet pungent odour of which had penetrated every fibre of their garments.

"Listen to the rain, leave ye!" said one of the women. "We'll have a wet walk home."

" 'Twill be midnight before we're there," said another.

"Ah, sure, the whole country will be up."

" 'Twill be like daylight with collogueing."

"There'll be no sleep in Farranchreesht tonight."

"Oh, Farranchreesht! Farranchreesht!" cried the young woman with the haggard face, the ravished lineaments of which were suddenly transfigured. "Farranchreesht and the sky over you, I wouldn't change places with the Queen of England this night!"

And suddenly Farranchreesht, the bare boglands with the hump-backed mountain behind, the little white houses and the dark fortifications of turf that made it seem the flame-blackened ruin of some mighty city, all was lit up within their minds. An old man sitting in a corner, smoking a broken clay pipe, thumped his stick upon the floor.

"Well, now," said Kendillon darkly, "wasn't it great impudence to her to come back?"

"Wasn't it now?" answered a woman.

"She won't be there long," he added.

"You'll give her the hunt, I suppose?" asked Moll Mor politely, too politely.

"If no one else do, I'll give her the hunt myself."

"Oh, the hunt, the hunt," agreed a woman. "No one could ever darken her door again."

"And still, Thade Kendillon," pursued Moll with her teeth on edge to be at him, "you swore black was white to save her neck."

"I did of course. What else would I do?"

"What else? What else, indeed?" agreed the others.

"There was never an informer in my family."

"I'm surprised to hear it," replied Moll vindictively, but the old man thumped his stick three or four times on the floor requesting silence.

"We told our story, the lot of us," he said, "and we told it well."

"We did, indeed."

"And no one told it better than Moll Mor. You'd think to hear her she believed it herself."

"God knows," answered Moll with a wild laugh, "I nearly did."

"And still I seen great changes in my time, and maybe the day will come when Moll Mor or her likes will have a different story."

A silence followed his words. There was profound respect in all their eyes. The old man coughed and spat.

"Did any of ye ever think the day would come when a woman in our parish would do the like of that?"

"Never, never, ambasa!"

"But she might do it for land?"

"She might then."

"Or for money?"

"She might so."

"She might, indeed. When the hunger is money people kill for money, when the hunger is land people kill for land. There's a great change coming, a great change. In the ease of the world people are asking more. When I was a growing boy in the barony if you killed a beast you made six pieces of it, one for yourself and the rest for the neighbours. The same if you made a catch of fish, and that's how it was with us from the beginning of time. And now look at the change! The people aren't as poor as they were, nor as good as they were, nor as generous as they were, not as strong as they were."

"Nor as wild as they were," added Moll Mor with a vicious glare at Kendillon. "Oh, glory be to You, God, isn't the world a wonderful place!"

The door opened and Magner, Delancey and the sergeant entered. Magner was drunk.

"Moll," he said, "I was lonely without you. You're the biggest and brazenest and cleverest liar of the lot and you lost me my sergeant's stripes, but I'll forgive you everything if you'll give us one bar of the 'Colleen Dhas Roo.' "

IV

"I'm a lonely man," said the drunk. "And now I'm going back to my lonely habitation."

"Me besht friend," he continued, "I left behind me—Michael O'Leary. 'Tis a great pity you don't know Michael, and a great pity Michael don't know you. But look now at the misfortunate way a thing will happen. I was looking for someone to console me, and the moment I turned me back you were gone."

Solemnly he placed his hand under the woman's chin and raised her face to the light. Then with the other hand he stroked her cheeks.

"You have a beauful face," he said, "a beauful face. But whass more important, you have a beauful soul. I look into your eyes and I see the beauty of your nature. Allow me wan favour. Only wan favour before we part."

He bent and kissed her. Then he picked up his bowler which had fallen once more, put it on back to front, took his dispatch case and got out.

The woman sat on alone. Her shawl was thrown open and beneath it she wore a bright blue blouse. The carriage was cold, the night outside black and cheerless, and within her something had begun to contract that threatened to crush the very spark of life. She could no longer fight it off, even when for the hundredth time she went over the scenes of the previous day; the endless hours in the dock; the wearisome speeches and questions she couldn't understand and the long wait in the cells till the jury returned. She felt it again, the shiver of mortal anguish that went through her when the chief warder beckoned angrily from the stairs, and the wardress, glancing hastily into a hand-mirror, pushed her forward. She saw the jury with their expressionless faces. She was standing there alone, in nervous twitches jerking back the shawl from her face to give herself air. She was trying to say a prayer, but the words were being drowned within her mind by the thunder of nerves, crashing and bursting. She could feel one that had escaped dancing madly at the side of her mouth but she was powerless to recapture it.

"The verdict of the jury is that Helena Maguire is not guilty." Which was it? Death or life? She couldn't say. "Silence! Silence!" shouted the usher, though no one had tried to say anything. "Any other charge?" asked a weary voice. "Release the prisoner." "Silence!" shouted the crier again. The chief warder opened the door of the dock and she began to run. When she reached the steps she stopped and looked back to see if she were being followed. A policeman held open a door and she found herself in an ill-lit, draughty, stone corridor. She stood there, the old shawl about her face. The crowd began to emerge. The first was a tall girl with a rapt expression as though she were walking on air. When she saw the woman she halted suddenly, her hands went up in an instinctive gesture, as though she wished to feel her, to caress her. It was that look of hers, that gait as of a sleep-walker that brought the woman to her senses. . . .

But now the memory had no warmth in her mind, and the something within her continued to contract, smothering her with loneliness and shame and fear. She began to mutter crazily to herself. The train, now almost empty, was stopping at every little wayside station. Now and again a blast of wind from the Atlantic pushed at it as though trying to capsize it.

She looked up as the door was slammed open and Moll Mor came in, swinging her shawl behind her.

"They're all up the train. Wouldn't you come?"

"No, no, no, I couldn't."

"Why couldn't you? Who are you minding? Is it Thade Kendillon?"

"No, no, I'll stop as I am."

"Here! Take a sup of this and 'twill put new heart in you." Moll fumbled in her shawl and produced a bottle of liquor as pale as water. "Wait till I tell you what Magner said! That fellow's a limb of the divil. 'Have you e'er a drop, Moll?' says he. 'Maybe I have then,' says I. 'What is it?' says he. 'What do you think?' says I. 'For God's sake,' says he, 'baptize it quick and call it whiskey.' "

The woman took the bottle and put it to her lips. She shivered as she drank.

" 'Tis powerful stuff entirely," said Moll with respect.

Next moment there were loud voices in the corridor. Moll grabbed the bottle and hid it under her shawl. The door opened and in strode Magner, and behind him the sergeant and Delancey, looking rather foolish. After them again came the two country women, giggling. Magner held out his hand.

"Helena," he said, "accept my congratulations."

The woman took his hand, smiling awkwardly.

"We'll get you the next time though," he added.

"Musha, what are you saying, mister?" she asked.

"Not a word, not a word. You're a clever woman, a re

markable woman, and I give you full credit for it. You threw dust in all our eyes."

"Poison," said the sergeant by way of no harm, "is hard to come by and easy to trace, but it beat me to trace it."

"Well, well, there's things they're saying about me!"

The woman laughed nervously, looking first at Moll Mor and then at the sergeant.

"Oh, you're safe now," said Magner, "as safe as the judge on the bench. Last night when the jury came out with the verdict you could have stood there in the dock and said 'Ye're wrong, ye're wrong, I did it. I got the stuff in such and such a place. I gave it to him because he was old and dirty and cantankerous and a miser. I did it and I'm proud of it!' You could have said every word of that and no one would have dared to lay a finger on you."

"Indeed! What a thing I'd say!"

"Well, you could."

"The law is truly a remarkable phenomenon," said the sergeant, who was also rather squiffy. "Here you are, sitting at your ease at the expense of the State, and for one word, one simple word of a couple of letters, you could be lying in the body of the gaol, waiting for the rope and the morning jaunt."

The woman shuddered. The young woman with the ravished face looked up.

" 'Twas the holy will of God," she said simply.

" 'Twas all the bloody lies Moll Mor told," replied Magner.

" 'Twas the will of God," she repeated.

"There was many hanged in the wrong," said the sergeant.

"Even so, even so! 'Twas God's will."

"You have a new blouse," said the other woman in an envious tone.

"I seen it last night in a shop on the quay," replied the woman with sudden brightness. "A shop on the way down from the court. Is it nice?"

"How much did it cost you?"

"Honour of God!" exclaimed Magner, looking at them in stupefaction. "Is that all you were thinking of? You should have been on your bended knees before the altar."

"I was too," she answered indignantly.

"Women!" exclaimed Magner with a gesture of despair. He winked at Moll Mor and the pair of them retired to the next compartment. But the interior was reflected clearly in the corridor window and they could see the pale, quivering image of the policeman lift Moll Mor's bottle to his lips and blow a long silent blast on it as on a trumpet. Delancey laughed.

"There'll be one good day's work done on the head of the trial," said the young woman, laughing.

"How so?" asked the sergeant.

"Dan Canty will make a great brew of poteen while ye have yeer backs turned."

"I'll get Dan Canty yet," replied the sergeant stiffly.

"You will, as you got Helena."

"I'll get him yet."

He consulted his watch.

"We'll be in in another quarter of an hour," he said. " 'Tis time we were all getting back to our respective compartments."

Magner entered and the other policemen rose. The sergeant fastened his collar and buckled his belt. Magner swayed, holding the door frame, a mawkish smile on his thin, handsome, dissipated face.

"Well, good night to you now, ma'am," said the sergeant primly. "I'm as glad for all our sakes things ended up as they did."

"Good night, Helena," said Magner, bowing low and promptly tottering. "There'll be one happy man in Farran-chreesht to-night."

"Come! Come, Joe!" protested the sergeant.

"One happy man," repeated Magner obstinately. " 'Tis his turn now."

"Come on back, man," said Delancey. "You're drunk."

"You wanted him," said Magner heavily. "Your people

wouldn't let you have him, but you have him at last in spite of them all."

"Do you mean Cady Driscoll?" hissed the woman with sudden anger, leaning towards Magner, the shawl drawn tight about her head.

"Never mind who I mean. You have him."

"He's no more to me now than the salt sea!"

The policeman went out first, the women followed, Moll Mor laughing boisterously. The woman was left alone. Through the window she could see little cottages stepping down through wet and naked rocks to the water's edge. The flame of life had narrowed in her to a pin-point, and she could only wonder at the force that had caught her up, mastered her and thrown her aside.

"No more to me," she repeated dully to her own image in the window, "no more to me than the salt sea!"

Patrick Kavanagh (1905-   )

Father Mat

I

                    In a meadow
Beside the chapel three boys were playing football.
At the forge door an old man was leaning
Viewing a hunter-hoe. A man could hear
If he listened to the breeze the fall of wings—
How wistfully the sin-birds come home!

It was Confession Saturday, the first
Saturday in May; the May Devotions
Were spread like leaves to quieten
The excited armies of conscience.
The knife of penance fell so like a blade
Of grass that no one was afraid.

Father Mat came slowly walking, stopping to
Stare through gaps at ancient Ireland sweeping
In again with all its unbaptized beauty:
The calm evening,
The whitethorn blossoms,
The smell from ditches that were not Christian.
The dancer that dances in the hearts of men cried:
Look! I have shown this to you before—
The rags of living surprised
The joy in things you cannot forget.

His heavy hat was square upon his head,
Like a Christian Brother's;
His eyes were an old man's watery eyes,
Out of his flat nose grew spiky hairs.
He was a part of the place,
Natural as a round stone in a grass field;
He could walk through a cattle fair
And the people would only notice his odd spirit there.

His curate passed on a bicycle—
He had the haughty intellectual look
Of the man who never reads in brook or book;
A man designed
To wear a mitre,
To sit on committees—
For will grows strongest in the emptiest mind.

The old priest saw him pass
And, seeing, saw
Himself a mediaeval ghost.
Ahead of him went Power,
One who was not afraid when the sun opened a flower,
Who was never astonished
At a stick carried down a stream
Or at the undying difference in the corner of a field.

II

The Holy Ghost descends
At random like the muse
On wise man and fool,
And why should poet in the twilight choose?

Within the dim chapel was the grey
Mumble of prayer
To the Queen of May—
The Virgin Mary with the schoolgirl air.

Two guttering candles on a brass shrine
Raised upon the wall
Monsters of despair
To terrify deep into the soul.
Through the open door the hum of rosaries
Came out and blended with the homing bees.
                         The trees
Heard nothing stranger than the rain or the wind
Or the birds—
But deep in their roots they knew a seed had sinned.

In the graveyard a goat was nibbling at a yew,
The cobbler's chickens with anxious looks
Were straggling home through nettles, over graves.
A young girl down a hill was driving cows
To a corner at the gable-end of a roofless house.

Cows were milked earlier,
The supper hurried,
Hens shut in,
Horses unyoked,
And three men shaving before the same mirror.

III

The trip of iron tips on tile
Hesitated up the middle aisle,
Heads that were bowed glanced up to see
Who could this last arrival be.

Murmur of women's voices from the porch,
Memories of relations in the graveyard.
On the stem
Of memory imaginations blossom.

               In the dim
Corners in the side seats faces gather,
Lit up now and then by a guttering candle
And the ghost of day at the window.
A secret lover is saying
Three Hail Marys that she who knows
The ways of women will bring
Cathleen O'Hara (he names her) home to him.
Ironic fate! Cathleen herself is saying
Three Hail Marys to her who knows
The ways of men to bring
Somebody else home to her—
"O may he love me."
What is the Virgin Mary now to do?

IV

               From a confessional
The voice of Father Mat's absolving
Rises and falls like a briar in the breeze.
As the sins pour in the old priest is thinking
His fields of fresh grass, his horses, his cows,
His earth into the fires of Purgatory.

It cools his mind.
"They confess to the fields," he mused,
"They confess to the fields and the air and the sky,"
And forgiveness was the soft grass of his meadow by the
    river;
His thoughts were walking through it now.

His human lips talked on:
"My son,
Only the poor in spirit shall wear the crown;
Those down
Can creep in the low door
On to Heaven's floor."

The Tempter had another answer ready:
"Ah lad, upon the road of life
'Tis best to dance with Chance's wife
And let the rains that come in time
Erase the footprints of the crime."
The dancer that dances in the hearts of men
Tempted him again:
"Look! I have shown you this before;
From this mountain-top I have tempted Christ
With what you see now
Of beauty—all that's music, poetry, art
In things you can touch every day.
I broke away
And rule all dominions that are rare;
I took with me all the answers to every prayer
That young men and girls pray for: love, happiness,
    riches—"
O Tempter! O Tempter!

V

As Father Mat walked home
Venus was in the western sky
And there were voices in the hedges:
"God the Gay is not the Wise."

"Take your choice, take your choice,"
Called the breeze through the bridge's eye.
"The domestic Virgin and Her Child
Or Venus with her ecstasy."

A Christmas Childhood

I

One side of the potato-pits was white with frost—
How wonderful that was, how wonderful!
And when we put our ears to the paling-post
The music that came out was magical.

The light between the ricks of hay and straw
Was a hole in Heaven's gable. An apple tree
With its December-glinting fruit we saw—
O you, Eve, were the world that tempted me

To eat the knowledge that grew in clay
And death the germ within it! Now and then
I can remember something of the gay
Garden that was childhood's. Again

The tracks of cattle to a drinking-place,
A green stone lying sideways in a ditch
Or any common sight the transfigured face
Of a beauty that the world did not touch.

II

My father played the melodion
Outside at our gate;
There were stars in the morning east
And they danced to his music.

Across the wild bogs his melodion called
To Lennons and Callans.
As I pulled on my trousers in a hurry
I knew some strange thing had happened.

Outside in the cow-house my mother
Made the music of milking;
The light of her stable-lamp was a star
And the frost of Bethlehem made it twinkle.

A water-hen screeched in the bog,
Mass-going feet
Crunched the wafer-ice on the pot-holes,
Somebody wistfully twisted the bellows wheel.

My child poet picked out the letters
On the grey stone,
In silver the wonder of a Christmas townland,
The winking glitter of a frosty dawn.

Cassiopeia was over
Cassidy's hanging hill,
I looked and three whin bushes rode across
The horizon—the Three Wise Kings.

An old man passing said:
"Can't he make it talk"—
The melodion. I hid in the doorway
And tightened the belt of my box-pleated coat.

I nicked six nicks on the door-post
With my penknife's big blade—
There was a little one for cutting tobacco.
And I was six Christmases of age.

My father played the melodion,
My mother milked the cows,
And I had a prayer like a white rose pinned
On the Virgin Mary's blouse.

If Ever You Go to Dublin Town

If ever you go to Dublin town
    In a hundred years or so
Inquire for me in Baggot Street
And what I was like to know.
    O he was a queer one
    Fol dol the di do,
    He was a queer one
    I tell you.

My great grandmother knew him well,
He asked her to come and call
On him in his flat and she giggled at the though'.
Of a young girl's lovely fall.
    O he was dangerous,
    Fol dol the di do
    He was dangerous
    I tell you.

On Pembroke Road look out for my ghost,
Dishevelled, with shoes untied,
Playing through the railings with little children
Whose children have long since died.
   O he was a nice man
   Fol dol the di do
   We all enjoyed him
   I tell you.

Go into a pub and listen well
If my voice still echoes there.
Ask the men what their grandsires thought
And tell them to answer fair.
   O he was eccentric,
   Fol dol the di do
   He was eccentric
   I tell you.

He had the knack of making men feel
As small as they really were—
Which meant as great as God had made them—
But as males they disliked his air
   O he was a proud one,
   Fol dol the di do
   He was a proud one
   I tell you.

If every you go to Dublin town
In a hundred years or so
Sniff for my personality,
Is it vanity's vapor now?
   O he was a vain one,
   Fol dol the di do
   He was a vain one,
   I tell you.

I saw his name with a hundred others
In a book in the library
It said he had never fully achieved
His potentiality.
    For he was slothful
    Fol dol the di do
    He was slothful
    I tell you.

He knew that posterity has no use
For anything but the soul
The lines that speak the passionate heart
The spirit that lives alone.
    O he was a lone one
    Fol dol the di do
    Yet he lived happily
    I tell you.

Louis MacNeice (1907-   )

Valediction

Their verdure dare not show ... their verdure dare not show ...
Cant and randy—the seals' heads bobbing in the tide-flow
Between the islands, sleek and black and irrelevant
They cannot depose logically what they want:
Died by gunshot under borrowed pennons,
Sniped from the wet gorse and taken by the limp fins
And slung like a dead seal in a boghole, beaten up
By peasants with long lips and the whisky-drinker's cough.
Park your car in the city of Dublin, see Sackville Street
Without the sandbags in the old photos, meet
The statues of the patriots, history never dies,
At any rate in Ireland, arson and murder are legacies

Like old rings hollow-eyed without their stones
Dumb talismans.
See Belfast, devout and profane and hard,
Built on reclaimed mud, hammers playing in the shipyard;
Time punched with holes like a steel sheet, time
Hardening the faces, veneering with a grey and speckled rime
The faces under the shawls and caps:
This was my mother-city, these my paps.
Country of callous lava cooled to stone,
Of minute sodden haycocks, of ship-sirens' moan,
Of falling intonations—I would call you to book
I would say to you, Look;
I would say, This is what you have given me
Indifference and sentimentality
A metallic giggle, a fumbling hand
A heart that leaps to a fife band:
Set these against your water-shafted air
Of amethyst and moonstone, the horses' feet like bells of hair
Shambling beneath the orange-cart, the beer-brown spring
Guzzling between the heather, the green gush of Irish spring.
Cursèd be he that curses his mother. I cannot be
Anyone else than what this land engendered me:
In the back of my mind are snips of white, the sails
Of the Lough's fishing-boats, the bellropes lash their tails
When I would peal my thoughts, the bells pull free—
Memory in apostasy.
I would tot up my factors
But who can stand in the way of his soul's steam-tractors?
I can say Ireland is hooey, Ireland is
A gallery of fake tapestries,
But I cannot deny my past to which my self is wed,
The woven figure cannot undo its thread.
On a cardboard lid I saw when I was four
Was the trade-mark of a hound and a round tower,
And that was Irish glamour, and in the cemetery
Sham Celtic crosses claimed our individuality,

And my father talked about the West where years back
He played hurley on the sands with a stick of wrack.
Park your car in Killarney, buy a souvenir
Of green marble or black bog-oak, run up to Clare,
Climb the cliff in the postcard, visit Galway city,
Romanticise on our Spanish blood, leave ten per cent of pity
Under your plate for the emigrant,
Take credit for our sanctity, our heroism and our sterile want
Columba Kevin and briny Brandan the accepted names,
Wolfe Tone and Grattan and Michael Collins the accepted
          names,
Admire the suavity with which the architect
Is rebuilding the burnt mansion, recollect
The palmy days of the Horse Show, swank your fill,
But take the Holyhead boat before you pay the bill;
Before you face the consequence
Of inbred soul and climatic maleficence
And pay for the trick beauty of a prism
In drug-dull fatalism.
I will exorcise my blood
And not to have my baby-clothes my shroud
I will acquire an attitude not yours
And become as one of your holiday visitors,
And however often I may come
Farewell, my country, and in perpetuum;
Whatever desire I catch when your wind scours my face
I will take home and put in a glass case
And merely look on
At each new fantasy of badge and gun.
Frost will not touch the hedge of fuchsias,
The land will remain as it was,
But no abiding content can grow out of these minds
Fuddled with blood, always caught by blinds;
The eels go up the Shannon over the great dam;
You cannot change a response by giving it a new name.
Fountain of green and blue curling in the wind

I must go east and stay, not looking behind,
Not knowing on which day the mist is blanket-thick
Nor when sun quilts the valley and quick
Winging shadows of white clouds pass
Over the long hills like a fiddle's phrase.
If I were a dog of sunlight I would bound
From Phoenix Park to Achill Sound,
Picking up the scent of a hundred fugitives
That have broken the mesh of ordinary lives,
But being ordinary too I must in course discuss
What we mean to Ireland or Ireland to us;
I have to observe milestone and curio
The beaten buried gold of an old king's bravado,
Falsetto antiquities, I have to gesture,
Take part in, or renounce, each imposture;
Therefore I resign, good-bye the chequered and the quiet hills
The gaudily-striped Atlantic, the linen-mills
That swallow the shawled file, the black moor where half
A turf-stack stands like a ruined cenotaph;
Good-bye your hens running in and out of the white house
Your absent-minded goats along the road, your black cows
Your greyhounds and your hunters beautifully bred
Your drums and your dolled-up Virgins and your ignorant
     dead.

Carrickfergus

I was born in Belfast between the mountain and the gantries
  To the hooting of lost sirens and the clang of trams:
Thence to Smoky Carrick in County Antrim
  Where the bottle-neck harbour collects the mud which jams

The little boats beneath the Norman castle,
  The pier shining with lumps of crystal salt;
The Scotch Quarter was a line of residential houses
  But the Irish Quarter was a slum for the blind and halt.

The brook ran yellow from the factory stinking of chlorine,
  The yarn-mill called its funeral cry at noon;
Our lights looked over the lough to the lights of Bangor
  Under the peacock aura of a drowning moon.

The Norman walled this town against the country
  To stop his ears to the yelping of his slave
And built a church in the form of a cross but denoting
  The list of Christ on the cross, in the angle of the nave.

I was the rector's son, born to the anglican order,
  Banned for ever from the candles of the Irish poor;
The Chichesters knelt in marble at the end of a transept
  With ruffs about their necks, their portion sure.

The war came and a huge camp of soldiers
   Grew from the ground in sight of our house with long
Dummies hanging from gibbets for bayonet practice
   And the sentry's challenge echoing all day long;

A Yorkshire terrier ran in and out by the gate-lodge
   Barred to civilians, yapping as if taking affront:
Marching at east and singing "Who Killed Cock Robin?"
   The troops went out by the lodge and off to the Front.

The steamer was camouflaged that took me to England—
   Sweat and khaki in the Carlisle train;
I thought that the war would last for ever and sugar
   Be always rationed and that never again

Would the weekly papers not have photos of sandbags
   And my governess not make bandages from moss
And people not have maps above the fireplace
   With flags on pins moving across and across—

Across the hawthorn hedge the noise of bugles,
   Flares across the night,
Somewhere on the lough was a prison ship for Germans,
   A cage across their sight.

I went to school in Dorset, the world of parents
   Contracted into a puppet world of sons
Far from the mill girls, the smell of porter, the salt-mines
   And the soldiers with their guns.

From Autumn Journal

Nightmare leaves fatigue:
  We envy men of action
Who sleep and wake, murder and intrigue
  Without being doubtful, without being haunted.
And I envy the intransigence of my own
  Countrymen who shoot to kill and never
See the victim's face become their own
  Or find his motive sabotage their motives.
So reading the memoirs of Maud Gonne,
  Daughter of an English mother and a soldier father,
I note how a single purpose can be founded on
  A jumble of opposites:
Dublin Castle, the vice-regal ball,
  The embassies of Europe,
Hatred scribbled on a wall,
  Gaols and revolvers.
And I remember, when I was little, the fear
  Bandied among the servants
That Casement[1] would land at the pier
  With a sword and a horde of rebels;
And how we used to expect, at a later date,
  When the wind blew from the west, the noise of shooting
Starting in the evening at eight
  In Belfast in the York Street district;
And the voodoo of the Orange bands
  Drawing an iron net through darkest Ulster,
Flailing the limbo lands—
  The linen mills, the long wet grass, the ragged hawthorn.
And one read black where the other read white, his hope
  The other man's damnation:

---

[1] Sir Roger Casement, hanged in London on August 3, 1916 for his participation in the rebellion of 1916.

Up the Rebels, To Hell with the Pope,
    And God Save—as you prefer—the King or Ireland.
The land of scholars and saints:
    Scholars and saints my eye, the land of ambush,
Purblind manifestoes, never-ending complaints,
    The born martyr and the gallant ninny;
The grocer drunk with the drum,
    The land-owner shot in his bed, the angry voices
Piercing the broken fanlight in the slum,
    The shawled woman weeping at the garish altar.
Kathaleen ni Houlihan! Why
    Must a country, like a ship or a car, be always femaie,
Mother or sweetheart? A woman passing by,
    We did but see her passing.
Passing like a patch of sun on the rainy hill
    And yet we love her for ever and hate our neighbour
And each one in his will
    Binds his heirs to continuance of hatred.
Drums on the haycock, drums on the harvest, black
    Drums in the night shaking the windows:
King William is riding his white horse back
    To the Boyne on a banner.
Thousands of banners, thousands of white
    Horses, thousands of Williams
Waving thousands of swords and ready to fight
    Till the blue sea turns to orange.
Such was my country and I thought I was well
    Out of it, educated and domiciled in England,
Though yet her name keeps ringing like a bell
    In an under-water belfry.
Why do we like being Irish? Partly because
    It gives us an edge on the sentimental English
As members of a world that never was,
    Baptised with fairy water;
And partly because Ireland is small enough
    To be still thought of with a family feeling,

And because the waves are rough
   That split her from a more commercial culture;
And because one feels that here at least one can
   Do local work which is not at the world's mercy
And that on this tiny stage with luck a man
   Might see the end of one particular action.
It is self-deception of course;
   There is no immunity in this island either;
A cart that is drawn by somebody else's horse
   And carrying goods to somebody else's market.
The bombs in the turnip sack, the sniper from the roof,
   Griffith,[1] Connolly,[2] Collins,[3] where have they brought us?
Ourselves alone![4] Let the round tower stand aloof
   In a world of bursting mortar!
Let the school-children fumble their sums
   In a half-dead language;
Let the censor be busy on the books; pull down the Georgian
    slums;
   Let the games be played in Gaelic.
Let them grow beet-sugar; let them build
   A factory in every hamlet;
Let them pigeon-hole the souls of the killed
   Into sheep and goats, patriots and traitors.
And the North, where I was a boy,
   Is still the North, veneered with the grime of Glasgow,
Thousands of men whom nobody will employ
   Standing at the corners, coughing.
And the street-children play on the wet
   Pavement—hopscotch or marbles;

---

[1] Arthur Griffith, first president of the Irish Free State (1922).

[2] James Connolly, one of the leaders of the rebellion of 1916.

[3] Michael Collins, one of the leaders in the Anglo-Irish war (1918-1921).

[4] Sinn Fein, the name of a nationalist newspaper edited by Arthur Griffith and the name of a political movement started by Griffith and others in 1905, means in Gaelic *Ourselves alone*.

And each rich family boasts a sagging tennis-net
 On a spongy lawn beside a dripping shrubbery.
The smoking chimneys hint
 At prosperity round the corner
But they make their Ulster linen from foreign lint
 And the money that comes in goes out to make more money.
A city built upon mud;
 A culture built upon profit;
Free speech nipped in the bud,
 The minority always guilty.
Why should I want to go back
 To you, Ireland, my Ireland?
The blots on the page are so black
 That they cannot be covered with shamrock.
I hate your grandiose airs,
 Your sob-stuff, your laugh and your swagger,
Your assumption that everyone cares
 Who is the king of your castle.
Castles are out of date,
 The tide flows round the children's sandy fancy;
Put up what flag you like, it is too late
 To save your soul with bunting.
Odi atque amo:[1]
 Shall we cut this name on trees with a rusty dagger?
Her mountains are still blue, her rivers flow
 Bubbling over the boulders.
She is both a bore and a bitch;
 Better close the horizon,
Send her no more fantasy, no more longings which
 Are under a fatal tariff.
For common sense is the vogue
 And she gives her children neither sense nor money
Who slouch around the world with a gesture and a brogue
 And a faggot of useless memories.

---

[1] I hate and I love.

W R. Rodgers (1909-   )

The Raider

There, wrapped in his own roars, the lone airman
Swims like a mote through the thousands of eyes
That look up at him ironing out the skies,
Frocked and fanged by fire, by nagging fingers
Of guns jagged and jogged, with shell-bursts tasselled.

Does ever the airman's eye, speeding on
To grim conclusion, alight and loiter
Curiously on the country below?
Or does his gaze easily dissolve
Upon the moving surfaces, and flow
Evenly away like rain on rivers?

Or, roaring back over our armoured rims,
Does his mind take in only the bloom and boom
Of bomb beneath him, noting how neatly
It mopped up a map-point town or snouted out
This tip or else that tap-root of resistance?

Yet, pity him too, that navigator
Who now in archipelago of steel
Nears that place where, hooked upon barbed air, he'll
Halt, hang hump-backed, and look into his crater.

Lent

Mary Magdalene, that easy woman,
Saw, from the shore, the seas
Beat against the hard stone of Lent,
Crying, "Weep, seas, weep
For yourselves that cannot dent me more

O more than all these, more crabbed than all stones,
And cold, make me, who once
Could leap like water, Lord. Take me
As one who owes
Nothing to what she was. Ah, naked.

My waves of scent, my petticoats of foam
Put from me and rebut;
Disown. And that salt lust stave off
That slavered me—O
Let it whiten in grief against the stones

And outer reefs of me. Utterly doff,
Nor leave the lightest veil
Of feeling to heave or soften.
Nothing cares this heart
What hardness crates it now or coffins.

Over the balconies of these curved breasts
I'll no more peep to see
The light procession of my loves
Surf-riding in to me
Who now have eyes and alcove, Lord, for Thee."

"Room, Mary," said He, "ah make room for me
Who am come so cold now
To my tomb." So, on Good Friday,
Under a frosty moon
They carried Him and laid Him in her womb.

A grave and icy mask her heart wore twice,
But on the third day it thawed,
And only a stone's-flow away
Mary saw her God.
Did you hear me? Mary saw her God!

Dance, Mary Magdalene, dance, dance and sing,
For unto you is born
This day a King. "Lady," said He,
"To you who relent
I bring back the petticoat and the bottle of scent."

Christ Walking on the Water

Slowly, O so slowly, longing rose up
In the forenoon of his face, till only
A ringlet of fog lingered round his loins.
And fast he went down beaches all weeping
With weed, and waded out. Twelve tall waves,
Sequent and equated, hollowed and followed.
O what a cock-eyed sea he walked on,
What poke-ends of foam, what elbowings
And lugubrious looks, what ebullient
And contumacious musics. Always there were
Hills and holes, pills and poles, a wavy wall
And bucking ribbon caterpillaring past
With glossy ease. And often, as he walked,
The slow curtains of swell swung open and showed,
Miles and smiles away, the bottle-boat
Flung on a wavering frond of froth that fell
Knee-deep and heaved thigh-high. In his forward face
No cave of afterthought opened; to his ear
No bottom clamour climbed up; nothing blinked.
For he was the horizon, he the hub,
Both bone and flesh, finger and ring of all
This clangourous sea. Docile, at his toe's touch
Each tottering dot stood roundaboutly calm
And jammed the following others fast as stone.
The ironical wave smoothed itself out

To meet him, and the mocking hollow
Hooped its back for his feet. A spine of light
Sniggered on the knobbly water, ahead.
But he like a lover, caught up,
Pushed past all wrigglings and remonstrances
And entered the rolling belly of the boat
That shuddered and lay still. And he lay there
Emptied of his errand, oozing still. Slowly
The misted mirror of his eyes grew clear
And cold, the bell of blood tolled lower,
And bright before his sight the ocean bared
And rolled its horrible bold eye-balls endlessly
In round rebuke. Looking over the edge
He shivered. Was this the way he had come?
Was that the one who came? The whole wieldy world
And all the welded welt that he had walked on
Burst like a plate into purposelessness.
All, all was gone, the fervour and the froth
Of confidence, and flat as water was
The sad and glassy round. Somewhere, then,
A tiny flute wriggled like a worm, O so lonely.
A ring of birds rose up and wound away
Into nothingness. Beyond himself he saw
The settled steeples, and breathing beaches
Running with people. But he,
He was custodian to nothing now,
And boneless as an empty sleeve hung down.
Down from crowned noon to cambered evening
He fell, fell, from white to amber, till night
Slid over him like an eyelid. And he,
His knees drawn up, his head dropped deep,
Curled like a question mark asleep.

The Net

Quick, woman, in your net
Catch the silver I fling!
O I am deep in your debt,
Draw tight, skin-tight, the string,
And rake the silver in.
No fisher ever yet
Drew such a cunning ring.

Ah, shifty as the fin
Of any fish this flesh
That, shaken to the shin,
Now shoals into your mesh,
Bursting to be held in;
Purse-proud and pebble-hard,
Its pence like shingle showered.

Open the haul, and shake
The fill of shillings free,
Let all the satchels break
And leap about the knee
In shoals of ecstasy.
Guineas and gills will flake
At each gull-plunge of me.

Though all the Angels, and
Saint Michael at their head,
Nightly contrive to stand
On guard about your bed,
Yet none dare take a hand,
But each can only spread
His eagle-eye instead.

But I, being man, can kiss
And bed-spread-eagle too;
All flesh shall come to this,
Being less than angel is,
Yet higher far in bliss
As it entwines with you.

Come, make no sound, my sweet;
Turn down the candid lamp
And draw the equal quilt
Over our naked guilt.

Spring

From my wind-blown book I look
Up and see the lazy rook
Rise and twist away,
And from every airy eave
The arrowy swallows wildly leave
And swoop as if in play.

Dark the daw with claw-wing sail
Swings at anchor in the gale,
And in the running grass
Daffodils nod and intervene
Like sud-flecks on a sea of green
Dissolving as they pass.

Mouldy and old the bouldered walls
Wake in the sun and warm their polls
And wag aubretia beards,
The snail-gaze of senility
Silvers each front, and backward they
Break wind and dree their weirds.

Bosoms of bloom that sob like moss
Beneath each jumpy breath, emboss
The bony orchard's breast;
And look, the leggy lilac canes
Are varicosed with ivy veins
Of envy coalesced.

There the hare, bound after bound,
Concertinas all the ground
As far as eye can spy it,
Like a fountain's dying spray
It falls in little frills away
Into a twitching quiet.

Still down the slow opposing slope
The intent ploughman draws his rope
Of parsimony fine,
Nor sees bold Icarus in his haste
Expend his spirit in a waste
Of aerobatic wine.

Icarus from his heady plane
Into depths of spinning brain
Bales out like a ball,
Pulls the ripcord, splits the sack
And lets the spilled silk splutter back
And speculative fall.

And hark, the lark sarcastic sings
To Icarus without his wings
Dawdling down the sky,
Indolent aeons have gone to make
Its gimlet bill, its song-gill's shake,
Its all-containing cry.

Part I

p. 3 *The Viking Terror*. Text in Whitley Stokes and John Strachan, *Thesaurus Palaeohibernicus* (Cambridge, 1903), II, 290.

    4 *A Pet Crane*. Myles Dillon, *Early Irish Literature* (Chicago, 1948), p. 156.

    4 *The Son of the King of Moy*. *Ibid.*, p. 155. Text in Kuno Meyer, "Bruchstücke der älteren Lyrik Irlands," *Preussische Akad. der Wissenschaften* (Berlin, 1919, no. 7), p. 69.

    4 *The Wife of Aed Mac Ainmirech, King of Ireland, Laments Her Husband*. Myles Dillon, *op. cit.*, p. 155. Text in *Thesaurus Palaeohibernicus*, II, 295.

    5 *A Love Song*. Myles Dillon, *op. cit.*, p. 155. Text in Kuno Meyer, "Bruchstücke der älteren Lyrik Irlands," p. 69.

    5 *The Drowning of Conaing*. Sean O'Faolain, *The Silver Branch* (New York, 1938), p. 66. Text in Julius Porkorny, *A Historical Reader of Old Irish* (Halle, 1923), p. 4.

    6 *The Deer's Cry*. Kuno Meyer, *Selections from Ancient Irish Poetry* (London, 1911), p. 25. Text in *Thesaurus Palaeohibernicus*, II, 354.

    9 *In Praise of Aed*. Robin Flower, *The Irish Tradition* (London, 1947), p. 27. Text in *Thesaurus Palaeohibernicus*, II, 295.

  10 *The Scribe*. Kuno Meyer, *Selections from Ancient Irish Poetry*, p. 99. Text in *Thesaurus Palaeohibernicus*, II, 290.

  10 *A Miserly Patron*. Myles Dillon, *op. cit.*, p. 155. Text in Julius Pokorny, *A Historical Reader of Old Irish*, p. 20.

  11 *Pangur Ban*. Robin Flower, *op. cit.*, p. 24. Text in *Thesaurus Palaeohibernicus*, II, 293.

  13 *The Vision of Ita*. Text and translation in Whitley Stokes, *The Martyrology of Oengus the Culdee* (London, 1905), p. 44. I have made some slight alterations in the translation.

  14 *He That Never Read a Line*. Robin Flower, *op. cit.*, p. 46. Text in *Zeitschrifte für celtische Philologie*, IX (1913), 470.

  14 *On A Dead Scholar*. Robin Flower, *op. cit.*, p. 43. Text in Whitley Stokes, *The Martyrology of Oengus the Culdee*, p. 198.

  15 *The Church Bell in the Night*. Kuno Meyer, *Selections from Ancient Irish Poetry*, p. 101. Text in Kuno Meyer, *A Primer of Irish Metrics* (Dublin, 1909), p. 21.

  15 *Starry Sky*. Sean O'Faolain, *op. cit.*, p. 29. Text in *Zeitschrifte für celtische Philologie*, I (1897), 327, ed. Kuno Meyer.

  16 *The Desire for Hermitage*. Sean O'Faolain, *op. cit.*, p. 34. Text in *Eriu*, II (1905), 55, ed. Kuno Meyer. O'Faolain has omitted nine quatrains. For a translation of the complete text see Ken-

---

[1] Unless it is otherwise indicated, the date of publication given for any item in the Bibliographical Notes is the date of first publication.

neth Jackson, *A Celtic Miscellany* (Cambridge, Mass., 1951), no. 34, p. 309.

p. 17   The Wish of Manchín of Liath. Kenneth Jackson, *A Celtic Miscellany*, no. 223, p. 308. Text in *Eriu*, I (1904), 39, ed. Kuno Meyer.

18   The Pilgrim at Rome. Kuno Meyer, *Selections from Ancient Irish Poetry*, p. 100. Text in *Thesaurus Palaeohibernicus*, II, 296.

18   Winter Has Come. Kenneth Jackson, *op. cit.*, no. 87, p. 139. Text in Kuno Meyer, "Bruchstücke der älteren Lyrik Irlands," p. 67.

19   The Ivy Crest. Robin Flower, *op. cit.*, p. 34. Text in *Thesaurus Palaeohibernicus*, II, 294.

20   Summer Is Gone. Sean O'Faolain, *op. cit.*, p. 55. Text in Kuno Meyer, *Four Old-Irish Songs of Summer and Winter* (London, 1903), p. 14.

21   May. Frank O'Connor, *The Fountain of Magic* (London, 1939), p. 19. Text in Kuno Meyer, *Four Old-Irish Songs of Summer and Winter*, p. 28.

23   A Song of Winter, Kuno Meyer, *Selections from Ancient Irish Poetry*, p. 57. Text in Kuno Meyer, *Four Old-Irish Songs of Summer and Winter*, p. 16.

25   To Crinog. Kuno Meyer, *Selections from Ancient Irish Poetry*, p. 37. Text in *Zeitschrifte für celtische Philologie*, VI (1908), 266, ed. Kuno Meyer.

27   The Old Woman of Beare. Frank O'Connor, *op. cit.* p. 9. Text in *Otia Merseiana* (The Publication of the Arts Faculty of University College, Liverpool), I (1899), 119.

32   I Should Like to Have a Great Pool of Ale. Kenneth Jackson, *op. cit.*, no. 227, p. 313. Text in *Celtica*, II (1952), 151, ed. David Greene.

33   St. Columcille the Scribe. Kuno Meyer, *Selections from Ancient Irish Poetry*, p. 87. Text in *The Gaelic Journal*, VIII (1897), 49.

34   A Storm at Sea. Robin Flower, *op. cit.*, p. 51. Text in *Otia Merseiana*, II (1900-01), 76, ed. Kuno Meyer.

36   The Praises of God. Kenneth Jackson, *op. cit.*, no. 119, p. 147. Text in *The Gaelic Journal*, IV (1889), 115, ed. Kuno Meyer.

36   The Blackbird. Kuno Meyer, *Selections from Ancient Irish Poetry*, p. 100. Text in Kuno Meyer, "Bruchstücke der älteren Lyrik Irlands," p. 66.

37   St. Columcille's Island Hermitage. Kenneth Jackson, *op. cit.*, no. 222, p. 307. Text in T. F. O'Rahilly, *Measgra Danta* (Cork, 1927), II, 120.

Part II

39   The Dream of Oenghus. Kenneth Jackson, *A Celtic Miscellany*, no. 39, p. 99. Text in F. Shaw, *The Dream of Oenghus* (Dublin, 1934), p. 43.

p. 44 *The Boyhood Deeds of Cuchulain.* Tom Peete Cross and Clark Harris Slover, *Ancient Irish Tales* (New York, 1936), p. 137. Text in E. Windisch, *Tain Bo Cuailgne*, Leipzig, 1905.

61 *The Tragic Death of Connla.* Text and translation in Kuno Meyer, "The Death of Connla," *Eriu*, I (1904), 113.

65 *Fand Yields Cuchulain to Emer.* Sean O'Faolain, *The Silver Branch*, p. 86. Text in A. G. Van Hamel, *Compert Con Culainn*, Dublin, 1933.

66 *Cuchulain's Lament for Ferdiad.* George Sigerson, *Bards of the Gael and the Gall* (New York, 1907), p. 119. Text in E. Windisch, *Tain Bo Cuailgne*, p. 597.

68 *The Death of Cuchulain.* Tom Peete Cross and Clark Harris Slover, op. cit., p. 333. Text in Kuno Meyer, *The Death-Tales of the Ulster Heroes*, Royal Irish Academy Todd Lecture Series, XIV, Dublin, 1906.

76 *The Story of Deirdre.* Kenneth Jackson, op. cit., no. 7, p. 49. Text in Vernam Hull, *Longes Mac N-Uislenn*, New York, 1949. Jackson's translation omits some short passages. Hull translates the complete text.

81 *The Colloquy of the Old Men.* Standish Hayes O'Grady, *Silva Gadelica* (London, 1892), I, 94 (text); II, 101 (translation). I use the version of Tom Peete Cross and Clark Harris Slover (op. cit., p. 457) in which modifications in O'Grady's translation are made for the sake of intelligibility and the text shortened by omissions.

95 *The Fianna.* Standish Hayes O'Grady, *Silva Gadelica*, I, 92 (text); II, 99 (translation).

96 *The Headless Phantoms.* Eoin MacNeill, *Duanaire Finn* (London, Irish Texts Society, VII, 1908), Part One, p. 28 (text), p. 127 (translation).

100 *The Bathing of Oisin's Head. Ibid.*, p. 14 (text), p. 111 (translation).

103 *Goll's Parting with His Wife. Ibid.*, p. 23 (text), p. 121 (translation).

105 *Oisin in the Land of Youth.* Michael Comyn, *The Lay of Oisin in the Land of Youth*, ed. Tomas O'Flannghaile (Thomas Flannery), London, 1896. Text and translation.

131 *The Voyage of Bran.* Text and translation in Kuno Meyer and Alfred Nutt, *The Voyage of Bran* (London, 1895), I, 3.

143 *Mad Sweeney.* Text and translation in J. G. O'Keefe, *Buile Suibhne Geilt, A Middle-Irish Romance* (London, Irish Texts Society, XII, 1913), p. 37ff., sections 26-41.

Part III

171 *Lamentation of Mac Liag for Kincora.* Poems of James Clarence Mangan, ed. D. J. O'Donoghue (Dublin, 1903), p. 49.

174 *At Saint Patrick's Purgatory.* Sean O'Faolain, *The Silver Branch*, p. 35. Text in *The Gaelic Journal*, IV (1889), 190.

p. 175 The Dead at Clonmacnois. T. W. Rolleston, Sea Spray: Verses and Translations (Dublin, 1909), p. 47. First published in Poems and Ballads of Young Ireland, ed. W. B. Yeats, Dublin, 1888.

176 On the Breaking-Up of a School. Osborn Bergin, Studies, XIII (1924), 85. Text and translation.

179 The Student. Frank O'Connor, The Fountain of Magic, p. 30. Text in T. F. O'Rahilly, Measgra Danta, I, 16.

180 Hugh Maguire. Frank O'Connor, The Fountain of Magic, p. 28.

182 Civil Irish and Wild Irish. Kenneth Jackson, A Celtic Miscellany, no. 182, p. 236. Text in The Irish Review, II (1912), p. 471, ed. Osborn Bergin.

184 Maelmora MacSweeney. Eleanor Knott, The Bardic Poems of Tadhg Dall O'Huiginn (London, Irish Texts Society, 1922), I, 180 (text); II, 120 (translation).

188 The First Vision. The Earl of Longford, The Dove in the Castle. A Collection of Poems from the the Irish (Dublin, 1946), p. 13. Text in Eleanor Knott, The Bardic Poems of Tadhg Dall O'Huiginn, I, 264.

192 The Second Vision. The Earl of Longford, op. cit., p. 18. Text in Eleanor Knott, op. cit., I, 268.

196 The Good Tradition. Robin Flower, The Irish Tradition, p. 165. The text is unpublished and survives in a manuscript in the British Museum. See Standish O'Grady and Robin Flower, Catalogue of Irish Manuscripts in the British Museum, London, II (1926), 6, no. 20.

197 The Flight of the Earls. Robin Flower, The Irish Tradition, p. 166. Text in Eriu, VIII (1916), 191, ed. Eleanor Knott.

200 Were Not the Gael Fallen. Robin Flower, op. cit., p. 172. The text is unpublished and survives in a manuscript in the Royal Irish Academy.

201 Who Will Buy a Poem? Kenneth Jackson, op. cit., no. 199, p. 265. Text in The Irish Review, III (1913), 82, ed. Osborn Bergin.

202 How Emain Macha Got Its Name. Text and translation in Patrick S. Dineen, The History of Ireland by Geoffrey Keating D. D. (London, Irish Texts Society), II (1908), p. 153.

204 Loingseach's Horse Ears. Ibid., p. 173.

205 The Death of Curaoi. Ibid., p. 221.

208 Mochua's Riches. Ibid., III (1908), 71.

209 St. Columkille. Ibid., p. 87.

214 Brian Boru. Ibid., p. 267.

Part IV

219 Against Blame of Women. The Earl of Longford, Poems from the Irish (Dublin, 1944), p. 1. Text in T. F. O'Rahilly, Danta Gradha (Cork, 1926), p. 4.

p. 220 *Do Not Torment Me, Woman*. Kenneth Jackson, *A Celtic Miscellany*, no. 48, p. 111. Text in T. F. O'Rahilly, *Danta Gradha*, p. 60.

221 *Reconciliation*. Kenneth Jackson, *A Celtic Miscellany*, no. 46, p. 109. Text in T. F. O'Rahilly, *Danta Gradha*, p. 24.

222 *He Praises Her Hair*. The Earl of Longford, op. cit., p. 9. Text in T. F. O'Rahilly, *Danta Gradha*, p. 17.

223 *No Sufferer for Her Love*. Robin Flower, op. cit., p. 150. Text in T. F. O'Rahilly, *Danta Gradha*, p. 10.

225 *Of Women No More Evil*. Robin Flower, op. cit., p. 149. Text in T. F. O'Rahilly, *Danta Gradha*, p. 3.

225 *He Praises His Wife When She Has Left Him*. Text and translation in Robin Flower, op. cit., p. 156.

226 *Dark Rosaleen*. D. J. O'Donoghue, *Poems of James Clarence Mangan* (Dublin, 1903), p. 3. Mangan based his translation on a text published by Samuel Ferguson in the *Dublin University Magazine* in 1834 and attributed to Costello of Ballyhaunis.

230 *Death's Warning to Beauty*. Robin Flower, op. cit., p. 140. Text in T. F. O'Rahilly, *Danta Gradha*, p. 138.

231 *He Charges Her to Lay Aside Her Weapons*. The Earl of Longford, *Poems from the Irish*, p. 3. Text in Patrick S. Dineen, *Danta Phiarais Feiriteir*, Dublin, 1903.

232 *The Harper*. Frank O'Connor, *The Fountain of Magic*, p. 33. Text in T. F. O'Rahilly, *Danta Measgra* (Cork, 1927), I, 7.

233 *The Woman of Three Cows*. D. J. O'Donoghue, *Poems of James Clarence Mangan*, p. 13.

235 *The Reverie*. Frank O'Connor, op. cit., p. 58. Text in Patrick S. Dineen and Tadhg O'Donoghue, *The Poems of Egan O'Rahilly* (London, Irish Texts Society, revised edition, 1911), p. 22.

236 *The Geraldine's Daughter*. D. J. O'Donoghue, *Poems of James Clarence Mangan*, p. 74. Text in Patrick S. Dineen and Tadhg O'Donoghue, op. cit., p. 168.

238 *A Sleepless Night*. Frank O'Connor, op. cit., p. 60. Text in Patrick S. Dineen and Tadhg O'Donoghue, op. cit., p. 26.

239 *A Grey Eye Weeping*. Frank O'Connor, op. cit., p. 62. Text in Patrick S. Dineen and Tadhg O'Donoghue, op. cit., p. 30. O'Connor has omitted three quatrains.

239 *Egan O'Rahilly and the Minister*. Kenneth Jackson, op. cit., no. 187, p. 241. Text in Patrick S. Dineen and Tadhg O'Donoghue, op. cit., p. 262.

241 *The Lament for Art O'Leary*. Frank O'Connor, op. cit., p. 75. Text in Shan O'Cuiv, *Cuine Airt I Laere*, Dublin, 1908, and in *The Gaelic Journal*, VII (1896), 18-23, ed. Osborn Bergin. O'Connor has omitted some verses. For a translation of the full text see Kenneth Jackson, *A Celtic Miscellany*, no. 221 p. 294.

p. 251 *Tara Is Grass. Collected Works of Padraic H. Pearse. Songs of the Irish Rebels and Specimens from an Irish Anthology* (Dublin, n. d.), p. 35. Text in T. F. O'Rahilly, *Burduin Bheaga* (Dublin, 1925), p. 9.

251 *The Convict of Clonmel.* Geoffrey Taylor, *Irish Poets of the Nineteenth Century* (London, 1951), p. 69.

252 *The Midnight Court.* Frank O'Connor, *The Midnight Court*, London, 1945. Mr. O'Connor has altered the text of his translation for the present edition. Gaelic text in *Zeitschrifte für celtische Philologie*, V(1904), 205, ed. L. C. Stern. The poem has been translated also by Arland Ussher (*The Midnight Court and the Adventures of a Luckless Fellow*, New York, 1926).

282 *I Am Raftery.* James Stephens, *Reincarnations* (New York, 1918), p. 75. Text in Douglas Hyde, *Abhrain & Danta*, Dublin, 1933.

283 *The County Mayo.* James Stephens, *op. cit.*, p. 29. Text in Douglas Hyde, *op. cit.*

284 *The Brow of Nephin.* Text and translation in Douglas Hyde, *Love Songs of Connacht* (London, 1905), p. 9.

285 *My Grief on the Sea. Ibid.*, p. 29.

286 *Ringleted Youth of My Love. Ibid.*, p. 41.

287 *I Shall Not Die for Thee. Ibid.*, p. 139.

Part V

289 *The Irish Dancer.* St. John D. Seymour, *Anglo-Irish Literature 1200-1582* (Cambridge, 1929), p. 98. The text is preserved in a 14th century English manuscript and was first published by W. Heuser, "Fragmente von unbekannten Spielmannsliedern des 14 Jahrhunderts, aus MS Rawl. D. 913," *Anglia*, XXX (1907), 175.

290 *A Rhyme-beginning Fragment.* St. John D. Seymour, *op. cit.*, p. 92. This and the following selection are preserved in a manuscript in the British Museum (Harley 913) which appears to have been put together and written, in part at least, in Ireland. Of the fifty-two items in the manuscript, seventeen are in Middle English, the others in Latin or Norman-French. Thirteen of the Middle English poems are connected by similarities of dialect and probably are the earliest specimens of the English language as it was written in Ireland. Since one of these bears the name of its author, Friar Michael of Kildare, the whole group has been associated with the Franciscan monastery in Kildare. First published by W. Heuser, "Die Kildare-Gedichte: die ältesten mittel-englischen Denkmäler in anglo-irischer Überlieferung," *Bonner Beiträge zur Anglistik*, Heft XIV (Bonn), 1904.

p. 290 *Cokaygne.* Text and footnotes are from St. John Seymour, *op. cit.,* p. 104, and George Ellis, *Specimens of the Early English Poets* (London, 1811), I, 83. See preceding note.

298 *An Anglo-Irishman's Complaint.* St. John Seymour, *op. cit.,* p. 99. The poem is preserved in the Book of Howth, a 16th century manuscript, first published in *Calendar of the Carew MSS in the Archepiscopal Library at Lambeth,* ed. J. S. Brewer and William Bullen, London, 1867-73. Seymour explains "without lease," in the second line, as meaning *without lying, truly,* and construes it as qualifying the next line. But possibly the phrase qualifies the first line of the poem and means "charters of peace" granted *without period of time.*

299 *A Modest Proposal. The Prose Works of Jonathan Swift,* ed. Temple Scott (London, 1925), VII, 207. First published 1729.

308 *Adventure in Cork. The Works of Oliver Goldsmith,* ed. J. W. M. Gibbs (London, 1884), I, 413. Although the authenticity of this letter has been doubted, since the text is based on a manuscript copy of the original, most authorities accept it as genuine. It is undated, but Gibbs suggests 1751 as the most likely date of its composition.

316 *The Croppy Boy.* This version—from Thomas Mac Donagh's *Literature in Ireland* (Dublin, 1916), p. 204—differs slightly from that published by Padraic Colum in *Anthology of Irish Verse* (New York, 1922). p. 103. William B. McBurney's "The Croppy Boy" is an altogether different poem.

317 *Oh, Breathe Not His Name. Irish Melodies and Songs by Thomas Moore,* with an introduction by Stephen Gwynn (London, The Muses Library, n.d.), p. 18. The *Melodies* came out in ten separate parts or numbers, the first two in 1808, the others respectively in 1810, 1811, 1813, 1815, 1818, 1824 and 1834. "Oh, Breathe Not His Name" was first published in 1808.

318 *The Harp That Once Through Tara's Halls. Ibid.,* p. 21. First published 1808.

318 *The Meeting of the Waters. Ibid.,* p. 34. First published 1808.

319 *The Song of Fionnuala. Ibid.,* p. 52. First published 1808.

320 *She Is Far From the Land. Ibid.,* p. 104. First published 1811.

321 *The Minstrel Boy. Ibid.,* p. 129. First published 1813.

321 *Dear Harp of My Country. Ibid.,* p. 170. First published 1815.

322 *The Hedge School.* William Carleton, *Traits and Stories of the Irish Peasantry* (London, 1869), I, 277-280. First published 1830.

327 *A Vision of Connaught in the Thirteenth Century.* D. J. O'Donoghue, *Poems of James Clarence Mangan* (London and Dublin, 1903), p. 94. First published 1846.

p. 330 *To My Native Land.* D. J. O'Donoghue, *op. cit.,* p. 107. O'Donoghue estimated the date of first publication as 1832.

332 *The Hunt.* Charles Lever, *Charles O'Malley, the Irish Dragoon* (Boston, 1894), I, 13-29. First published 1841.

348 *The Abdication of Fergus Mac Roy.* Samuel Ferguson, *Lays of the Western Gael and Other Poems* (London, 1888), p. 28. First published 1865.

354 *The Burial of King Cormac. Ibid.,* p. 47. First published 1865.

358 *The Wedding of the Clans.* Aubrey De Vere, *The Sisters, Inisfail, and Other Poems* (London, 1861), p. 177.

360 *The Fairies.* William Allingham, *Poems* (London, 1850), p. 87.

362 *Aghadoe.* John Todhunter, *The Banshee and Other Poems* (London, 1888), p. 84. "Aghadoe" appeared first in *Poems and Ballads of Young Ireland,* ed. W. B. Yeats and others, which was published earlier in the same year.

366 *The Nameless Dun.* William Larminie, *Fand and Other Poems* (Dublin and London, 1892), p. 35.

367 *The Murrigan.* George Moore, *A Story-Teller's Holiday* (New York, 1929), p. 60. First published 1918 and revised for republication in 1929.

375 *The Rising of the Moon.* Lady Gregory, *Seven Short Plays* (New York, n.d.), p. 75-91. First produced at the Abbey Theatre, Dublin, March 9, 1907.

385 *The Grave of Rury.* T. W. Rolleston, *Sea Spray: Verses and Translations* (Dublin, 1909), p. 19.

386 *Poisson d'Avril.* E. Œ. Somerville and Martin Ross, *Some Experiences of an Irish R. M.* (London, Everyman's Library, 1944), p. 205. First published 1908.

398 From the Preface to *John Bull's Other Island. Selected Plays of Bernard Shaw* (New York, n.d.), p. 445-474. First published 1907.

428 *Cuchulain's Fight with the Sea. The Collected Poems of W. B. Yeats* (New York, 1951), p. 33. First published 1892 under the title "The Death of Cuchullin" and subsequently revised.

432 *The Folly of Being Comforted. Ibid.,* p. 76. First published 1902.

432 *To a Shade. Ibid.,* p. 108. First published 1913.

433 *In Memory of Major Robert Gregory. Ibid.,* p. 130. First published 1918.

437 *Sailing to Byzantium. Ibid.,* p. 191. First published 1927.

439 *Leda and the Swan. Ibid.,* p. 211. First published 1924.

439 *Among School Children. Ibid.,* p. 212. First published 1927.

442 *The Wild Old Wicked Man, Ibid.,* p. 307. First published 1938.

444 *The Statues. Ibid.,* p. 322. First published 1939.

p. 446 Truth. AE (George Russell), Collected Poems (London, 1920), p. 133.

446 The Twilight of Earth. Ibid., p. 183. First published 1904.

448 On Behalf of Some Irishmen Not Followers of Tradition. Ibid., p. 229.

450 A Prisoner. Selected Poems (London, 1935), p. 128. First published 1925.

450 The King of Ireland's Son. Nora Hopper, Selected Poems, London, 1906. The poem exists in three different versions. Although that which appeared in Ballads in Prose—it was inserted in a prose tale—was published first (1894), Yeats suspected that the longer and inferior version which appeared two years later in Under Quicken Bows actually represented an earlier draft of the poem. Still another version—the best of the three and the one which is most frequently quoted—appeared in Selected Poems, published the year of the poet's death.

451 Deirdre of the Sorrows, Act III. The Complete Works of John M. Synge (New York, 1935), p. 249-268. First produced at the Abbey Theatre, Dublin, January 13, 1910.

467 The Crab Tree. The Collected Poems of Oliver St. John Gogarty, (New York, 1954), p. 48. First published 1927.

468 Ringsend. Ibid., p. 37.

469 Exorcism. Ibid., p. 45.

470 To the Liffey with the Swans. Ibid., p. 49. First published 1923.

471 Per Iter Tenebricosum. Ibid., p. 191.

471 Verse. Ibid., p. 3.

472 To the Maids Not to Walk In the Wind. Ibid., p. 106. First published 1923.

472 To W. B. Yeats, Who Says That His Castle of Ballylee Is His Monument. Ibid., p. 25.

473 Leda and the Swan. Ibid., p. 144.

477 The Old Age Pensioner. Joseph Campbell, Irishry (Dublin, 1913), p. 31.

478 The Unfrocked Priest. Ibid., p. 44.

480 I Am the Mountainy Singer. Joseph Campbell, The Mountainy Singer (Boston, 1919), p. 11.

481 I Am the Gilly of Christ. Ibid., p. 30.

482 As I Came Over the Grey, Grey Hills. Ibid., p. 49.

483 I Will Go With My Father A-Ploughing. Ibid., p. 115.

484 The Herb-Leech. Ibid., p. 119.

485 The Raid. Sean O'Casey, Inishfallen, Fare Thee Well (London, 1949), p. 44-60.

503 A Drover. The Collected Poems of Padraic Colum (New York, 1953), p. 84. First published 1904.

p. 504 *A Poor Scholar of the 'Forties*. Ibid., p. 120. First published 1904.

505 *The Wind*. James Stephens, *Collected Poems* (London, 1926), p. 106.

506 *The College of Surgeons*. Ibid., p. 118.

506 *Check*. Ibid., p. 170.

507 *The Crest Jewel*. Ibid., p. 252.

509 *Ivy Day in the Committee Room*. James Joyce, *Dubliners* (New York, The Modern Library, n.d.), p. 148. First published 1914.

526 *Night and Morning*. Austin Clarke, *Night and Morning*, Dublin, 1938.

527 *Tenebrae*: Ibid.

528 *The Straying Student*. Ibid.

530 *An Old Air*. F. R. Higgins, *The Dark Breed* (London, 1927), p. 34.

531 *Song for the Clatter-Bones*. F. R. Higgins, *The Gap of Brightness* (New York, 1940), p. 14.

532 *The Wild Sow*. Liam O'Flaherty, *The Short Stories of Liam O'Flaherty* (London, 1937, 1948), p. 102-106. First published 1924.

536 *A Difficult Question*. Kate O'Brien, *The Land of Spices* (New York, 1941), p. 100-108.

543 *My Grander*. Sean O'Faolain, *Bird Alone* (New York, 1936), p. 17-22.

547 *In the Train*. Frank O'Connor, *Bones of Contention* (London, 1936), p. 59.

563 *Father Mat*. Patrick Kavanagh, *A Soul for Sale. Poems* (London, 1947), p. 3.

568 *A Christmas Childhood*. Ibid., p. 13.

570 *If Ever You Go to Dublin Town*. *The Irish Times*, March 21, 1953.

572 *Valediction*. Louis MacNeice, *Poems 1925-1940* (New York, 1940), p. 76. First published 1935.

576 *Carrickfergus*. Ibid., p. 129.

578 *from Autumn Journal*. Ibid., p. 212. First published 1939.

582 *The Raider*. W. R. Rodgers, *Awake and Other Poems* (London, 1941), p. 39.

582 *Lent*. W. R. Rodgers, *Europa and the Bull and Other Poems* (London, 1952), p. 34.

584 *Christ Walking on the Water*. Ibid., p. 42.

586 *The Net*. Ibid., p. 44.

587 *Spring*. Ibid., p. 91.